ROBERT GAMBLES

AMBERLEY

For Brian, Peter and Ian

First published as *Breaking Butterflies* in 2006

This edition first published 2013

Amberley Publishing
The Hill, Stroud
Gloucestershire, GL5 4EP

www.amberley-books.com

British Library Cataloguing in Publication Data.
A catalogue record for this book is available from the British Library.

ISBN 978 1 4456 1337 6 (print)
ISBN 978 1 4456 1349 9 (ebook)

Typeset in 10pt on 12pt Sabon.
Typesetting and Origination by Amberley Publishing.
Printed in the UK.

Contents

Acknowledgements

This study of historical anecdotes drawn from 2,000 years of English history is the distillation of innumerable notes and jottings compiled over several decades, during which time I have accumulated many obligations. It is with pleasure that I can acknowledge the help given by so many friends and colleagues (some of whom are no longer with us); their interest and their contributions were much appreciated. Research in more recent times by a new generation of professional historians and biographers has made possible a more accurate interpretation of many of these traditional tales – it is impossible adequately to express my debt to these writers who have shed so much new light on their subject and have guided me to important and often obscure sources – and here I would pay tribute to those dedicated librarians in all parts of the country who have been unfailingly helpful in providing information, books and documents not usually in great demand. In recent years, when I have been unable to visit distant libraries myself, I have been fortunate to have had assistance (and critical assessment) from my sons Brian and Peter, who have found time in busy lives to consult material in major libraries on my behalf; without their help a number of the chapters in this study could not have been written.

I also wish to acknowledge the contribution of my granddaughter Elizabeth, who so successfully produced a corrected version of this study on disc. I owe a debt of gratitude, too, to my editors Nicola Gale and Emily Brewer, whose enthusiastic support, unwavering patience and editorial expertise were invaluable at every stage.

Words now seem inadequate to express all that I owe to the loving support and critical appraisal of my late wife Hannemor, who encouraged me when the going was difficult and reminded me of unfinished business when the files began to gather dust.

Preface

We can conjure up the past in many different ways. We can imagine ourselves in another age as we wander through the ruins of a medieval abbey or castle, or stroll through the sumptuous rooms of an aristocratic mansion. We can wonder at the astonishing ingenuity of mankind in every age as we peer at displays of technological inventiveness from the stone axe to the computer; we can create works of literature and art – historical dramas, films, novels, son-et-lumière productions, paintings of street scenes, landscapes and people; or we can listen to ballads, poems, songs and stories telling of the lives and real or imagined adventures of kings, queens, nobility and knights errant, or of men and women not unlike ourselves.

We can also study history analytically, engaging in detailed and scholarly research, putting every aspect of a past society and its institutions under the microscope of academic rigour. Even the well-known anecdotes of history, including those of dubious provenance, may be profitably studied in this way; some might reinforce or add colour to a historically correct perception of a particular individual or event. Others, on the contrary, may have been deliberately contrived or fabricated to conceal or distort the truth about a historical character or incident. Was Alfred the Great really so absent-minded as actually to allow the cakes to burn? Did King Cnut really believe that he could turn back the tide? Was Fair Rosamund tortured and murdered by bad Queen Eleanor? Was King John so utterly villainous as to murder his own nephew? Was Robert Bruce inspired by the perseverance of a spider? Did Francis Drake ignore the approaching Armada in order to finish a game of bowls? Did Nelson disobey his Commander's order at the Battle of Copenhagen? Was Queen Victoria never amused?

These stories have been part of the reality of history for generations of children and they were, once upon a time, among the most vivid memories of childhood. Yet for over a century, most academic historians dismissed them as no more than fictitious inventions, irrelevant to the serious business of historical studies. In his long-forgotten *A History of England Before the Norman Conquest*, Sir Charles Oman, commenting on the story of King Alfred and the cakes, wrote, 'It is useless to spend time "breaking a butterfly"; the quaint tale is only worth mentioning because it has achieved such a worldwide popularity.'

In the 2,000 years of recorded English history there is a luminous cloud of these butterflies, all once uncritically accepted or rejected, but few were actually caught and their colourful hues examined. I have cast a net in this cloud and tried to catch just a few of these will-o'-the-wisps that haunt every age of our history, and attempted to trace their origins and test their truth. Yet ... who breaks a butterfly upon a wheel? These intriguing tales are part of our historical heritage and, once examined, should be left free to fly: the story of Eve and the apple in the Garden of Eden will live on however many times we are reminded that no apple tree is mentioned in the Book of Genesis.

Preface to This Edition

The publication of this new edition has offered the opportunity to make a few amendments and additions to the text in the light of recent research and the greatly appreciated advice of the late Professor Patrick Collinson. The book has also been given a new and more appropriate title.

Robert Gambles
Kendal 2013

Introduction

Storys to rede ar delitabill
Suppos that thai be nocht bot fabill
[Stories are a pleasure to read even if they are no more than fables]

John Barbour's opening lines to his poem 'Brus', celebrating the life of Robert Bruce, were echoed almost 600 years later by an elderly lady recalling, in the 1930s, memories of history lessons in her Victorian schooldays:

My English history was derived from a little book in small print that dealt with the characters of the kings at some length. I heard how one was ruthless alike to friend and foe, and how another was so weak that the sceptre fell from his nervous grasp. I seemed to see it falling. The book had no doubts or evidence or sources, but gave all the proper anecdotes about cakes, the peaches and new ale, never smiling again, the turbulent priest, and the lighted candle. I am glad that I had these at the credulous stage, and in this unhesitating form. They were much more glowing than if they had been introduced by the chilling words 'It is said that...' Not as a lesson, but for sheer pleasure, did I browse in *A Child's History of Rome*, a book full of good stories that spared none of the details about Regulus in the barrel, the death of Gracchus, Marius in the pond, and Sulla's cold-blooded slaughters.[1]

This was in the 1870s but almost everyone who was of primary-school age in the mid-twentieth century might also recall that, even then, all the proper anecdotes were an essential feature of history lessons. Mrs Markham's enduringly popular *History* may have been long superseded by Heather Marshall's *Our Island Story*, and the tales stripped of much moralising undergrowth, but they were still at the heart of a child's vision of the past – and are even now wistfully recalled (e.g. by Lady Antonia Fraser and Andrew Marr, BBC Radio 4, December 2003).

All this has changed. The teaching of history has become the shuttlecock of current political ideologies and the *dernier cri* in educational theory. In the urgent rush to improve literacy and numeracy, history has been relegated to a lowly position in the curriculum and little time is set aside for children simply to listen to stories, the surest introduction to the pleasures of reading, not only of history but of the whole of literature. Only the intuitive insight of skilled teachers and enlightened parents can now offer children this golden opportunity.

Medieval chroniclers, Tudor scholars, Stuart diarists, eighteenth- and nineteenth-century novelists and historians have all bequeathed to posterity a rich heritage of imaginatively reconstructed history. Most of them were unfamiliar with the concept of 'scientific history', which places emphasis on original sources, factual accuracy and a strict methodology. Their primary aim was to present history as a graphic and colourful story, a picturesque pageant of dramatic events, heroic deeds and personal crises. The chroniclers who compiled vividly embroidered accounts of the death of Fair Rosamund or the rescue of Richard the Lionheart, sought to vilify Richard III or dramatise the death of Sir Philip Sydney, or invented the fable of Isaac Newton and the apple tree or George Washington and the cherry tree were not so very different from those journalists of the present day, who luridly report the real or imagined lives of public figures and 'celebrities'. Perhaps 'a good story' is a necessary feature of a literate society. It may be significant that some of the most popular film and television productions in recent years have been dramatised versions of the 'period' novels of some of our best 'storytellers', notably Jane Austen, Walter Scott, Charles Dickens, George Eliot and John Galsworthy, with some of Shakespeare's historical plays and a few colourful interpretations of the civil wars between Cavaliers and Roundheads not far behind. The large audiences for expertly researched and theatrically presented programmes on historical and archaeological themes represent something more than sentimental nostalgia. We live in a society in which this popular appreciation of history is seen to flourish and in which there is a wider understanding that history may – quite legitimately – be written from a number of perspectives; this would seem to signal not only an innate curiosity about the past but perhaps also an inexpressible need to create a new understanding of our national identity, in an age when we have lost our imperial supremacy and self-confidence and when even the concept of British nationhood is challenged.

We have yet to come to terms with the events that radically changed our society in the second half of the twentieth century, but 200 years ago there occurred an even more fundamental dislocation of a long-established way of life. The French Revolution and the social and political upheaval that accompanied it; the social and technological transformation brought about by the agricultural and industrial revolutions; the doubling of the population in less than a hundred years; the religious and intellectual challenges of Methodism and the Romantic movement and the emergence of Britain as a dominant imperial power all came together in the early years of the nineteenth century to create a turmoil in the nation's traditional structures and beliefs, such as had not been experienced since the Reformation of the sixteenth century had marked the end of the Middle Ages and the flowering of Elizabethan England as a sovereign nation state. Just as in the reign of Elizabeth I there was a growing awareness of an English national identity, so in the reign of Victoria similar instincts were at work striving to find in the past a distinctive English character and distinctive English institutions and traditions worthy of the country's new leadership of the world. There was a need for a national history that would enshrine what were felt to be the essential virtues of the English character, which had created the English nation. The rapid growth of a wealthy and educated bourgeois class, proud of England's pre-eminence and of the part they had played in achieving it, gave a special impetus to the demand for books and magazines, particularly works of history and novels with a historical setting. The writings of Walter Scott, Jane Austen, Harrison Ainsworth and Charles Dickens found a wide and enthusiastic public.

Two studies of the historical literature produced by this romantic interest in the past, one at each end of the twentieth century, touched upon the philosophy that shaped it. In 1901 Katie Magnus in *The First Makers of England* stated her belief that 'the seeds of our national character are to be sought in the lives of the heroes of early England, from whom we trace the beginnings of our best habits and institutions'.[2] Almost one hundred years later, the authors of *Myth and Nationhood* reflected that 'the concept of a Nation ... cannot be sustained without a suitable past ... In order to create a convincing representation of the 'nation', a worthy and distinctive past must be rediscovered and appropriated. An invented history is therefore crucial to the development of nationalism.'[3]

The pattern was set by David Hume, whose multi-volume *History of England*, published between 1754 and 1762, became the sourcebook for almost every nineteenth-century history textbook. Hume's work – and the popular abbreviated version produced by J. S. Brewer in 1880, known as *The Student's Hume* – was by far the most influential history book of the century and, although it lost favour as the new 'scientific history' gained ground, it remained at the heart of the history taught in British schools until the early years of the twentieth century. The secret of Hume's success was a readable and coherent narrative liberally embellished with anecdotes of kings, queens and 'heroic' figures, which had been handed down through the centuries to form a body of established tradition that was perceived to be essentially and indisputably English. There was a romantic revival of interest in Celtic history in the mid-nineteenth century but it was generally accepted that the history of Britain was subsumed into the history of England, a view positively promoted by Sir Walter Scott.

In the middle decades of the nineteenth century, there was an unparalleled outpouring of history books for both children and adults, almost all of them lavishly furnished with versions of the traditional anecdotes. Among these were such popular publications as Lady Maria Callcott's *Little Arthur's History of England*, Charles Dickens's *A Child's History of England*, Mrs Markham's *History of England* ('Mrs Markham' was the pseudonym used by Elizabeth Penrose, 1780–1837), Anne Rodwell's *The Child's First Steps to English History*, May Beverley's *Romantic Passages in English History* and *Tales and Stories from History* by Agnes Strickland, a slight successor to her equally popular twelve-volume *Lives of the*

Queens of England. These histories were read aloud to both children and adults – Lady Callcott's 'Little Arthur' was her grandson, just one of many children who learned their history as a bedtime story or a daytime interlude – and adult reading groups often chose history as their favoured subject: in her novel *Heartsease* (1854), Charlotte Yonge describes how her circle of ladies met 'to finish the volume of Miss Strickland's *Queens* which they were reading together'. Dickens's dramatic public readings of his novels were a notable feature of the social life of his time. Also widely read were the works of such distinguished mid-century historians as James Froude, J. R. Green and Thomas Babington Macaulay, and for all of these history had an immediacy of purpose – to establish the virtues and continuity of the English nation and its institutions, to celebrate the victories of English arms over a succession of enemies, to extol the merits of English 'heroes' and to deplore the deeds of those who had tried to oppose the progress of the English people towards political and religious freedom and independence. Family loyalty, personal integrity, courage and self-sacrifice were praised as commendable private virtues; patriotism, heroism and devotion to civic or national duty were emphasised as public virtues. Macaulay himself described his *History of England* as the history of physical, of moral and of 'intellectual improvement' and he aimed to write it in such a compelling narrative that it would 'replace the last fashionable novel upon the table of young ladies'.

Historical anecdotes played a significant part in teaching these virtues. The more medieval they were the better, as this added the spice of romance made familiar through popular reading of Scott's Waverley novels and the tales of King Arthur and Robin Hood. Almost all the best-known anecdotes were culled from the medieval centuries, as this was seen as a shadowy time of sinister events and romantic adventures, when the virtuous won their rewards and the wicked received their just deserts. It was also seen as the seed time when those great institutions that England had given to the world were conceived – trial by jury, elected parliaments, constitutional monarchy, a national Church, local government through parishes, boroughs and shires, and the principles of individual liberty, which, it was believed, were enshrined in Magna Carta.

This 'picturesque' version of English history captured the imagination of Victorian England so comprehensively that for many it became the true authentic history, infinitely preferable to what Catherine Morland in *Northanger Abbey* had dubbed 'real solemn history'. Gilbert à Beckett in his *Comic History of England* attempted to expose the dubious nature of this popular history but he had to admit that this was a forlorn quest: 'The public, being accustomed to falsehood would regard the absence of even the most flagrant hoax as a curtailment of the fair proportion of history.'[4] Even Thackeray, who was usually very critical of invented picturesque history, had to admit that 'out of the fictitious book I get all the expressions of the life of the time; of the manners of the moment, the dress, the pleasures, the laughter, the ridicules of society ... Can the heaviest historian do more for me?'[5]

Thackeray himself made a notable contribution to this brand of historical writing in his novel *Henry Esmond*. Set in the reign of Queen Anne, this was a literary triumph even in an age of classical historical novels: Scott's *Ivanhoe*, Dickens's *Tale of Two Cities*, Ainsworth's *Boscobel* and *Tower of London*, Kingsley's *Hereward the Wake*, Marryat's *Children of the New Forest*, Bulwer-Lytton's *Last of the Barons* – a random selection to which one ought to add Tennyson's *Idylls of the King*, which transformed the hitherto 'Celtic' King Arthur into a genuine Saxon hero, 'the verray parfit knight' of Victorian sentiment. Robin Hood, for centuries a folk hero of the medieval forests and a lovable rogue, was recast, to join Hereward the Wake, as a champion of native English resistance to the Norman invader. The shadowy figure of Maid Marian was given real substance by Thomas Love Peacock in 1819 and her popular image – still familiar in modern pantomime – was set in stone thirty years later by J. H. Stocqueller in his novel *Maid Marian, the Forest Queen*.

This imaginative vision of the past was not confined to traditional stories or folklore. Historians themselves were apt to portray historical characters as 'good' or 'bad': William Rufus, King John, Edward II, Richard III represented all that was 'bad'; King Alfred, Richard I, Henry V and Elizabeth I were exemplars of all that was 'good'. Even the scholarly John Lingard was tempted to include alleged verbatim conversations between Charles Stuart, in flight from defeat at Worcester in 1651, and the Penderel family in order to support his contention that English Catholics were largely unswerving in their loyalty to the Stuart cause at that time.[6] Thomas Bowdler's expurgated version of Gibbon's *Decline and Fall of the Roman Empire* was hailed as a great improvement on the original, as it was now suitable for family reading. Similar 'improvements' were inflicted on Malory's *Morte d'Arthur*, but only after four drastic expurgations was it considered to be a proper guide to moral conduct. Thomas Percy's collections of old ballads were subjected to 'ingenious conjectural emendations' to the original texts, which 'left them in such a state that they could be read with pleasure'.[7]

This was, in fact, all that most readers asked of their history. Jane Austen's Miss Tilney expressed it well:

> I am fond of history and am well content to take the false with the true
> ... If a speech be well drawn up, I read it with pleasure, by whomsoever
> it may be made – and probably with much greater if the production of
> Mr Hume or Mr Robertson [William Robertson (1721–93), Principal
> of Edinburgh University, author of a number of history books highly
> regarded in their time], than if the genuine words of Caractacus, Agricola
> or Alfred the Great.[8]

History should be written so that it could be read with pleasure; otherwise it became, as Catherine Morland said, 'very tiresome'.

In the final decades of Victoria's reign a sea change took place in the study of history and in attitudes to historical sources and historical writing. Romance was out and 'real solemn history' was in. This was apparent at various levels of historical studies: in academic circles, historians such as William Stubbs, Edward Freeman and J. H. Round, and the publication of important State papers, brought a new dimension to medieval studies that left no place for picturesque anecdotes; throughout the shires, amateur historians and archaeologists were delving into local records and into the earth in the now fashionable search for 'facts' about the past; at Cambridge, Lord Acton and his posse of learned historians were engaged in producing the massive and authoritative *Cambridge Modern History*, the declared aim of which was to tell history as it actually happened – not a work Miss Morland would have enjoyed; in the schools, Mrs Markham was facing a challenge from new examination textbooks bearing such soulless titles as *A School History of England* or *A Catechism of English History*, mostly unillustrated and furnished with lists of events, dates, battles and the reigns of kings. The bell tolled for 'traditional' history but, as our London Child of the 1870s reminded us, 'all the proper anecdotes' were still very much a part of school history – and would remain so for another two or three generations.

In a perceptive lecture delivered in the 1950s, Robert Birley suggested that with so much emphasis on 'scientific history' historians had become more like archaeologists, concerning themselves more and more with 'the essential substructure of society' and less with the actual life of individuals, which with its 'twists and turns produce[s] dramatic episodes, tragic or comic, pathetic or just plain exciting, and moments which test men and women so that their true character is displayed'.[9]

This is, of course, precisely why these traditional stories held such a strong appeal. The defiant courage of Caratacus in Rome, the simple humanity of King Alfred, the tragic folly of the sinking of the White Ship, the knightly valour and romance of Richard the Lionheart, the wicked deeds of 'bad' King John, the selfless devotion of Eleanor of Castile, the compassion of Queen Philippa at Calais, the bizarre fate of the Duke of Clarence, the gentlemanly courtesy of Philip Sidney at Zutphen, the calculated nonchalance of Francis Drake as the Armada approached, Oliver Cromwell's agonising dilemma, the pathos of James Wolfe's poetic journey to death and glory, the insouciant heroism of Lord Nelson, the formidable dedication of Florence Nightingale – all these and many others make good stories and, for children especially, they can often be the introduction to 'real, solemn history' in the same way as familiar nursery rhymes can spark an interest in poetry and literature or, as Sir Philip Sidney himself succinctly expressed it, they are 'the first light given to ignorance, and the first nurse, whose milk little and little enables them to feed afterwards of tougher knowledge'.

This does not mean that these traditional tales should not be subjected to the processes of analysis in an attempt to ascertain their origins, their veracity and their value to historical studies. Nor should they be dismissively cast aside and consigned to history's dustbin simply because, as Sir Charles Oman wrote, 'they have achieved such world-wide popularity'. Professor Frank Barlow more recently advised that 'the modern historian should not be too puritanical ... To exclude all the best yarns serves no good purpose. They are often the closest we can get to the truth of the matter, metaphors which provide authentic local colour.'[10]

A 'scientific' methodology is, of course, unequivocally essential in the search for the truth about the past; it underpins the whole structure of historical studies and historical writing. The debate whether history is art or science was always sterile: it is clearly both but the historian's material is the work of human beings who were not so very different from ourselves even if they lived in a society very different from our own. The 'facts' of history are not as incontrovertible as the 'facts' of science for they rely on an evaluation of sources compiled by individuals endowed with all the flaws, as well as all the gifts, of the human mind; and in their interpretations it is inevitable that historians bring to bear these same gifts and flaws. History, then, is not so much a definitive account of the past as an interpretation of the past based on all the information we can discover about it. To assemble and analyse the detail in these sources demands imagination and a systematic methodology; the literary presentation of a historical interpretation can be 'dry as dust' and 'very tiresome' or

> a glimpse through the curtain of old night into a brilliantly lighted scene of living men and women, not mere creatures of fiction and imagination, but warm-blooded realities even as we are ... people will read history if it fascinates them. It is therefore the duty of historians to make it as fascinating as possible, or at any rate not to conceal its fascination under a heap of learning which ought to underlie but not to overwhelm written history.[11]

It would, therefore, seem to be (to use Professor Barlow's word) 'puritanical' for historians to reject or exclude historical anecdotes if they make history more interesting, and many recent authoritative studies have incorporated them with advantage, even with judicious professional reservations as to their possibly apocryphal nature.

Such tales can readily take their place in Clio's house of many mansions. As Elgar said of music, history is in the air all round us – these enduring yarns of human strengths and weaknesses, of mystery, catastrophe and agonising dilemma can help us to reach out and catch it.

The poet Horace gave a sound guide to writers of history more than 2,000 years ago:

> Omne tulit punctum qui miscuit utile dulci.
> Lectorum delectando pariterque monendo.
>
> [He has won every point who has mixed profit with pleasure
> By delighting his reader at the same time as instructing him.][12]

1

Caratacus in Rome, AD 51

The Britons defended themselves and their country with great bravery; but their imperfect skill in the art of war could not withstand the Roman power and discipline. After fighting many battles, the Romans at length took prisoner a British king named Caractacus, and his family. They were all sent to Rome; and the king, with his wife and two daughters were made to walk through the streets, loaded with chains, while the emperor and empress and all the people, were assembled to look at them, as if they had been so many wild animals. Poor Caractacus, as you may suppose, was very indignant at this treatment, and made such a moving speech to the emperor … that he immediately ordered his chains to be taken off, and treated him with great kindness ever after.

Mrs Markham's *History of England*

In AD 40 the Roman Emperor Gaius (better known as Caligula) assembled an invasion force at Boulogne and erected a magnificent lighthouse; he then called off the whole operation.[1] This sudden change of mind may have been no more than the capricious whim of a mercurial Caesar, but the military exercise itself was a signal that the unfinished business of Britannia was once more a high priority in the imperial strategy of the Roman Empire. Three years later, under another, more rational Emperor, the nettle was finally grasped and the Claudian invasion was launched with conquest firmly in mind.

The choice of date was not accidental. For much of the first century the British tribes had been of little concern in Rome. Under the guidance of Cunobelinus, the leader of the Catuvellauni tribe, there had been a long period of coexistence with Rome, with diplomatic and commercial relations creating a non-threatening situation, in which Rome could complete its settlement of Gaul, and Cunobelinus could extend his sway over the southern tribes of Britain.

By AD 43 this British quiescence had come to an end. Cunobelinus had achieved a vague overlordship over the Atrebates and the Trinovantes in the south and east of Britain without precipitating conflict with Rome – he was even described by Suetonius as King of the Britons[2] – although there was a 'diplomatic incident' in 39/40 when Gaius refused to extradite Adminius, a son of Cunobelinus who had fled his father's wrath, most probably for supporting the pro-Roman element in British tribal politics. Shortly after this, Cunobelinus died to be succeeded by two other sons, Togodumnus and Caratacus, who immediately caused alarm in Rome by pursuing a policy of almost aggressive expansion of Catuvellaunian influence, northwards towards the Humber, south of the Thames and westwards into the territory of the Dobunni. When Verica, the pro-Roman 'king' of the Atrebates was driven out and sought refuge in Gaul, Togodumnus and Caratacus demanded his return, a diplomatic indicator that they now considered their 'Britain' to be a kingdom to be reckoned with.

Rome could not regard with equanimity the prospect of such a potential threat so close to a still-unsettled Gaul and this, together with other, perhaps more transparent motives, decided Claudius to turn the full power of the Roman legions on to the tribes of Britain.

They were, of course, successful; it was inevitable that the highly trained, battle-hardened, disciplined and well-equipped Roman military machine would overcome the largely untrained, ill-disciplined, poorly equipped, divided tribal units that opposed it. Yet even the great Aulus Plautius found a worthy foe in Caratacus, and it was only after several years of hard fighting that conquest was finally achieved.

This prolonged British resistance was acknowledged by the Romans to be inspired by the personal leadership, military skills and single-minded dedication of Caratacus, who organised line after line of defence and, with his demonic charioteers and ramshackle infantry, tested the Roman generals in a succession of battles fought against all the odds. Put to flight by the initial onslaught, he then engaged the invaders along the River Medway in that rare feature in ancient warfare, a two-day battle, before being forced to retreat when a surprise attack decimated the horses of his elite charioteers. Further resistance among the Essex marshes cost the Romans significant losses, and Togodumnus his life. It was a spirited but futile attempt to turn back an irresistible tide; the venture was also undermined by the hostility Caratacus met from other British tribes resentful of his arrogant claims to overlordship and even anticipating that, when Britain became a Roman province, they would share all the urban opulence and consumer benefits so visibly enjoyed by the rest of Western Europe.

They were quickly disillusioned, it would seem. Within a few years the Iceni and the Trinovantes rose in unsuccessful revolt against their new masters, but Caratacus was far away in the west preparing to resist the Roman advance into the hilly homelands of the Silures in South Wales and the Ordovices in central Wales. It seems likely that he may also have been responsible for the great defensive earthworks on Minchinhampton Common in the Cotswolds, intended perhaps to check the Romans there;[3] but Vespasian had decisively demonstrated at Maiden Castle in Dorset that such once-formidable defence-works were no answer to the disciplined power of the Roman cohorts. Caratacus saw that his best hope now lay in the mountains of Wales, and by the year 49 he had succeeded in establishing himself as leader of an alliance of the Silures and the Ordovices – and a significant number from other British tribes. It is a tribute to the forceful personality of Caratacus that he could bring together the peoples of tribes who were usually so antagonistic to one another. Tacitus commented that 'all who feared the Roman peace joined him'.[4] In AD 51 the stage was set for the final battle.

Caratacus chose his ground well. The exact site is not known but it was almost certainly above the River Severn – Dolforwyn and Cefncarnedd both fit the description given by Tacitus – on a steep, craggy hill with stone ramparts at weak points and a stone-walled fort on the summit. The Roman commander, Ostorius, and his legionaries viewed this apparently impregnable position with some concern: Caratacus was now regarded as an opponent to be treated with the utmost respect, and the fighting spirit of the Britons he led here was dauntingly clear. However, the river proved to be easily fordable and the first onslaught took the Romans to the walls of the fortress. Here they were fought to a standstill and they had to employ the well-drilled tactic of the testudo, linking their shields overhead, before they could begin to demolish the stonework and break through to surround and destroy any further resistance. Superiority in numbers, tactics, training and equipment ensured Ostorius an overwhelming victory. Caratacus escaped in the final melee but his wife, daughter and brother were taken prisoner.

Caratacus made his way to the north where the Brigantes tribe had shown stubborn opposition to the Roman advance and, given his implacable hostility to the invader, he almost certainly hoped to be able to carry on the struggle in the northern hills. Such hopes were quickly dashed, for Brigantian affairs were now controlled by the pro-Roman Queen Cartimandua and no longer by her anti-Roman husband Venutius. Caratacus was promptly handed over to the Romans, and he and his family were despatched as prisoners of war to Rome.

Tacitus claimed that Caratacus was 'the most outstanding Briton in the field of military science', and the Emperor, Senate and military establishment in Rome agreed. The capture of the man who had defied the might of the Roman army for so long was hailed as a special triumph, and Claudius intended to reap all the glory. The people of Rome were summoned to see the processional spectacle as, first, petty British tribal vassals were paraded in chains followed by the spoils of war won in Britain; next came the disconsolate figures of Caratacus's wife, daughter and brothers; and finally the British leader himself, defiantly refusing to entreat for mercy. Such parades in the past had usually ended in the execution of the captives and no-one expected this occasion to be different: not even the great French hero, Vercingetorix, had been spared. According to Tacitus, however, Caratacus stepped onto the dais before the Emperor and delivered the following speech:

> 'Had my lineage and rank been accompanied by only moderate success, I should have come to this city as a friend rather than a prisoner, and you would not have disdained to ally yourself peacefully with one so nobly born, the ruler of so many nations. As it is, humiliation is my lot, glory yours.
>
> I had horses, men, arms, wealth. Are you surprised I am sorry to lose them? If you want to rule the world, does it follow that everyone else welcomes enslavement? If I had surrendered without a blow before being brought before you, neither my downfall nor your triumph would

have become famous. If you execute me, they will be forgotten. Spare me, and I shall be an everlasting token of your mercy.'

Claudius responded by pardoning him and his wife and brothers. Then the Senate met. It devoted numerous complimentary speeches to the capture of Caratacus. This was hailed as equal in glory to any previous exhibition of a captured king. Ostorius received an honorary Triumph.[5]

It was a common convention for historians in ancient times to put speeches into the mouths of important figures on such occasions and it is impossible to know precisely what Caratacus did or did not say.[6] Tacitus himself wrote that Caratacus 'spoke in these terms' so he is not claiming that his report is a verbatim account. We may accept as fact that Caratacus did make a speech and that he was subsequently pardoned by Claudius and lived out his life in Rome as a free man.

Historical source material for the life of Caratacus is very sketchy and, in consequence, his role in inspiring British resistance to the Roman invasion has received less recognition than it deserves. It is only in comparatively recent times that historians have begun to appreciate that Celtic society was much more sophisticated in its culture and achievements than was formerly realised. Admiration for the urban civilisation of Rome and the remarkable feats of engineering the Romans accomplished – and the wealth of written and archaeological artefacts they left behind them – created a, perhaps unconscious, prejudice against the 'primitive' societies they overwhelmed. Sellar and Yeatman expressed it succinctly in *1066 and All That*: 'The Roman Conquest was a Good Thing, since the Britons were only natives at that time.' Caratacus may have been impetuous, arrogant and ultimately unsuccessful but he was a man of indomitable spirit, a born leader of men and a personality of immense power and charisma. He clearly believed with all his being that whatever material benefits might accompany the *Pax Romana* they were not compatible with the soul of Celtic society and would destroy it. In the speech he made as a captive in Rome it is easy to imagine that he spoke with even more heartfelt passion than is found in the version recorded by Tacitus. Only a great man could fling into the Emperor's face the words 'If you want to rule the world, does it follow that everyone else welcomes enslavement?'

2

St Gregory:
Not Angles but Angels, *c.* 574–78

The Angles and Saxons lived as heathens in their new country for more than a hundred years. And now I will tell you how God gave them the word of life and turned them from their false gods. Soon after the Angle and Saxon kings had settled themselves quietly in Britain, a good many boys were taken from Britain to be made servants in Rome. Most of these were Angles, and it happened that as they were standing together an Abbot named GREGORY saw them, and he thought they were very beautiful, and asked where they came from and who they were. He was told they were Angles, from Britain, but that they were not Christians. He was sorry for this, and said if they were Christians they would be Angels not Angles.

Now Gregory did not forget this; but when he was made Bishop of Rome, he sent for a good man named AUGUSTINE, and asked him if he would go to Britain and teach these people to be Christians.

Maria Callcott, *Little Arthur's History of England*

All versions of this famous story are derived from that given by Bede in his *Ecclesiastical History of the English People*, which was completed in 731 and is still one of the most popular history books ever written. King Alfred declared it to be one of the books 'most necessary for all men to know'. Thirty years earlier an anonymous monk of Whitby had written an apparently well-informed *Life of Gregory*, which is perhaps 'the earliest piece of Latin writing of the Anglo-Saxon period'.[1] This work also described Gregory's meeting with the Angles in the marketplace in Rome. Both authors were apparently repeating an oral tradition concerning an incident that had occurred well over a century earlier. As with all orally transmitted stories, while the gist of the tales survives they acquire additional detail and picturesque embroidery as time goes by. Bede and the monk of Whitby were thus presenting slightly different versions of the same oral tradition but Bede seems not 'to have known the Whitby Life which contains a number of stories about Gregory afterwards universally known and told there for the first time but unused by Bede'.[2] The two accounts of the marketplace encounter in Rome are essentially the same, but it is Bede's version that has become part of our popular historical literature.

There have been many editions of Bede's *History*, notably those of John Smith published in 1722 and Charles Plummer in 1896. The twentieth century contributed a revised and updated translation using, for the first time, an eighth-century manuscript now in St Petersburg. This edition presents Bede's story of Gregory and the Anglian boys as follows:

We must not fail to relate the story about St Gregory which has come down to us as a tradition of our forefathers. It explains the reason why he showed such earnest solicitude for the salvation of our race. It is said that one day, soon after some merchants had arrived in Rome, a quantity of merchandise was exposed for sale in the market place. Crowds came to buy and Gregory among them. As well as other merchandise he saw some boys put up for sale, with fair complexions, handsome faces, and lovely hair. On seeing them he asked, so it is said, from what region or land they had been brought. He was told that they came from the island of Britain, whose inhabitants were like that in appearance. He asked again whether those islanders were Christian or still entangled in the errors of heathenism. He was told that they were heathen. Then with a deep-drawn sigh he said, 'Alas that the author of darkness should have men so bright of face in his grip, and that minds devoid of inward grace should bear so graceful in outward form.' Again he asked for the name of the race. He was told that they were called Angli. 'Good', he said, 'they have the face of angels, and such men should be the fellow-heirs of the angels in heaven'. 'What is the name of the kingdom from which they have been brought?' He was told that the men of the kingdom were called Deiri. 'Deiri', he replied, 'De ira? good! snatched from the wrath of Christ and called to his mercy. And what is the name of the king of the land?' He was told that it was Aelle; and playing on the name, he said, 'Alleluia! the praise of God the Creator must be sung in those parts'. So he went to the Bishop of Rome and of the apostolic see, for he himself had not yet been made pope, and asked him to send some ministers of the word to the race of the Angles in Britain to convert them to Christ. He added that he himself was prepared to carry out the task with the help of the Lord provided the pope was willing. But he was unable to perform this mission, because although the pope was willing to grant his request, the citizens of Rome would not permit him to go so far away from the city. Soon after he became pope he fulfilled the task he had so long desired. It is true that he sent other preachers, but he himself helped their preaching to bear fruit by his encouragement and prayers. I have thought it proper to insert this story into this Church History, based as it is on the tradition which we have received from our ancestors.[3]

There is no contemporary evidence for this famous anecdote, not even in Gregory's own extensive writings, and because of this and the difficulty of reconciling Gregory, the austere and earnest monk and author of so many erudite works of theological analysis, with the perpetrator of spontaneous puns in the marketplace in Rome, some modern historians regard the whole episode as apocryphal or ignore it entirely. This scepticism derives, perhaps, from a cautious disinclination to acknowledge the validity of oral traditions as a form of acceptable historical evidence even if, in eighth-century Britain, Bede himself was prepared to do so: 'I have put together this account of the history of the Church in Britain and of the English people in particular, gleaned either from ancient documents or from tradition or from my own knowledge.'[4] In his version of the story of Gregory and the Anglian boys, he makes it quite clear that it is 'based on the tradition which we have received from our forefathers'.

It is worth noting, too, that many monkish writings seem to suggest that the making of enigmatic puns, often very bad ones, was an occupational eccentricity; a similar quirky mind was almost certainly responsible for the tag 'Non Angli sed Angeli', 'Not Angles but Angels', which so neatly and famously summarises Bede's account of Gregory's comment in the marketplace. Even serious and erudite scholars and public figures have been known to indulge in whimsical wordplay in informal conversation; Aristotle himself comments on their appropriate usage.[5] He would not have expected Gregory to refer to such an incident in his later writings. The lack of contemporary evidence is rarely an infallible clue to the veracity of a historical anecdote. More pertinent is the reference to the boys' fair hair and complexions: these would not be likely to be worthy of special comment if the story had originated in Northumbria, where such features were common among the Anglian population, but to an enquiring Italian they would be a curiosity. The monk of Whitby – and Bede too – were almost certainly relating an actual incident that, so the former tells us, took place during the pontificate of Benedict I, that is, between 574 and 578.

It is true that a modern historian might prefer not to include such inherited oral traditions in his work; but while Bede was undoubtedly a meticulous historian, scrupulous in his use of all the material available to him, he was also a teacher, primarily a Christian teacher concerned with spreading Christ's message to all those, particularly in Britain, who were still 'in darkness'. Just as we introduce children to a wider knowledge and understanding of our culture by sharing their delight in storytelling, fairy tales, fantasy and the marvellous, so the early Christian Church looked upon stories, however improbable, from the lives of the saints, and accounts of the miracles attributed to them, as stepping stones toward true faith. Those who listened to these stories were, like children, enchanted and enthralled and subtly prepared for further education. It is also undeniable that most of these anecdotes are delightful in themselves, captivating for both young and old alike. Their literal truth may never be fully established but, as far as the tale of Gregory and the fair-headed boys from Anglia are concerned, the balance may well be in favour of accepting it as based on an actual incident. The judgement of Sir Frank Stenton should be allowed to stand: 'There is no need to reject this famous story, for it contains nothing that is improbable, and it belongs to the oldest stratum of tradition about Gregory's life.'[6]

No shadow of doubt needs to be cast over Bede's emphasis on Gregory's commitment to the conversion of Britain. When, in 597 as Pope Gregory, he sent Augustine on his mission to Britain, he was fulfilling a personal desire that had been in his mind for twenty years. However, political considerations also entered into his plans.

The loss of Britain as a province of the Roman Empire had always been regarded as a particular humiliation, and its recovery by and for the Roman Church would have obvious political advantages. In addition, the collapse of the Empire had left a vacuum in the West which Gregory intended that the Church should fill. The power and dominance in Europe of the medieval papacy had its origins in the vision and policies of Gregory the Great: the conversion of Britain was part of this vision – without Gregory's advice, encouragement and personal intervention, Augustine's mission could easily have ended in ignominious failure.

Patrick Wormald, the twentieth century's pre-eminent historian of Anglo-Saxon England, attached unusual importance to Bede's lengthy account of the story of Gregory and the Angles. He maintained that Bede's historical writings played a decisive 'role in defining English national identity[7] and that his incorporation of the Gregory anecdote in his *History of the English People* was a significant reason for the adoption of 'English' (rather than Germanic 'Saxon') as the national language.

3

Edmund, King of East Anglia: His Martyrdom, 870

In 870 [the Danes] defeated and took prisoner Edmund, the King of East Anglia, to whom they proposed that he should renounce the Christian faith and rule under their supremacy. As this proposal was rejected with scorn and horror, the Danes bound the king naked to a tree, scourged and wounded him with arrows and finally beheaded him. The constancy with which Edmund met his death caused him to be canonised as a saint and martyr.

J. S. Brewer, *The Student's Hume*

The oldest source for the story of King Edmund is the Anglo-Saxon Chronicle, compiled within twenty years of the event. From this we learn that in the autumn of 865 (the chronicle began its year on 24 September so this is entered under 866) 'a great heathen army came to England and took up winter quarters in East Anglia; and there they were supplied with horses and the East Angles made peace with them'. This now-mounted force then left to campaign in Northumbria and Mercia before returning to East Anglia. Under the year 870, the chronicle records that 'in that year the raiding army rode across Mercia into East Anglia, and took up winter quarters at Thetford. And that winter King Edmund fought against them; and the Danes had the victory and killed the king, and conquered all that land'.

This severely factual, dispassionate account, quite unspecific on the manner of Edmund's death, would lead one to assume (as, indeed, Bishop Asser assumed)[1] that he was a casualty of the battlefield, were it not for the unusual fact that within little more than a single generation Edmund had come to be honoured as a saint in East Anglia, and a cult relating to his martyrdom had already begun to emerge. A series of coins bearing the legend SC EAMUND REX (SC means 'sanctus', i.e. holy) appeared during the reign of Edward the Elder (899–924), a sure indication that belief in the king's sainthood was firmly held by men who could have been witnesses to his death at the hands of the Danes only some forty years earlier.[2]

Just over a hundred years passed before a detailed account of Edmund's death appeared, written in the typically florid style characteristic of so many Lives of the saints but with claims to authenticity that lend credibility to the facts it relates. This is the *Passio Sancti Edmundi*, compiled in the late 980s by Abbo of Fleury at the request of the monks of Ramsey Abbey. An account of an event written so long afterwards would usually be treated with extreme caution by historians but, in a prefatory letter addressed to Dunstan, Abbo reminds the archbishop that he (Abbo) heard Dunstan tell the story to the Bishop of Rochester, the Abbot of Malmesbury and others, and that Dunstan had stated that he himself had heard it many years before when it was related to King Athelstan by an old man who swore on oath that, as a young man, he had been King Edmund's armour-bearer on the day when he was put to death.

We know with some certainty that Dunstan was born around 909 and that he was at the court of King Athelstan by his late teenage years, that is about fifty-five years after Edmund's death. The young armour-bearer would then probably be about seventy-five and so quite capable of recalling such a dramatic event in his life. Dunstan would be approximately that age, too, when Abbo heard him regale the bishop and the abbot with the story. The 116 years that elapsed between 870, when Edmund died, and 986, the likely date when Abbo heard the story from Dunstan, can readily be spanned by two human memories. Doubts about the armour-bearer's memory must not be ignored, but where such a barbarous event is concerned the memory would be deeply embedded in the mind and, as a modern psychiatrist has stated, such 'memories, when fixed, are notoriously difficult to erase (indeed they are the most durable features – other, perhaps, than scar tissue – acquired during a person's lifetime)'.[3]

If, therefore, we cut through the rhetoric and verbose embellishments of Abbo, it seems likely that we might have a fairly accurate account of what the armour-bearer actually said concerning the martyrdom of his king. This task was most effectively performed a few years after Abbo by Archbishop Aelfric, who in his *Lives of the Saints* produced a version that is as close as we are likely to get to what really transpired in East Anglia on 20 November 870.[4]

There are a few discrepancies between Abbo's account of the movement of the Danish armies and that given by the Anglo-Saxon Chronicle; the only one of real significance here is between the chronicle's firm statement that Edmund was defeated in battle at Haegelisdun (Hellesdon) and Abbo's omission of this, a deliberate hagiographical device to depict Edmund as a peace-loving Christian, the innocent victim of heathen barbarism. Edmund was taken prisoner during the battle and negotiations appear to have taken place, during which Ivar, the Viking leader, offered to spare Edmund if he would agree to accept Danish supremacy over his kingdom and abandon his Christian faith. Rejecting his bishop's advice to surrender or flee, Edmund replied that he would submit only if Ivar became a Christian. Edmund was seized, stripped and bound and brought before Ivar, who ordered him to be scourged and tied to a tree. He was then made the target for Danish arrows 'until he bristled with them like a hedgehog or a thistle. Finally, in accordance with Viking custom, the king was beheaded.'[5]

Roger of Wendover, writing in the early thirteenth century, adds certain details to Abbo's story that appear to be derived from Scandinavian sources. They do not change in any significant way the manner of Edmund's death, but they do introduce the mysterious figure of Ragnar Lothbroc, for whose existence there is no historical evidence.[6]

According to this account, Lothbroc, a royal Dane, was driven out to sea and eventually landed in East Anglia where he was received by King Edmund. During his visit, Lothbroc's great skill in hawking and hunting aroused the jealousy of one of Edmund's men, called Bern (Beorn), who killed Lothbroc and hid his body in a wood. When the body was discovered, Bern was cast out to sea to perish but he survived and came to land in Denmark, where he told Lothbroc's sons, Ivar and Ubba, that Edmund had killed their father. This led to a revenge attack on East Anglia and, with slight variations, the story of the battle and the death of Edmund is again repeated. The additional detail is added that after the king's beheading, at Bern's suggestion, his head was disposed of in the same wood where the body of Lothbroc was found. As the very existence of Lothbroc as a real person is doubtful, and as Wendover adds nothing of significance to Abbo's account of Edmund's death, we are again left with the Anglo-Saxon Chronicle and the armour-bearer's memory as the most reliable historical evidence for this event.

Wendover complicated the story further by his statement that Edmund was buried at the Suffolk village of Hoxne on the banks of the River Waveney. It seems probable that he based this on the 1101 charter for a Norwich priory, which granted to the priory the church and chapel of St Edmund of Hoxne 'where the same martyr was killed', and in Wendover's own lifetime the Bishop of Norwich had done much to enhance the prestige of St Edmund's chapel at Hoxne, which Domesday Book had recognised as the episcopal see for Suffolk. There is, however, no reliable evidence to link Hoxne with Edmund's death: the Anglo-Saxon Chronicle refers to Haegelisdun, which Domesday Book gives in its natural linguistic development as Hailesduna; this has to be Hellesdon and not Hoxne.

Yet Hoxne has acquired over the centuries all the customary legends and folk tales associated with sites of important shrines and saintly occurrences. An oak tree, alleged to be the very tree to which Edmund was bound while he was shot to death with arrows, was venerated for many centuries until it suddenly disintegrated on 11 September 1848, and, most remarkable of all, a letter to the *Bury Post* at that time claimed that the writer had recovered from the hollow trunk of the tree the 'point of an arrow ... about 4½ or 5 feet from the ground ... the annual ring or layer showing the growth of more than 1000 years.'[7] There is also an inexhaustible spring of water flowing from the spot near where, as local superstition believes, Edmund's head was thrown after his execution: this, the editor sardonically comments, 'may, we have no doubt, be explained by natural causes'. Other legends of St Edmund abound in Hoxne and, whatever the historical evidence may be, Hoxne is unlikely to be replaced by Hellesdon as the 'traditional' site of the awesome events of 20 November 870. Edmund's body was taken to a specially built round chapel in Bury in the tenth century and transferred to the new minster erected there during the reign of Cnut (1016–35). This shrine was destroyed at the Dissolution in 1538, but Edmund's relics were rescued and preserved in Toulouse; they now rest, it is claimed, in Arundel, Sussex.

The New Oxford Dictionary of National Biography (2004), acknowledges that 'some of Abbo's statements may well be true', but describes his account of Edmund's martyrdom as 'a patchwork of hagiographical topoi', the precursor of later hagiographers who created 'a detailed and romantic legend, a piece of attractive literature but not sober history'.

Even so, the early development of his cult cannot be ignored, as it suggests very cogently that a basis of fact lies within the traditional story of his death.

Note: Much of the detail in this chapter is derived from the thorough analysis of the historical background to the subject by Dorothy Whitelocke in her article 'Fact and Fiction in the Legend of St Edmund', *Proceedings of Suffolk Institute of Archaeology* (Vol. 31, 1970) to whom acknowledgement is made.

4

King Alfred:
Did He Burn the Cakes? 878

The King was obliged to disguise himself as a common peasant and to take refuge in the cottage of one of his cowherds who did not know his face. Here, King Alfred, while the Danes sought him far and near, was left alone one day by the cowherd's wife, to watch some cakes which she had put to bake upon the hearth. But being at work on his bows and arrows ... his noble mind forgot the cakes and they were burnt ... The cowherd's wife scolded him well when she came back ... 'You will be ready enough to eat them by-and-by, and yet you cannot watch them, idle dog'.

Charles Dickens, *A Child's History of England*

This, probably the most familiar of all historical anecdotes, first appeared in 1574 when Matthew Parker, Queen Elizabeth's Archbishop of Canterbury, produced the first printed edition of the *Life of King Alfred*, written by Bishop Asser during Alfred's own lifetime. The simple humanity and charm of the story evoked such a popular response that it soon replaced another well-known Alfredian legend associated with the king's retreat to the Isle of Athelney. This was derived from the twelfth-century chronicle of William of Malmesbury and told of a vision of St Cuthbert seen by Alfred in his hiding place, inspiring him to renew his campaign to defeat the Danish invader of his kingdom.[1] This, like many other legends recounted by the early chroniclers, may well have been culled from the confusion of religious, historical and ballad literature that survived from Anglo-Saxon England.

Matthew Parker contributed further to this confusion by including in his edition of Asser's Life of King Alfred extensive extracts from a chronicle known to us as the Annals of St Neots but referred to by Parker as the 'Life of St Neot'. Thus, his account of the story of Alfred and the cakes, from which all subsequent versions are derived, runs as follows[2]:

At this time King Alfred, of whom we have already had much to say, was leading a hazardous life in great difficulties with a few of his nobles and also some soldiers and vassals among the woods and swamps of the county of Somerset. For he was destitute except for what he could get openly or by stealth by raiding the heathen or even the Christians who had submitted to heathen rule. And, as we read in the 'Life of St Neot', he lay in hiding with a certain cowherd. Now it happened one day a countrywoman, the wife of that cowherd, decided to bake some loaves as the king was sitting by the hearth seeing to his bows and arrows and other gear. When the unfortunate woman saw the loaves burning at the fire, she ran up quickly and took them away, upbraiding the invincible king and saying:

'Hi! man, when you see the loaves burning, why can't you turn them round? You'll be glad enough to eat them when they are ready'.

The 'Life of St Neot' referred to by Parker has not survived but other works from various sources all refer to such a chronicle, and all have versions of the Alfred story, differing chiefly in their literary style. In each version, however, the famous 'cakes' that the cowherd's wife was preparing are referred to as loaves (*panes* or *solidam farinam*) and it would seem certain that the herdsman's wife was, indeed, baking bread.

The real difficulty in any attempt to determine the origin of the tale of Alfred and the 'cakes' lies in unravelling the tangle of fact, fiction and dubious chronology that is so often a feature of early chronicles and of the Lives of saints in particular. The Annals of St Neots and other related chronicles state that St Neot died just before 878; they also agree that he was ordained at Glastonbury by Bishop Aelfheah of Winchester, but the only two bishops of Winchester of that name belong to the tenth century (934–51 and 984–1005 respectively). As we also know that the relics of St Neot were transferred from Cornwall at some time between 978 and 1020, it would seem that St Neot lived in the tenth century rather than as a contemporary and kinsman of King Alfred, as the legend would have it.

The original, now lost Life of St Neot may well have been the source of the story of Alfred and the 'cakes', but it appears that the tale had nothing to do with the saint himself. Historians strongly suspect that it was a spurious interpolation included in the author's account of the saint's life: in his 1904 edition of Asser's Life of King Alfred, W. H. Stevenson commented that the story may have been 'a tradition connected with Alfred that the author of the 'Life of St Neot' dragged into his compilation when wearied of filling in gaps of his hero's life from his imagination'.[3]

The first written version of this early tradition occurs in an Old English homily on St Neot, which appears to predate all other Lives of the saint. It is written in Old English rather than Latin and so was almost certainly compiled before the Conquest, probably in the early eleventh century and possibly earlier still, but it is clearly reporting a much older tradition. This version of the story of the 'cakes' differs in some respects from the later and more enduring version:

Alfred ... came safely to Athelney and begged for protection in the house of a herdsman and, moreover, willingly served him and his disagreeable wife. It happened one day that the herdsman's wife heated her oven and the king sat by it, warming himself at the fire, the household not knowing that he was the king. Then the disagreeable wife suddenly started up and, in a sharp voice, said to the king, 'See that you turn the loaves ['hlafes' means 'bread'] so that they do not burn; for I notice everyday that you are a great eater'. He was at once obedient to the disagreeable wife, because of necessity he had to be.[4]

This presents the story less dramatically than later versions and consequently it has a deeper ring of truth. It also confirms that the herdsman's wife was baking loaves of bread rather than cakes as we understand those confections. Throughout Northern Europe at that time bread was baked on a griddle as 'haver-bread', or flat oatcakes, and this has to be the origin of the 'cakes' in the story. Finally, in this version there is no suggestion that Alfred did, in fact, allow the bread to burn: the housewife instructed him to see that they did not burn and, we are told, he obeyed her orders, because, in the circumstances, he had to be careful to do so.

Final proof of this simple story is not to be expected and its vigorous survival for at least a thousand years owes much to the high esteem in which Alfred has always been held in the annals of English kingship. He is the only English monarch to bear the title 'Great'; he is the only king in English history before 1066 to be part of popular general knowledge; during the seventeenth century he was credited with the creation of those English institutions that concerned the rights of the common man – trial by jury, a code of common law, the principle that the king should govern with advice (the Witenagemot), the encouragement of education and literacy – all based on an enlightened royal government. The real and imagined achievements of Alfred were grafted onto a legendary reputation that portrayed him as the model king and the model Englishman. Such a paragon among men would certainly not have burned the bread he was asked to keep an eye on, but this temporary absence of mind gave him a familiar quality of human vulnerability, with which everyone could sympathise.

It may be of some significance that the same story appears in the Old Norse saga of Ragnar Lodbrok (Ragnar Hairy Breeks), a legendary (and probably mythical) Viking leader of that era. The tale related that he, too, 'burned the loaves' he had been asked to watch, a moment of weakness in a man of 'heroic' achievements. It is possible that the Danes in the Danelaw used this story as propaganda against Alfred in their conflict for supremacy in England and that it had no vestige of truth, but without supporting evidence this must be no more than speculation.

5

King Edgar:
The Commendation at Chester, 973

He was completely governed by St Dunstan, and other vehement monks, who, in return, wrote the history of his life, and praised him as the best king who had ever lived. We are not able, at this distance of time, to know how much of this praise he deserved. We are told that justice was so well and wisely administered in his time, that travellers had no longer any fear of robbers; and that he was so much courted and honoured that eight kings rowed him in his royal barge on the river Dee. It appears certain that he attended diligently to the maritime affairs of his kingdom; and that he left so large a fleet that the Danes never returned to molest him.

Mrs Markham's *History of England*

Mrs Markham's cautious assessment of King Edgar worthily reflects the limited extent of historical knowledge of his reign in the early nineteenth century. As Professor Stenton commented more than a century later, 'his reign is singularly devoid of incident'[1] but assiduous research over many years has helped towards a much fuller knowledge and understanding of these sixteen years of unusual tenth-century peace in Britain.

The years of Edgar's reign (959–75) were marked by a lull in the attacks on England from the Norwegian and Danish Vikings, whose attempts to overrun the whole country had been thwarted by the military exploits of Saxon kings from Alfred to Athelstan. Edgar was able to consolidate the achievements of his predecessors, and successfully established their claim to imperial dominion over all Britain. He is usually regarded as the first king of all England.

It would be wrong, however, to suggest that the 'peace' of Edgar's reign was achieved merely by resting on the laurels won by his forbears. Within Britain, the relationships between the several political entities were very fragile and it was among the outstanding achievements of these turbulent centuries that Edgar succeeded in reconciling not only the sensitive kings and princes of Scotland and Wales to his supremacy but, more importantly, the haughty earls of the Danelaw, who were given virtual freedom to govern themselves. Edgar 'was the first to recognise in legislation that the Danish east of England was no longer a conquered province but an integral part of the English realm'.[2] In return, they formally recognised Edgar's overlordship. This relationship was confirmed by a ceremony of homage known as commendation, a term frequently found in Domesday Book.

The famous meeting at Chester in 973 was arranged to mark such an act of commendation. It was a theatrical occasion staged to demonstrate, with visual emphasis, Edgar's unquestioned supremacy. Three manuscripts of the Anglo-Saxon Chronicle record that Edgar arrived in Chester with his impressive fleet to receive the pledge of six kings to serve him by land and sea.[3] This is given strong contemporary support by Aelfric, Abbot of Eynsham and a close friend of Bishop Aethelwold, who, with Dunstan, helped to direct Edgar's policies. In his Life of St Swithin, Aelfric, in a passage contrasting the misery of the reign of Aethelred II with the peace and stability of Edgar's time, firmly states that 'all the kings of this island, of Cumbrians and Scots, eight kings, came to Edgar once upon a time on one day, and they all bowed to Edgar's government'.[4]

This convincing contemporary evidence for the story is amplified by an account written just over a century later in the chronicle attributed to Florence of Worcester, who died in 1118. It is here that the famous rowing on the River Dee is first recorded. Florence asserts that the eight kings were Kenneth II, King of Scots; Malcolm, King of the Cumbrians; Maccus, king of many islands; Dufnal (Dunmail), King of Strathclyde; Jacob, King of Gwynedd; Huwel (son of Idwal, an earlier King of Gwynedd and rival claimant to Jacob); Siferth and Juchil, all of whom, except the last two, can be identified, a fact which lends credence to the chronicler's list. As Stenton commented, 'No Anglo-Norman writer, inventing a list of names with which to garnish an ancient annal, could have come as close as this to fact or probability.'[5]

There seems little doubt, therefore, that these kings and princes did gather at Chester in 973 to acknowledge Edgar's supremacy, and historically this is the essential importance of the occasion. We can be less certain about the episode of the rowing although the balance of probability would suggest that it did, in fact, take place as a dramatic and symbolic act to demonstrate, in public, the pledges given in the privacy of Edgar's palace at Chester. The Worcester Chronicle relates that, with Edgar at the rudder, the royal barge was rowed by the eight kings and princes from the palace to the priory church of St John and back again.[6] In an age when the nature of royal authority was so essentially personal, and therefore extremely fragile, such symbolic gestures assumed a greater importance than in later centuries, when the power of the monarch was firmly established. We should, perhaps, not overlook the report that, just before the events at Chester, there had taken place at Bath (among the remains of Imperial Rome) a ceremony of enormous significance in the history of the English monarchy, a ceremony charged with symbolism. This was Edgar's long-delayed Coronation, with its historic binding of Crown and Church, the swearing of the Coronation Oath, and the symbolic rituals of anointing and investiture with the regalia of ring, sword, crown, sceptre and rod. Acts of homage were associated with the ceremony, too, and so all the events at Chester readily fit into the picture and the rowing of the royal barge on the Dee begins to appear more like historical fact and less like a chronicler's fanciful embellishment.

There was symbolism, but also a shrewd political pragmatism, in Edgar's introduction of an advanced monetary system. In 973 he ordered all coins then in circulation to be called in, melted down and re-struck as uniform pennies, which were to be the common currency throughout the Kingdom of England. All dies were cut in London and distributed to forty local mints, the number of which was constantly added to. No manorial or episcopal mints were permitted as in some European countries; the only legal currency was that in the king's name and this was subject to change at regular intervals to guard against forgery and debasement. Edgar's institution of a national coinage under royal control set the pattern for the English currency for several centuries. It was a powerful tool – and symbol – in the process of gaining acceptance of the concept of a united English Kingdom.[7]

Edgar's reign is also notable for the development of a new and vigorous monastic culture and for his encouragement of the regeneration of the Church, known as the tenth-century reform, all achieved by his close working relationship with men of outstanding ability and commitment, such as St Dunstan and St Aethelwold. This, and the stability brought to the country by sixteen years fortuitously free from foreign attacks (which also greatly assisted Edgar's other policies), made his reign seem like a golden age, the high point of the Anglo-Saxon monarchy, particularly when it was succeeded by a long period of weak and disputed kingship and by the resumption of constant and ultimately successful Viking invasions. It is ironic that, within fifty years of the act of homage to King Edgar, Cnut, a Danish Viking, should be king over all England, and that he, too, should receive symbolic homage as he was rowed in his barge on the River Ouse close by the powerful (and invulnerable) island-abbey of Ely where, according to the ancient song,

Merry sungen the monkes in Ely
When Cnut King rowed by.

The New Oxford Dictionary of National Biography (2004) draws attention to the fine differences in the chronicle accounts of the meeting at Chester. The Anglo-Saxon Chronicle states that the kings and princes 'made a treaty' with Edgar; Aelfric's chronicle claims that they 'did homage' to him; Henry of Huntingdon notes that they only 'pledged loyalty that was due to him as lord'. The importance of the whole occasion is stated to be in the awesome demonstration of English sea power.

6

King Cnut:
Turning Back the Tide, 1020s

One day as they were walking upon the seashore, the nobles began, as usual, to tell Canute how powerful he was.

'All England obeys you,' they said.

'And not only England, but Denmark, Norway and Sweden.'

'Should you desire it, you need but command all the nations of the world, and they will kneel before you as their king and lord.'

'You are king on sea and land. Even the waves obey you.'

Now this was foolish talk, and Canute, who was a wise man, did not like it. He thought he would teach these silly nobles a lesson. So he ordered his servants to bring a chair.

When they had brought it, he made them set it on the shore close to the waves. The servants did as they were told, and Canute sat down, while the nobles stood around him.

Then Canute spoke to the waves. 'Go back,' he said, 'I am your lord and master, and I command you not to flow over my land. Go back and do not dare to wet my feet.'

But the sea, of course, neither heard nor obeyed him. The tide was coming in, and the waves rolled nearer and nearer, until the king's feet and robe were wet.

Then Canute rose, and turning sternly to his nobles said, 'Do you still tell me that I have power over the waves? Oh! Foolish men, do you not know that to God alone belongs such power. He alone rules earth and sky and sea, and we and they alike are His subjects and must obey Him.'

The nobles felt how foolish they had been, and did not try again to flatter Canute in such a silly way. From that day, too, Canute never wore his crown, but placed it upon a figure of Christ in the minster at Winchester, as a proof of his humility.

H. T. Marshall, *Our Island Story*

On 30 November 1016, Edmund Ironside, son of Aethelraed the Unraed (the Anglo-Saxon Chronicle referred in 1011 to Aethelraed as 'un-raed': lacking in counsel, indecisive. His nickname, 'unready', is an obvious corruption of this), died suddenly at the age of thirty-five, and Cnut the Dane was recognised as King of all England. With the consent of the bishops, abbots and ealdormen Cnut gained control over the entire kingdom and, with his claims to Denmark and Norway, he had suddenly become, at the age of twenty-two, the most powerful ruler in Northern Europe. 'He was the first Viking leader to be admitted into the civilised fraternity of Christian kings.'[1]

Cnut had been baptised into the Christian Church at the age of five or six and he seems to have adopted his new faith with a genuine enthusiasm; he was shrewd enough to note that in England the Church was already a national institution, established for several centuries and with powerful influence throughout the kingdom through its system of dioceses, abbacies and councils, all enforcing its body of canon law and all with 300 years of authority behind them. The Church was the strongest institution in the land and, little more than fifty years earlier, in the reign of King Edgar, had sealed the bond between the English Church and the English monarchy, which was to last for all succeeding generations. The Church anointed the monarch at the coronation ceremony in irrefutable acknowledgement that he was the agent of God appointed to protect and promote the interests of the Christian Church. Cnut's own Coronation gave his claim to the throne 'a much-needed aura of legitimacy ... Once crowned, his position had divine sanction, was regarded by the Church as sacrosanct, and so was considerably strengthened.'[2] There is no reason to cast doubt on the sincerity of Cnut's Christian faith, but he was already well versed in the exigencies of *realpolitik* and he accepted that, certainly in eleventh-century England, a strong monarchy and a strong Church went hand in hand.

It is not easy to assess the piety of the actions of medieval monarchs, precisely because of this bond between religion and politics in English history. The monastic chroniclers naturally make much of acts of piety shown by these kings and, conversely, made a special point of commenting critically on any monarch who, they considered, had notably failed in this respect. William the Conqueror's reign was stained with blood and cruelty, but this was, it seems, redeemed by his patronage of the Church; his successor, William Rufus, less charitable towards the Church, was roundly condemned for his catalogue of sins, especially blasphemy, immorality, avarice, personal extravagance and also his long hair and trendy clothes. Orderic Vitalis, William of Malmesbury and others found a clear link between all this and the king's apparent lack of respect for the Church.

Contemporary chroniclers had no such problem with Cnut. Professor Stenton commented many years ago, 'It is Cnut's distinction as a ruler that from the beginning of his reign he set himself to win the respect of the English church',[3] a sound political judgement at the time and followed up with numerous acts of piety to cement a relationship highly beneficial to both parties. David Hume, a sceptical critic of moral postures, while fully acknowledging that Cnut built churches, endowed monasteries, enriched the ecclesiastics and bestowed revenues for the support of chantries, as well as undertaking a pilgrimage to Rome, which brought notable benefits to English pilgrims, cast doubt on the merits of this form of religious devotion. Cnut, he concluded, 'instead of making compensation to those whom he had injured by his former acts of violence, employed himself entirely in those exercises of piety which the monks represented as the most meritorious', but he conceded that 'by this spirit of devotion, no less than by his equitable and politic administration, he gained, in good measure, the affection of his subjects'.[4] It would, perhaps, be an equitable judgement to say that Cnut's religious devotion was genuine, but that as a practical and pragmatic politician he knew full well the value of any public demonstration of piety.

Thus we may reasonably conclude that the monk of St Omer, who compiled the contemporary chronicle known as Encomium Emmae, was recording actual events in his description of Cnut's pious acts on his way to Rome in 1027, and that Symeon of Durham's story of Cnut walking barefoot for the final few miles of his pilgrimage to the church of St Cuthbert had a trustworthy basis of fact.[5] A similar humility may be read into the well-known story of the gift of a golden, jewelled cross presented by Cnut and his wife Emma to the New Minster in Winchester – the contemporary drawing of this event (preserved in the 'Liber Vitae' of New Minster and dated around 1020) depicts an angel holding the crown over Cnut's head and pointing upwards to a figure of Christ in Majesty, the clear inference being that the king's authority is derived from God and is therefore sacrosanct, but also that his power is less than God's.

The same spirit of planned piety might easily have inspired the most famous of all the stories illustrating Cnut's acts of religious devotion and humility; and if a contemporary chronicle had survived that contained this story, it would have been more readily accepted as an account of an actual event. This is, of course, the tale of how Cnut attempted to turn back the tide, a story that has entered the English language as a figure of speech. Unfortunately, no contemporary chronicle refers to this incident, which first appeared in Henry of Huntingdon's 'Historia Anglorum', written just a hundred years later. Henry is an important source for Anglo-Norman history, but he was inclined to embroider the stories he collected from years before his own lifetime. The story of Cnut and the waves was a perfect instrument for him to emphasise his undeviating disdain for worldly vanities. Cnut is portrayed as a wise monarch demonstrating in a most dramatic way the shallow folly of his courtiers' flattery.[6] It is unfortunate that, in telling his story, Henry of Huntingdon gives no indication of precisely where this piece of theatre took place.

Several places have claimed to be the scene where Cnut played out his little drama with the tide. Geoffrey Gaimar, the twelfth-century Anglo-Norman chronicler, located it on the banks of the River Thames;[7] Gainsborough in Yorkshire has also been suggested, but since the citizens of this town murdered Cnut's father, Swein, it seems unlikely that Cnut held his court there; a strong tradition in Sussex favours the then-important port of Bosham, much patronised by royalty and a popular point of embarkation. The pre-Conquest church there acquired great wealth from royal bounty, and tradition maintains that a royal chapel there contained the tomb of a daughter of Cnut who died in childhood.

None of these traditions can be substantiated and there is a similar lack of verifiable evidence to aid an assessment of the entire story. It is such a remarkable demonstration of Cnut's political piety that one would expect to find it in a contemporary chronicle such as the Encomium Emmae but here there is no reference to it. On the other hand, however much he was given to embellishing them, Henry of Huntingdon has never been accused of inventing his anecdotes. It seems certain that he was able to consult chronicles, then in existence but long since lost, and also other manuscripts that have survived but only with drastic editing. The lost texts of the Anglo-Saxon Chronicle and the surviving text of the Worcester Chronicle are oft-quoted examples. If we do not believe that Henry of Huntingdon dreamt up the entire story a hundred years after Cnut's lifetime, then this may be a possible explanation for its omission from the contemporary sources now available to us. In the context of this mystery a closer look at the illustration in the 'Liber Vitae' of New Minster referred to above might be helpful. Henry of Huntingdon stated that after failing to turn back the tide Cnut never wore his crown again but placed it on a crucifix. In the drawing the crown appears to be about to be removed from Cnut's head by an attendant angel, whose pointing finger is suggesting that the power invested in the crown is derived from God. Symbols were of immense significance in religious artistry throughout the Middle Ages and the symbolism of the king's surrender of his crown to adorn a crucifix would be well understood. Our monkish chronicler would almost certainly have been acquainted with the record and the significance of this ostentatious event.

David Hume's account of this story in his *History of England* (1761) was drawn from Henry of Huntingdon and this is the version that has come down to us:

> Some of his flatterers breaking out one day in admiration of his grandeur, exclaimed that everything was possible for him: upon which the monarch, it is said, ordered his chair to be set on the sea-shore, while the tide was rising; and as the waters approached, he commanded them to retire, and to obey the voice of him who was lord of the ocean. He feigned to sit for some time in expectation of their submission;

but when the sea still advanced towards him, and began to wash him with its billows, he turned to his courtiers, and remarked to them, that every creature in the universe was feeble and impotent, and that power resided with one Being alone, in whose hands were all the elements of nature; and who could say to the ocean, 'Thus far shalt thou go and no farther'; and who could level with his nod the most towering piles of human pride and ambition.[8]

This, and many another of Cnut's numerous acts of piety, can readily be seen as planned and deliberate with an important political purpose, for, whatever his personal commitment to the Christian Church, he was above all an adroit politician with a perceptive insight into the many problems he had to deal with. He was a foreigner on the throne of England; he belonged to the race of Vikings who had ravaged and plundered England for 200 years; he had murdered Aethelred's son and a number of English noblemen and sent the sons of Edmund Ironside to Sweden with orders that they were to be put to death; he had levied a crippling Danegeld first on London and then on the whole country; and he had had the effrontery to marry Emma, Aethelred's widow. Yet he ruled the kingdom for almost twenty years, and, secured by a Danish army and aristocracy, he gave it a period of stability such as it had not enjoyed for generations. He seemed acutely aware of the strength of English conservatism, and introduced no radical changes but reinforced the strong monarchy created by the late Saxon kings, continued the alliance between Church and king and consolidated the ancient laws of the kingdom by his Code, which at the time was favourably received 'as a restatement of the good customs of the past by a king who was strong enough to enforce them'.[9] Cnut was also nominal ruler of the kingdoms of Denmark and Norway and, although his success in governing either of these turbulent countries was limited, it was his control of the great trade route through the Channel and the North Sea, and via the Kattegat into the Baltic, that gave him importance in the courts of Europe and brought England and Scandinavia into permanent contact with the rest of the Continent. Concessions from the papacy for English churchmen and greater protection for English pilgrims, the cession of the province of Schleswig to Denmark by the emperor and the marriage of Cnut's daughter, Gunnhild, to the emperor's son were all indicators of Cnut's diplomatic skills and political importance as overlord of the North. Cnut grasped from the outset of his reign that his royal power, at home and abroad, could be greatly enhanced by close collaboration with the Church and by apparently stage-managed acts of piety. This is not to imply that Cnut's religious faith was no more than skin-deep but, as a modern interpreter of his reign has commented, it does suggest that he fully understood that 'good religion could be good politics, good politics could require good religion, and there can be no doubt that Cnut threw himself into certain aspects of his role with zest'.[10]

The story of Cnut's challenge to the tide may or may not be apocryphal but it is certainly totally consistent with all the other tales of his public acts of piety, with which the chronicles regale us, and it is indisputably part of our language and literature.

The New Oxford Dictionary of National Biography (2004) makes the philosophical comment that the king had been encouraged to identify himself with Christ and 'thus, paradoxical as it may seem, Cnut's acts of piety were really statements about the elevated nature of his power'.

7

Lady Godiva:
Her Ride Through Coventry, *c.* 1041

It is related of this lady that in order to free the inhabitants of Coventry from a heavy tax laid on them by her husband, she readily consented to a very extraordinary condition, on which the earl promised to ease them of their burden, namely, that she should ride stark naked from one end of the town to the other. This condition gave the burghers little hope of being relieved. But Godiva performed it, covering her body with her hair, and commanding all persons to keep within doors, and from their windows, on pain of death. Notwithstanding this severe penalty, there was one who could not forbear giving a look, out of curiosity, but it cost him his life. In memory of this event, there is a statue of a man looking out of a window, always kept in a certain house in Coventry.

Paul de Rapin de Thoyras, *The History of England*, first published 1723–25, 4th edition, translated by N. Tindal, 1761

'+ Ego Godiva Comitissa diu istud desideravi' ('I Countess Godiva have long wished for this'). Thus did Godiva, wife of Leofric, Earl of Mercia, literally make her mark on history as her name was appended to the charter that founded her Abbey of Spalding in Lincolnshire. In earlier years she had made generous benefactions to the monastery at Stow, near Lincoln, and to religious houses at Worcester, Evesham, Chester, Much Wenlock, Leominster, Burton-upon-Trent and, most notably, at Coventry where, together with her husband, she bestowed such lavish gifts of gold, jewels and holy relics, that the medieval chronicler William of Malmesbury wrote that 'the very walls seemed too narrow for all this treasure'. Even earlier in her life, before her marriage to Leofric, she may have given land from her East Anglian estates to the monastery at Ely. Godiva – or Godgifu, to accord her her Old English name – was, in her own right, a woman of substantial wealth, influence and status, and, as the wife of one of the three most powerful earls in the kingdom, she was one of the most eminent women of Anglo-Saxon England, ranking alongside Aethelflaed, Lady of the Mercians and daughter of Alfred the Great, and Emma, Queen successively of King Aelthelred II and King Cnut – and ultimately, for quite incongruous reasons, more famous than either of these.

Godgifu married Leofric sometime before 1040 when he was already a key figure in the years of political instability caused by the disputed succession to the throne on the death of Cnut. There is evidence to suggest that their marriage was a successful partnership. Both had a sense of family honour and loyal service to Church and Crown combined with a generous perception of the Christian duties of the rich and powerful. Leofric was shrewd in his political judgements and moderate in his counsels, firm in action but magnanimous in victory, and he always upheld the dignity and authority appropriate to one of the king's chief advisers. There is no shred of evidence to support the Victorian portrayal of Leofric as a callous, overbearing tyrant utterly indifferent to the plight of the poor or to the humiliation of his wife, as he is depicted in Tennyson's popular 1842 poem 'Godiva', notably in one dramatic passage, where Godiva pleads with her husband to relieve the people of Coventry of the tax he is alleged to have imposed upon them:

> She told him of their tears,
> And prayed him, 'If they pay this tax, they starve'
> Whereat he stared, replying, half-amazed,
> 'You would not let your little finger ache
> For such as these?' – 'But I would die,' said she.
> He laughed, and swore by Peter and by Paul;
> Then filliped at the diamond in her ear;
> 'Oh ay, ay, ay, you talk!' – 'Alas!' she said,
> 'But prove me what it is I would not do.'
> And from a heart as rough as Esau's hand,
> He answered, 'Ride you naked through the town,
> And I repeal it'; and nodding, as in scorn,
> He parted, with great strides among his dogs.[1]

Tennyson's poem proved to be a landmark in the Victorian transformation of the Godiva legend. Henceforward the story had little affinity with its alleged historic origins or with the accretions of the later Middle Ages. Godiva was idealised both as an embodiment of all the feminine virtues and as a model for the first champions of women's rights – Josephine Butler even identified Godiva with those Victorian women who risked opprobrium through their social work among London's prostitutes. The famous naked ride through Coventry was the subject of paintings by Sir Edwin Landseer and John Collier, both of whom placed a discreet emphasis on Godiva's nudity but managed to convey both shame and sacrifice. In Coventry itself, the traditional Godiva processions were once more revived but this time the atmosphere was more carnivalesque, although much was done to further popular acquaintance with the latest version of the Godiva legend by sales – numbered in tens of thousands – of ballads such as the 'Coventry Garland', which portrayed Godiva as a saintly heroine, Leofric as an overbearing, supercilious husband and Peeping Tom as a despicable villain, whose terrible punishment was no more than he deserved. Even the historic legend was rapidly fading as more and more emphasis was put on the moralistic and erotic aspects of the story. The twentieth-century film industry seized upon the story: Maureen O'Hara in the 1955 film *Lady Godiva* fulfilled exactly the popular image of Godiva as a naked beauty with long blonde hair riding through the town on a horse, but on this occasion she was performing this historic deed at the behest of an arrogant Norman in order to 'prove' the loyalty of the Saxons. Other films and a number of dramas, pantomimes, ballads, poems and songs have perpetuated the Godiva legend, but the original medieval story has long been overlaid with irrelevance and trivialisation. In North America, Godiva's image is best known as the logo of 'Godiva chocolatier', while in Britain her most recent manifestation appeared in a powerful late poem by Sylvia Plath, in which 'white Godiva' on her horse Ariel is no longer a naked wife forced into a humiliating horseback ride but 'God's lioness' furiously galloping like an arrow into the sunrise – 'the red eye, the cauldron of the morning'. As a recent study observed, the real eleventh-century Godgifu 'would never be able to imagine, not in a thousand years, what others have fantasised through the legend of Lady Godiva'.[2]

The only certain historical facts in the story of Godiva are that she was a real person who was born in the early part of the eleventh century and died in 1067, that she was a wealthy landowner in her own right, wealth which she used to endow and make generous benefactions to churches and monastic foundations in various parts of her estates, notably the abbey at Coventry, which she founded in partnership with her husband and where both were buried side by side. She was the wife of Leofric, Earl of Mercia, a man of wise counsel in the country's affairs at a time of political uncertainty, and who was careful to maintain the authority and dignity of both the Crown and his own position. Their son, Aelfgar, was a man of little political judgement, who was fortunate to be allowed to succeed to his father's earldom; their granddaughter, Ealdgyth, married Harold Godwineson and so in 1066 became the last Queen of Anglo-Saxon England.

It is remarkable that there is no reference in any contemporary chronicle to the incident of the naked ride, for most medieval chroniclers avidly noted down any item of 'news' that came their way. The story suddenly appears 200 years later in the St Albans Chronicles known as the Flores Historiarum and the Chronica Majora, compiled by Roger of Wendover and by Matthew Paris, his successor as the abbey's resident historian in 1235. These two chroniclers were once treated as authoritative sources but modern historians now treat them with caution, as their unreliability has been convincingly demonstrated. It is now accepted that factual accuracy was not a prime consideration and that both these chroniclers, Matthew Paris especially, were much given to imaginative embellishment of any story they found.[3] Nevertheless, their version of events was to be the principal source for most subsequent medieval chroniclers. William of Malmesbury, writing 100 years before Roger of Wendover and Matthew Paris, referred to Godiva only as the saintly wife of Leofric, but the St Albans chroniclers produced this startling addition to her biography:

Countess Godiva, renowned for her piety, anxious that the town of Coventry should be relieved of the burden of a heavy tax, pleaded with her husband on many occasions to free the town of this obligation; and when the count rebuked her for being so persistent in asking for something which would be damaging to his authority, he firmly ordered her not to raise the matter again; but with feminine obstinacy she persevered in her pleading, until she finally received this answer from her exasperated husband: 'Mount your horse naked,' he said 'and ride across the town's marketplace from one end to the other, with all the people assembled, and when you return you shall have what you ask for.' And to this Godiva replied, 'And, if I am willing to do this, will you give me your permission? to which he replied, 'I will.' Then the Countess, dear to God, escorted by two soldiers, mounted her horse naked as agreed, and released her hair from the fastenings on her head and let it fall to cover her whole body, with only her shining white legs visible; and so she rode across the marketplace seen by no-one and returned joyfully to her husband who was astounded by this amazing feat. Count Leofric released the people of Coventry from their obligations and confirmed the town's charter with his own seal.[4]

This is an astonishing and fascinating story, as its subsequent history shows, but if it is exposed to historical scrutiny its veracity is immediately called into question. Godiva had absolutely no necessity to plead with Leofric to free the citizens of Coventry from a tax he had imposed: Coventry was Godiva's own estate; she alone had the right to levy a tax on the town, so she had no cause to plead with her husband as the chronicle describes. The concept that a woman could hold land directly from the king, and quite independent of her husband, was familiar to Anglo-Saxon society. It is possible that the tax referred to was the much-resented 'heregeld', a levy imposed by the Danish King of England, Harthacnut, in 1041 for the support of his army and ships, but even if this were true Godiva would have had to appeal to the king for relief and not to Leofric. Coventry in the mid-eleventh century was not a 'town' large enough to have a marketplace, but a village with a population of probably little more than 300; its principal building, dominating the village, would have been the monastery, an improbable scene for Godiva's alleged horseback ride. By the date of the St Albans Chronicle it had grown rapidly and had a population of some 5,000, but even then it had to wait another century before it received a charter; so the reference to Leofric's 'confirming' Coventry's charter is an anachronism. Finally, all that we know of Leofric's character is inconsistent with the manner in which he is portrayed in this account. He was acutely conscious that, at a time of political uncertainty, the authority and dignity of the king and his representatives had to be seen to be upheld and, as Professor Frank Barlow briskly commented, 'Leofric, Earl of Mercia, a religious and loyal man, is unlikely to have permitted or subjected his wife to such a humiliating ordeal ... As one of the most eminent men of his time he would not have demeaned either his wife or himself by being associated with such an event.'[5]

This is the view taken by all modern historians and, it would seem, by many of the principal medieval chroniclers, for it is curious – and significant – that the story of Godiva's ride is not mentioned in such early chronicles as those of Simeon of Durham, Henry of Huntingdon, John of Worcester, Orderic Vitalis, William of Malmesbury, Roger of Hoveden and Walter of Coventry – all of whom were writing in the century between around 1120 and 1220.

The problem still remains of discovering how it was possible for such a story to have suddenly come to light, with so many details already in place, in the year 1250. We may safely assume that Matthew Paris provided imaginative embellishment when he came to chronicle his version, but we cannot assume that he invented the entire story. For a possible answer to this question we have to look ahead several hundred years to the 1560s and the chronicle of Richard Grafton, in which he refers to a lost chronicle written by Geoffrey, prior of the monastery at Coventry between 1216 and 1235. According to Grafton, the Godiva legend appeared in this missing document and he published his own paraphrase of Geoffrey's account. It is perhaps worth noting that, at the time when Geoffrey was prior, the monastery at Coventry was struggling to recover from its ransacking by Hugh, Bishop of Chester, in 1189, when much damage was done and most of the charters pertaining to the foundation were destroyed, in particular those (some forged) that detailed the privileges and exemptions from various obligations formerly granted to the monastery. The town – now with a flourishing market – was also seeking to reaffirm similar privileges and, lacking a charter or other urban status, was striving after its own identity, separate from the religious foundation in its midst. Geoffrey was, it appears, very much occupied with this dual problem. In 1241 a new Prior of Coventry and a number of his monks spent a whole year in residence at the abbey of St Albans where Matthew Paris was now chronicler and it was only a few years later that his version of the Godiva legend appeared and rapidly became widely known. We do not know how trustworthy Grafton's work is – John Stow, his contemporary chronicler, accused him of garbling his sources – but he had a profound effect on the subsequent history of the Godiva legend. For he introduced new material into the (by his day) well-established basic details of the story, which he claimed were derived from Geoffrey of Coventry. From Grafton we learn that, before embarking on her ride, Godiva called a meeting of 'all those that were Magistrates and rulers of the said City of Coventry' to explain the conditions imposed on her by Leofric but added that 'for the reverence of womanhood' she would only agree to the ride if

> straight commandment should be given throughout all the city, that every person should shut in their houses and windows, and none so hardy to look out into the streets nor remain in the streets, upon a great pain, so that when the time came of her outriding none saw her, but her husband and such as were present with him, and she and her gentlewoman to wait upon her, galloped through the town, where the people might hear the treading of her horse, but they saw her not.[6]

It is curious that there are such significant differences between two almost contemporary chronicles, and this must cast doubt on the trust we can place in either of them as to the origin or veracity of the story they have to tell.

Students of ancient folklore have pointed to certain similarities between the Godiva story as told in the thirteenth-century chronicles and traditional tales from Celtic and Nordic mythology. The Celtic goddess Epona, the Welsh goddess Rhiannon and the Norse heroine Aslaug, of Ragnar Lodbrok's Saga, were all associated with legends having links, however tenuous, with the conventional story of Lady Godiva, notably in certain fertility cults involving a woman, clothed or naked, riding a horse in a ceremony designed to bring benefits to the community. At the time when Roger Wendover and Matthew Paris were writing, there was a keen interest in these ancient legends, largely inspired by the romances of chivalry then popular throughout Western Europe and sure to be known to the much-travelled and much-visited monks in the monasteries of England and France. One of the important developments of early medieval literature was the transfer of these traditional stories from the oral to the written form, and authors made the most of this unprecedented opportunity to give full rein to their literary imagination. There is a stark contrast between the bare bones of factual information given in, for example, the Anglo-Saxon Chronicle or the sedate prose of the Venerable Bede and the embellished journalism of Matthew Paris or Henry of Huntingdon.[7]

The comment of Professor Donaghue in his recent study of the Godiva legend effectively summarises the historian's problems in this matter: 'In the absence of any other explanation, it is best to assume that at some point between 1067 and about 1200 someone, for unknown reasons, created the fiction of Godiva's ride in the form made familiar by the St Albans chronicle.'[8]

Grafton's sixteenth-century 'discovery' that, before Godiva made her ride, an edict had been issued ordering everyone to stay indoors and no one should be 'so hardy to looke out into the streetes … upon great paine', marked the development of a new stage in the evolution of the legend. John Brompton, abbot of Jervaulx in 1436, had already modified the St Albans account by dispensing with Godiva's gentlewoman and military escort and all the assembled townsfolk, leaving her a lone, naked figure riding across an empty marketplace. Grafton gave this the 'authority' of the lost chronicle of Prior Geoffrey in the form of a magisterial edict. It was almost inevitable that once a ban was placed on spying on the lady a rogue citizen would be invented who had defied it.

And so the legend of 'Peeping Tom' was born. A small statue made of oak and dating from the early sixteenth century still exists in Coventry and is said to be a representation of this 'voyeur'. It was an essential participant in the Coventry 'Godiva processions' from their beginning in 1678. For some time, he was known only as 'the Peeper'; Daniel Defoe, on his tour through Great Britain, wrote of 'the poor fellow that peep'd out of the window to see her', but a ballad of 1723 gave him an occupation: 'a poor taylor, who would needs be peeping, and was struck blind'. This was a less severe punishment than that stated in Paul de Rapin's *History of England*, published at about the same date, where we read that 'there was one who could not forbear giving a look, out of curiosity, but it cost him his life'. In 1765 he was given a name: in the Coventry archives for that year appears an item for expenses for a new wig and for the repainting of the statue of Peeping Tom, a name that was quickly incorporated into English idiom as the expression for a furtive voyeur.

The Victorians were fascinated by the various strands of the legend. Their apparent preoccupation with the figure of the naked Godiva had a strong erotic interest – even the queen expressed a close interest in the way Sir Edwin Landseer had portrayed her in his painting *Lady Godiva's Prayer*, while John Collier's youthful Godiva was shown sitting *astride* her horse, historically correct but distinctly shocking in 1898. The same age also brought a steady stream of ballads, plays, poems, satires, sculptures and even peep shows – all based on aspects of the story but steadily moving further away from its historical setting.

The twentieth century continued this process, making full use of the new medium of cinematic film to emphasise the erotic and the voyeuristic elements in the fantasy legend that the Godiva story had by then become. Nothing better illustrates the prodigious distance now existing between the historic Godiva of Mercia and the modern bizarre interpretations of the Godiva legend than a short story by Alberto Moravia, in which a husband fantasises about his wife playing out Godiva's naked ride with her long hair partly covering her body and bribes her to agree to do this in return for the gift of a special stallion she has shown a particular wish to own. He is so enthralled that he remains unaware that the horse she is riding is circling nearer and nearer to where he is standing. Suddenly it rears up to kick him on the head, killing him instantly. Leofric and Peeping Tom are merged, as perhaps they were in Adam van Noort's painting of 1586, which when it was cleaned of centuries of grime in 1976 revealed a bearded man looking out of an upstairs window as Godiva rode across the square. This was assumed to be Leofric himself.

This, too, is artistic licence. Leofric, Earl of Mercia, an honourable man, the son and grandson of honourable men and with a high sense of the responsibilities of his high office, would never have agreed to the humiliation of either his wife or himself in this way. Rather he would wish to see her arrayed in public with all the trappings of her noble station – a gown of finest fabric, jewelled necklaces and adornments, her hair raised or divided into two tresses and crowned with a gold coronet glittering with jewels and pearl pendants. It has been truly said that 'the legend of Godiva's ride has never really been about the eleventh century woman named Godgifu'.[9]

The New Oxford Dictionary of National Biography (2004) notes two recent and very different developments in the evolution of the Godiva legend: a revival of the traditional Coventry Godiva Procession was staged to mark the centenary of the motor car in 1996; and the Godiva International Award was established to be given to a woman of international reputation in the field of social welfare.

8

William II (Rufus):
Death in the New Forest, 1100

One day when he was hunting in the New Forest ... he had a gentleman named Walter Tyrrel with him, who was reckoned skilful in shooting with a bow and arrow. This gentleman, seeing a fine deer run by, wished to show the king how well he could shoot; but he was a little too eager, and his arrow, instead of going straight to the deer, touched a tree, which turned it aside, and it killed the king, who was standing near the tree. But the truth is that it was never known who shot the arrow that killed the king. Some poor men found William's body lying in the forest, and carried it to Winchester, where it was buried.

Maria Callcott, *Little Arthur's History of England*

This simply told story of the death of William Rufus appears, with imaginative variations, in almost every narrative of English history. It is, as E. A. Freeman wrote in his monumental history of the reign of William Rufus, 'one of those events in English history which are familiar to every memory and come readily to every mouth'.[1] Most people will also have learned that Rufus was a thoroughly unpleasant character and that 'his death was a Good Thing'.[2]

Historical interpretation of William II was almost uniformly hostile until modern times. The nineteenth-century outpouring of history books for children and the general reader did not, for reasons of propriety, refer in detail to the perceived moral shortcomings of William and his court, which were considered too depraved to be utilised as moral teaching. When 'accurate scientific' history became the fashion in the latter half of that century, this aspect of William's reign, which featured so largely in the contemporary chronicles then being so assiduously edited by men of academic distinction, exercised an exaggerated influence on the interpretation of the period and certainly of the man.

The usually austere Anglo-Saxon Chronicle set the tone in its entry for 1100: 'On the morning after Lammas Day the king William was shot with an arrow in hunting by a man of his, and afterwards brought to Winchester and buried in the bishopric ... he was hated by well-nigh all his nation, and abhorrent to God, just as his end showed.'

Here we find echoes of William's fraught relations with the Church and the monastic foundations. The king provoked much ill feeling by his determination to establish the principle that his bishops and abbots owed allegiance and service primarily to him rather than to the papacy; he deliberately left abbacies, and occasionally bishoprics, vacant in order to take their estates into his own hands – by the end of his reign some 15 per cent of the royal revenue was derived from this source.[3] Almost all men of religion, notably the Archbishop of Canterbury, Anselm, were openly critical of what they considered to be the dissolute and grossly immoral conduct of William and his court and the effeminate fashions they indulged in. Three eminent monkish chroniclers of the time – Eadmer of Canterbury, William of Malmesbury and Orderic Vitalis of Evroul – wrote at length of William's oppression of the Church and of his dissolute life. They condemned the sexual immorality of the court and especially homosexuality, which the king apparently not only tolerated but practised; they deplored the fashion among the nobility of wearing the hair long, often curled with tongs and held in place by a headband; they cast censorious eyes on tight-fitting, thigh-revealing tunics and luxurious robes, while the taste for effeminate shoes with long, curled and pointed toes was considered to be especially degenerate. Orderic, in a passage of vitriolic passion, accuses the king of obscene fornication and incessant adultery, setting an example of foul lewdness to his subjects; he was accompanied by effeminates and catamites when he met his death and was mourned only by the mercenary knights, lechers and common harlots who had lost their paymaster.[4]

This was not the stuff of children's story books, but the tale of the king's sudden and mysterious death certainly was, for it had all the fascination of suspected murder as well as the moral lesson of a villain receiving his just deserts. All the important chroniclers of the early twelfth century relate their version of the events in the New Forest on 2 August 1100, and all are agreed that in William's death there is no need to look beyond the avenging hand of God: whoever shot the fatal arrow was only carrying out God's intention to save His Church from further despoliation at the hand of this unrepentant sinner.

Eadmer was writing at the time of the event; William of Malmesbury and Florence of Worcester some twenty years later; Orderic Vitalis more than thirty years later and John of Salisbury in the 1140s – all provide descriptive detail interspersed with personal commentary to flesh out the bare bones of the story as first told in the Anglo-Saxon Chronicle, which gives the only simple version of what happened. The comments and embroideries added by these creative writers do not fundamentally change it.

The hunting season for the red stag opened on 1 August and on the following day the king was at his hunting lodge in the New Forest with an entourage of relatives, such as his brother Henry, close friends, notably Walter Tirel, and various prominent officials and feudal magnates. The method of hunting at that time was the 'battue': the deer were driven into a forest glade or a specially made corral, where the huntsmen were stationed at butts (trysts) placed at bends in the enclosed area, often opposite one another, from where they shot their arrows at the animals as they passed through.[5] It was customary for the party to be ready at dawn but, for reasons that are unknown, William on this occasion delayed the proceedings until after the midday meal. This was such an unusual departure from custom that the chroniclers found it necessary to put forward various explanations, which included the king's alleged hangover from the previous night's indulgences and the arrival of a messenger from the Abbot of Gloucester relating that a monk had experienced a vision warning that God intended the king's imminent death because of his ill treatment of the Church, an omen which William greeted with mockery and contempt. The chroniclers made the most of this with vivid descriptions and verbatim reports of words allegedly spoken: the king is said to have shown the abbot's letter to Walter Tirel with the comment, 'You carry out this sentence', to which Tirel is said to have replied, 'I will, indeed, my lord.'

The hunting party then dispersed to their 'trysts', the king accompanied by Walter Tirel, who seems to have stood opposite him. The low evening sun shining in their eyes may have affected the accuracy of their aim and William's shot at a stag inflicted only a partial wound; as he watched his quarry run on, Tirel took aim at a second stag but his arrow hit the king in the chest (whether it glanced off a tree or not is unknown). William fell forward, thus driving the arrow fatally into his body. When Tirel saw that the king was dead, he leapt onto his horse and fled the scene, as did everyone else, leaving the body to be picked up by servants and local 'rustics' to be taken on a cart to Winchester Cathedral, where it was buried under the tower with minimal rites.

William of Malmesbury, writing twenty years after the event,[6] is the first chronicler to name Tirel as responsible for William's killing, as part of a lively account of the whole disaster; and it was this version that was subsequently followed by all later writers, with their own imaginative variations. The exact truth of what happened cannot be discovered. Tirel himself always maintained, even on his deathbed, that he was innocent of the crime, and many were (and are) willing to accept that, whether he actually loosed the arrow which hit the king or not, he was not guilty of criminal intent. In default of any reliable evidence to the contrary, we have to conclude that the death of William Rufus was an accident, the type of shooting accident which was not at all uncommon in deer hunts of medieval times: Richard of Normandy, William's nephew, met his death in this manner, as did the Earl of Hereford in 1143. No one, it seems, set off in pursuit of Tirel; there are no accusations of murder; it was an accident of the hunt; as far as most of William's contemporaries are concerned, the voice of God had spoken.[7]

The conspiracy theory of history intruded into the story in the late nineteenth century, when in 1895 J. H. Round, the eminent historian of feudal England, commented on the link between Walter Tirel and the Clare family, who had had an uneasy relationship with William II since the baronial rebellions of 1088 and 1095. The Clares were among the ten wealthiest families in England and had estates in France too; they were prominent at William's court but appear to have been closer to the king's brother Henry.

Gilbert and Roger of Clare were among the hunting party in the New Forest on 2 August 1100 – Walter Tirel was their brother-in-law and renowned for his skill in shooting a deadly arrow. To a man, they abandoned the body of their king and fled to their estates. Furthermore, once he was established on the throne, Henry treated the family of Clare with marked favour. All this was considered by Round, and others who followed him to point to a plot to kill the king. In the mid-twentieth century the *Oxford History of England* authoritatively pronounced that 'there is, at the least, enough evidence to arouse the suspicion that the sudden end of Rufus was the result of a conspiracy formed and organised among members of the house of Clare, a conspiracy of which Henry himself was aware'.[9]

This theory was comprehensively taken apart by C. W. Hollister, the most recent biographer of Henry I,[10] but conspiracy as an explanation of the mysteries of history and politics is a tenacious cult with reputable historians to support it. The *Journal of Medieval History* confidently stated in 1977 that 'most writers on this period (except C. W. Hollister) believe that William II was murdered either on the orders of his brother or by dissidents who supposed that their interests would be better served with Henry on the throne'.[11] However, other leading authorities on the period will have none of this: Barlow comments that there is not a shred of good evidence for the theory and Hollister adds that 'the likeliest explanation for the killing is simply, as everyone supposed at the time, that it was a hunting accident'.[12]

Perhaps Lady Callcott's version of William's demise as told to Little Arthur is about right after all.

The New Oxford Dictionary of National Biography (2004), commenting on the death of Rufus, states that 'there is no good reason to think that it was anything but a (fairly common) hunting accident'.

9

Henry I:
The Loss of the *White Ship*, 1120

He [Henry I] was returning to England with a numerous train and many ships; one of which, called the White Ship, was allotted to the prince and his retinue. The prince had ordered some wine to be given to the ships crew, of which they drank so freely that many of them were intoxicated. The rest of the fleet had meanwhile sailed, and Fitzstephen, the commander of the White Ship, crowding all his sails, and plying all his oars, to overtake them, the vessel suddenly struck upon a rock called the Catte Raze. A boat was immediately let down, into which the prince and some of the young nobles were hurried; and they might have reached the shore in safety, had not the prince insisted on going back to rescue his illegitimate sister, the Countess of Perche, whose shrieks he heard from the ship, where all was terror and confusion. As soon as the boat approached the vessel, so many persons jumped into it, that it instantly sunk, and every creature perished. Thus died the prince with many of the young nobles, and several ladies of rank. Of three hundred persons who were on board, the only one who escaped was a butcher of Rouen, of the name of Bertould, who, by clinging to the mast, contrived to keep his head above water till the next morning when he was picked up by some fishermen. The captain had also clung to the mast, but when told by the butcher that the prince had perished, he would not survive so great a disaster, and threw himself headlong into the sea.

Mrs Markham's *History of England*

For three days, no-one dared to carry the intelligence to the King. At length, they sent into his presence a little boy, who, weeping bitterly, and kneeling at his feet, told him that the *White Ship* was lost with all on board. The King fell to the ground like a dead man, and never, ever afterwards was seen to smile.

Charles Dickens, *A Child's History of England*

This story is also told at great length in H. T. Marshall's *Our Island Story*.

The sinking of the *White Ship* was the most catastrophic maritime disaster of the medieval centuries (there were other medieval shipwrecks in the Channel, when similar numbers were lost – e.g. in 1170 and 1177 – but none with the same historic significance). More than 300 passengers were drowned, including nearly 200 members of the Anglo-Norman nobility, most important among them being eighteen-year-old Prince William Adelin, whose death meant that there was no obvious heir to the English throne. It also destroyed what William of Malmesbury described as Henry's 'brilliant and carefully crafted peace' with Louis VI of France. All depended on the newly celebrated marriage of Prince William and Matilda of Anjou. It had taken four years to achieve this settlement; the consequences of its sudden wreck on a half-submerged rock off Barfleur were, for England, a disputed succession and nineteen years of civil war and anarchy.[1]

Such a disaster could not fail to inspire the pen of every chronicler of the age, and the historian is able to draw on many accounts to reconstruct the events of that dramatic shipwreck almost 900 years ago. Orderic Vitalis and William of Malmesbury give the fullest versions, but Symeon of Durham, Eadmer and Hugh the Chanter of York also wrote useful accounts, while Henry of Huntingdon embellished it all with his usual dramatic prose and flights of fancy.[2]

From these sources we can recreate with plausible accuracy the full story of the *White Ship* disaster. The version given by Mrs Markham summarises all the essential facts.

Charles Dickens also gave a lengthy account in his *Child's History of England*, but included much detail that belongs to the novelist's imagination, as, for example, his reference to the gay young nobles and beautiful ladies wrapped in mantles of varied colours, dancing and singing in the moonlight on the ship's deck. There was no moon on that night, a stiff breeze was blowing across the water and it was, after all, the end of November. He also includes a verbatim account of a long and improbable conversation between the captain of the *White Ship* and Burold, the butcher from Rouen, which, we are asked to believe, took place as they clung to a spar and struggled for their lives in the ice-cold water. Burold's dramatic tale of the captain deliberately drowning himself when he realised the extent of the disaster is repeated by some chroniclers but is surely too melodramatic to be convincing.

So far-reaching were the consequences of this catastrophe that Orderic Vitalis wrote that those nearest to the king were so fearful of how he would react when he heard of it that at first none of them dared to tell him. Eventually a young boy was persuaded to throw himself weeping at Henry's feet to break the news to him. 'Immediately Henry fell to the ground, overcome with anguish.'[3] The loss of his son and heir, and all that depended on him, would in itself have caused overwhelming personal grief, but he had also lost his natural daughter, Matilda, and most of his closest and most loyal advisers, including Richard, Earl of Chester, and Ralph the Red, the formidable Norman baron who had done so much to defend Henry's Normandy castles against French incursions. Furthermore, the hard-won peace, on which Henry had spent so much effort and so many years to bring about was now in ruins. He had to devote most of the remaining fifteen years of his reign trying to repair the damage.

It is small wonder that one of the best-known and firmly entrenched traditions of Henry I is that, after this devastating misfortune, 'he never smiled again'. This legend was given scholarly support when, in 1970, Sir Richard Southern, who found nothing but gloom in this 'unloveable reign', questioned the evidence of two twelfth-century writers who give sunny accounts of life at Henry's court in these years. Walter Map was a collector of historical anecdotes and interesting detail, and he portrayed a typical day at Henry's court as a morning spent on official business followed by a short siesta and an afternoon devoted to sports, 'hilarity and decent mirth', while Geoffrey Gaimar enthused about the many occasions of 'love and gallantry, And woodland sports and jests, Of feasts and splendour, Of lavish gifts and riches'. Henry of Huntingdon tells us that, in the final years of his life, Henry spent much of his time in his favourite city of Rouen, where his grandsons, the future Henry II and Geoffrey, were born in 1133 and 1134. 'Sunning himself in the pride and joys of a grandfather, he passed perhaps the happiest months of his life.' Furthermore, Henry had married in 1121; his second wife was Adeliza of Louvain, whom many contemporary chroniclers portray as young and beautiful, nubile, intelligent and warm-hearted. It is difficult to agree with Sir Richard Southern that 'it is hard to see what there was to joke about' or to understand why Henry should have had nothing to smile about.[4]

In fact, no contemporary, nor any late medieval or early modern, chronicler makes any reference to Henry's inability to smile. Even in the mid-seventeenth century Sir Richard Baker's Chronicle of the Kings of England does not give this story, which appears for the first time in the *History of England* by Paul de Rapin de Thoyras, published in 1727, which (in its English translation) became the standard and most widely read history of England until David Hume's famous work some thirty years later. De Rapin, referring to the loss of the *White Ship*, wrote that 'this unexpected accident made such an impression on the king that he was never after seen to smile'.[5] It was not until the mid-nineteenth century, however, that the legend became embedded in popular, 'traditional' historical anecdote, with the publication of a poem by the minor poetess, Felicia Hemans, chiefly celebrated for her lines on 'The Stately Homes of England' and 'The Boy Stood on the Burning Deck'. Her poem on the tragedy of the *White Ship* with the title and refrain 'He Never Smiled Again' was designed to appeal to the lugubrious sentimentality of the age; the first verse sets the tone:

The bark that held a prince went down,
The sweeping waves rolled on;
And what was England's glorious crown
To him that wept a son?
He lived – for life may long be borne
Ere sorrow breaks its chain; –
Why comes not death to those who mourn? -
He never smiled again!

The story of the loss of the *White Ship* is a well-documented historical event; the tale of Henry's unsmiling face is a myth.

10

Henry I: Death from 'a Surfeit of Lampreys', 1135

On 25th November while staying for the hunting in the Forêt de Lyons … he was seized with acute indigestion, brought on, it is said, by a meal of lampreys which always disagreed with him and from which his doctor had expressly ordered him to refrain. Fever set in and he died a week later on 1st December.

A. L. Poole, *From Domesday Book to Magna Carta*

I must tell you the cause of his death; for I think it is a good lesson to all of us. He had been told by the physicians that he ought not to eat too much, but one day a favourite dish was brought to his table (I have heard that it was potted lampreys), and he ate such a quantity that it made him ill, and so he died, after he had been king thirty-five years.

Maria Callcott, *Little Arthur's History of England*

Henry I left England for the last time in August 1133. His departure was accompanied by a total eclipse of the sun and a rare earthquake that shook the Channel coast. His progress through Normandy was a political, military and personal success, but it was marked by a series of natural disasters with great loss of life from floods, snowstorms, heatwaves, fires and lightning strikes. Medieval folk held a firm belief that unusual occurrences in the natural world were portents of events to come and, with hindsight, the chroniclers made much of these omens in their accounts of Henry's unexpected death in 1135. Orderic Vitalis, in particular, portrays in dramatic detail all these events leading up to an 'eyewitness' account of the king's last hours. Henry, we are told, arrived at Lyons-la-Fort tired from his long exertions against feudal lords of doubtful loyalty, but anticipating an active day's hunting on the following day. He fell ill during the night; his condition steadily worsened and a few days later he died.[1]

Orderic does not indicate the nature of the king's illness, nor does he express an opinion on the likely causes of it. The first appearance of the famous story of the lampreys occurs in Henry of Huntingdon's *Historia Anglorum*, written shortly after 1135. This chronicler is generally regarded as reliable for the period of his own lifetime and most historians have accepted, with only muted caution, his statement that Henry

> partook of a dish of lampreys, which were always harmful to him, and which he always liked. For, when his doctor forbade him to eat them, the king paid no attention to this wholesome advice, as it is said, 'We ever strive for the forbidden thing and yearn for things denied us' [quotation from Ovid's *Amores*].[2]

The Archdeacon of Huntingdon's moral sermon is loudly echoed by Lady Callcott 700 years later in the version she read to her grandson, but in this later account there is a veiled reference to the famous 'surfeit', which legend insists was responsible for Henry's demise. It was Robert Fabyan's 1516 chronicle that first introduced this when he erroneously alleged that this was to be found in Ranulph Higden's fourteenth-century Polychronicon: 'Ranulphe saythe he took a surfet by etynge a lamprey and therof died.'[3] What Ranulph actually said was 'He hadde i-ete of a lamprey while he was olde and he loved it alway, though it greved him evermore.'[4] Even so, for many storytellers, and certainly for those who wished to teach or preach, a moral lesson was a prerequisite of any good story. Lady Callcott made the most of Henry's fatal indulgence – an indulgence that appears to have been no more than eating food that had always disagreed with him and that he had been advised not to touch, a human weakness common to all ages and not confined only to medieval kings. None of the contemporary chroniclers refers to the morally reprehensible indulgence implied by the word 'surfeit'. King John, too, was portrayed by generations of historians as a hard, ruthless and generally unpleasant character and he likewise met a well-deserved end, according to the traditional story, from a 'surfeit' – in his case of too many peaches and too much new cider. He may well have overindulged in the hospitality of the citizens of King's Lynn but the poor man died in all the agonies of dysentery. Historical anecdotes can sometimes be unkind to unpopular monarchs.

The political consequences of Henry I's death were disastrous for the peoples of his Anglo-Norman possessions. In Normandy, the news that the heavy hand of their ruler need no longer be feared was greeted by an outburst of lawlessness; Orderic Vitalis devotes many pages to a description of the ravages committed against churches, monasteries, tombs, farms, villages and towns. Normandy, wrote Henry of Huntingdon, was 'set on fire'. In England, the disputed succession to Henry's throne resulted in almost twenty years of civil war and baronial conflict, a time when it was said that God and his angels slept. Henry's weakness for lampreys has much to answer for; for we may be reasonably certain that this was, indeed, the cause of his death, even if we can discount the anecdotal surfeit.

Lampreys were in medieval times commonly found in the rivers of England and Normandy. Lampreys and eels quite often figure as items in the payments of feudal dues: the Isle of Ely was subject, appropriately enough, to an annual levy of 100,000 eels due to the Crown, while in 1300 a feudal tenant had to produce 'a carte-lode of grete lamprees and of eles' in payment of his annual dues. Clearly these fish were regarded as a delicacy and, even when they had almost disappeared from English waters, a Victorian Natural History noted that 'lampreys reach this country packed in jars with vinegar ... and bay leaves'. These eel-like fish are rarely seen in Britain now; only in Loch Lomond are they found in significant numbers.

The New Oxford Dictionary of National Biography (2004) points out that the problem was 'not that he ate too many lampreys but that his physician had advised him not to eat any at all – the surfeit legend has no basis in historical record'.

11

Thomas Becket:
'The Turbulent Priest', 1170

Thomas Becket, Henry II's Archbishop of Canterbury and the 'turbulent priest' of the story, was murdered in his cathedral on 29 December 1170. The king and the archbishop had been at loggerheads for several years over the respective rights and responsibilities of the Crown and the Church but both had seen the wisdom of patching up their differences. Unfortunately, Becket was self-centred, self-important, inept and provocative in his manner of proceeding in public affairs, and Henry had inherited not only the Angevin determination to maintain the dignity and prerogatives of the Crown, especially in relations with the Church, but also, in full measure, his family's notorious fiery and unpredictable temper. It was during one such fraught episode that a singularly tactless (or mischievous) courtier remarked to the fuming monarch, 'While Becket lives you will have neither peace nor quiet nor see good days'. Henry is said to have responded angrily and imprudently with the famous words 'Will no-one rid me of this turbulent priest?' This outburst led directly to the murder of the archbishop a few days later.

Medieval chroniclers and later biographers give their own variants on the actual words the king is said to have uttered, but the substance is essentially the same. The version given in J. C. Robertson's edition of *Materials for the History of Thomas Becket* is notably less succinct and memorable than the bitter taunt of the traditional 'turbulent priest' outburst: 'What miserable drones and traitors have I nurtured and promoted in my household who let their Lord be treated with such shameful contempt by a low-born clerk?' There seems little doubt that Henry did use some ill-considered words, for he later admitted responsibility for the archbishop's death but denied that he had ever intended it. This was not the first occasion on which Henry's anger had led him to mouth such reckless sentiments. Five years earlier, there had been another bitter moment when Becket went so far as to threaten the king with excommunication and, according to the contemporary chronicler John of Salisbury, who was present at the time, Henry, in a tearful rage, declared that 'they were all traitors who could not summon up the zeal and loyalty to rid him of the harassment of one man'. In 1170, his outburst was overheard by four knights of the household, enemies of Becket, who were, as Henry's associate and biographer William FitzStephen alleges, 'eager to win [the king's] favour'. These four headstrong opportunists hastened to Canterbury with no clear purpose in mind other than to force Becket to submit to the king. It was only when Becket put up a vigorous resistance to their attempts to drag him from the church that, in mindless panic, his assailants wildly slashed out with their swords and killed him. We may never know the precise words uttered by Henry in his rage but, even if he did not intend it, they led directly to the murder of his 'turbulent priest'.

Historians have derived their accounts of the murder of Thomas Becket on the version given by two men who were present at the scene. As so often happens with eyewitness accounts, these differ in detail but agree on the general course of events. William FitzStephen was Becket's clerk and remained with him until he died; Edward Grim was a visitor to the cathedral and intervened in the struggle to try to help Becket, being was wounded in the process. Their accounts are included in J. C. Robertson's monumental collection of *Materials for the History of Thomas Becket* (1859) but the precise words of the traditional 'turbulent priest' story do not appear in any of these chronicles although all agree that Henry's outburst included some such remark.

12

Fair Rosamund, 1176

There is a pretty story told of this reign, called the story of Fair Rosamund. It relates how the king doted on Fair Rosamund who was the loveliest girl in all the world; and he had a beautiful bower built for her in a park at Woodstock; and how it was erected in a labyrinth, and could only be found by a clue of silk. How the bad Queen Eleanor, becoming jealous of Fair Rosamund, found out the secret of the clue, and one day appeared before her with a dagger and a cup of poison, and left her to the choice between these deaths. How Fair Rosamund, after shedding many piteous tears and offering many useless prayers to the cruel Queen, took poison and fell dead in the midst of the beautiful bower, while the unconscious birds sang gaily all around her.

Now there was a Fair Rosamund, and she was (I dare say) the loveliest girl in the world, and the king was certainly very fond of her, and the bad Queen Eleanor was certainly made jealous. But I am afraid – I say I am afraid because I like the story so much – that there was no bower, no labyrinth, no silken clue, no dagger, no poison. I am afraid Fair Rosamund retired to a nunnery near Oxford, and died there peaceably.

Charles Dickens, *A Child's History of England*

There was, indeed, a Fair Rosamund: she was the daughter of Walter de Clifford, lord of extensive estates in Pembrokeshire, the Welsh Marches and other counties, and the recipient of a grant of land from King Henry II in 1174 specifically 'pro amore Rosamundae filiae suae'.[1] She was the great love of Henry's life – he and Queen Eleanor had been estranged and even at war with each other for many years – and, certainly in his eyes, she was Rosa mundi, the Rose of the World, for not surprisingly he thought that she surpassed all women in beauty, an opinion dutifully endorsed by the early chroniclers and, centuries later, by Thomas Hearne, who in 1718 described her as 'the masterpiece of nature and the most complete beauty of the age'.[2] She may well have been a great beauty but neither Henry, in his infatuation, nor Hearne, 600 years later, can be regarded as impartial witnesses. Hearne portrayed her as a paragon – highly educated, lively and vivacious, brilliant in conversation, fond of music and literature and skilled in such feminine arts as embroidery and fine needlework – Hearne refers to an embroidered cope at Buidwas Abbey bearing the legend 'Rosamund Clifford propriis manibus me fecit' ('made by Rosamund Clifford with her own hands'). Historical fact and probability may go thus far with the traditional story of Rosamund, but despite his cautious (and justifiable) doubts about the rest of his 'pretty story' Dickens knew full well that it was too good a tale to be banished from popular folk history by a few inconvenient facts unearthed by the new generation of academic historians.

The principal point of controversy surrounding Rosamund is the manner of her death, believed to have occurred in 1176. It is part of the drama of her story that she was 'murdered' by 'bad' Queen Eleanor, an act transformed by much macabre detail into a medieval melodrama.

The first version of this appeared in the fourteenth century in the French Chronicle of London, where an elaborate tale is told of the fatal meeting between Eleanor and Rosamund at the 'bower' Henry had built for her at Woodstock. No contemporary chronicle refers to this confrontation, but ninety years afterwards we are given a detailed account of how Eleanor poured abuse on Rosamund, stripped her of her clothes, left her to roast naked between two fires and then stabbed her with a dagger and left her to bleed to death in a bath of scalding water. Subsequent chroniclers changed and added to this inherently improbable and gruesome tale, but none seemed to question that Eleanor had murdered Rosamund.

The case for the queen's defence is clear. She had waged war on the king on behalf of her sons and, following her defeat and capture, she was imprisoned in 1173 and there she remained until some years after Rosamund's death. As W. L. Warren pointed out in his study of Henry II, 'since the tales relate to a period when

Eleanor was in fact a closely guarded prisoner it is difficult to believe that they are anything more than romantic fantasies'.[3]

Most medieval chroniclers, apparently, also took this view: Roger of Hoveden and William of Newburgh, among the more reliable chroniclers, assume that Rosamund died a natural death and are more concerned with the details of her tomb. It was not until 200 years after the event that the London Chronicle added more colourful material to the legends surrounding Rosamund's last years.

In 1516 Robert Fabyan's chronicle introduced the elaborate story of Rosamund's bower at Woodstock. Henry is supposed to have had constructed an underground sanctuary for his mistress described by Fabyan as 'an house wrought lyke unto a knot in a garden called a maze'. This labyrinth was so complex that it was necessary, for those who did not know its secret, to be guided by means of a clew or thread. Fabyan tells a tale that Eleanor discovered where Rosamund's 'bower' was hidden and found her way to Rosamund by this 'clewe of threde or silke and delte with her in such a manner that she lyved not long after'.[4] This fantasy was gratefully repeated by almost all later versions of the Rosamund legend.

Some years later the poisoned cup was added to the story. In his *Reliques of Ancient English Poetry*, published in 1765, Thomas Percy included a ballad, dated 1611 and entitled 'The Confession of Queen Eleanor', in which the cup of poison referred to by Dickens made its first appearance. In the course of the ballad the queen confesses to the murder:

> I poysoned Fair Rosamund
> All in fair Woodstock's bower[5]

And so the legend passed into the repertoire of nineteenth-century historical anecdotes.

Thomas Hearne, believing, as did the contemporary chroniclers, that Rosamund died a natural death, was more concerned with relating the events that followed. Both King Henry and Rosamund's family had made generous benefactions to the nunnery at Godstow, near Oxford, and the nuns there buried Rosamund before the High Altar. Her tomb was adorned with silk hangings and bathed in the soft light of lamps and candles, with constant prayers for her soul all in accordance with the king's benefaction.[6]

The quiet dignity of this memorial to the king's great love was shattered in 1191 when Godstow nunnery received a visit from the austere Hugh, Bishop of Lincoln. He ordered the elaborate adornments to be taken down and the body removed from the church to the cemetery outside, 'for she was a harlot'.[7] This was duly done, but contemporary chroniclers agree that in due course the nuns once more removed the tomb and placed it in the sanctuary of their chapter house, this time wrapping the body in leather and lining the coffin with lead. A new tombstone bore the simple inscription 'Tomba Rosamundae'. Thomas Hearne imaginatively describes the tombstone as having elaborate carvings of red and green roses and a stone sculpture of 'the cup which she drank the poison given her by the queen'.

As a further token of his love, Henry had a cross erected at each place on the way between Woodstock and Godstow, where Rosamund's body rested. In the 1530s, Leland reported that 'Close to Godstow there is a cross with the Latin inscription "May he who passes by this symbol of salvation make a prayer, and beseech Rosamund to grant pardon for his sin"'. Leland also refers to Rosamund's tomb having been 'taken up recently' and 'when the coffin was opened a very sweet smell emanated from it'.[8]

Ranulf Higden, writing some hundred years after the event, states that Rosamund's tombstone bore the Latin inscription

Hic jacet in tumulo Rosa mundi, non Rosa munda,
Non redolet sed olet quae redolere solet.[9]

This typically complex epitaph appears to be an attempt to contrast Rosamund's remarkable beauty with her unchastity and to distinguish between her fragrance in life and her unpleasant smell in death. Perhaps Thomas Hearne in 1718 has produced the most useful translation:

Here lies in the grave Rose of the World but not the clene rose,
She smelleth not swete, but stynketh ful foule
That sumtyme smelled ful swete.[10]

A book entitled *Dives et Pauper*, dated 1493, purports to tell the story behind the inscription:

> We read that in England was a King that had a concubine whose name was Rose, and for her great beauty he called her Rosamund, Rosa mundi, that is to say, Rose of the World. For he thought that she passed all women in beauty. It befell that she died and was buried while the King was absent. And when he came back, for the great love that he had to her, he would see the body in the grave, and when the grave was opened, there sat a horrible toad upon her bosom between her breasts, and a foul adder was twined round the middle of her body. And she stank so that neither the King nor anyone else could stand to look upon such a horrible sight.

The author then adds, 'This is a simple story, invented by commentators to fright women from committing adultery.'[11] 'Sic transit gloria Rosamundae.'

It was inevitable that such a story should appeal in the eighteenth century to the producers of drama and opera with sinister and mysterious plots. Two operas appeared – Thomas Clayton's in 1707 and Anton Schweitzer's in 1780 – but both were disastrous failures (in both operas Rosamund was drugged and not poisoned). A play by Chezy survived for two performances only in 1823 but, perhaps to make amends for the many scurrilous fictions heaped on Rosamund's name, the charming *Incidental Music to Rosamund* written for this play by Franz Schubert has survived. If Hearne was right, Rosamund would have loved it.

While much of detail in the story of Fair Rosamund is literary invention, it is certain that Henry did have built at Woodstock a secret bower where he and Rosamund could meet. *The New Oxford Dictionary of National Biography* (2004) refers to a Pipe Roll of 1231, which has reference to 'Rosamund's Chamber' with gardens, an orchard, a spring (Rosamund's Well) and a bower for secret meetings, all most probably laid out for Henry II. In the seventeenth century, John Aubrey produced a sketch of Everswell, adjoining the Palace of Woodstock, showing a complex of buildings with gardens, pools and a cloister.

13

Richard I and Blondel, 1193

In old times a beautiful story was told about the way the English found out where Richard was. It was this. Richard had a servant called Blondel, who loved his master much. When Richard did not come home, Blondel became very anxious, and went in search of him. He travelled from one castle to another for some time, without finding his master. At last, one evening, when he was very tired, he sat down near the castle of Trifels to rest, and while he was there he heard somebody singing, and fancied the voice was like the king's. After listening a little longer, he felt sure it was, and then he began to sing himself, to let the king know he was there; and the song he sang was one the king loved. Some say the king made it. Then Richard was glad, for he found he could send to England, and let his people know where he was.

Maria Callcott, *Little Arthur's History of England*

H. T. Marshall's *Our Island Story* tells this story in great detail, including a full version of Blondel's song from Grétry's opera.

Richard I, known throughout history as the Lionheart, presented himself to the world as the epitome of knightly chivalry. Tall and athletic, imperious and fearless, and never more so than when mounted on his magnificent horse, Fauvel, and fully armed in his high Rhenish helmet, his overall chain mail and his two-handed battleaxe, a red cross blazoned on his white surcoat and a lion rampart roaring across his red shield. In an age when war was a way of life, Richard was the hero of Europe's war-obsessed nobility. Before he was thirty he had displayed impressive military prowess in a series of fratricidal conflicts across France, from Normandy and Anjou to Poitou and Aquitaine, campaigns in which he had also shown ruthless leadership, military skill, savage cruelty and unpredictable generosity. All this was again demonstrated in his war against the great Muslim Sultan, Saladin, in the Third Crusade, from which he emerged a legend in all the courts of Europe and with the acknowledged respect of his Muslim foes.

Richard was not quite the paragon of Chaucer's 'verray parfit gentil knyght' for, as the chronicler Gerald of Wales observed, 'he cared for no success that was not reached by a path cut by his own sword and stained with the blood of his adversaries';[1] and a modern historian bluntly comments, 'He was lion-hearted but soulless ... Men respected his skill and his strategic sense but there was little for which to love him.'[2] Romantic heroes are perhaps most appreciated at a distance: Richard might have seemed heroic under the walls of Jerusalem and romantic in captivity by the Danube, but Englishmen had to live with the reality of penal taxation to pay for their absent king's adventures, and his death, as the chronicler tells us, was greeted with relief.[3]

Yet Richard, Coeur de Lion, remains one of the most romantic figures of English history, and the Third Crusade one of its epic stories, portrayed and romanticised in the contemporary panegyric *The Journey of the Crusaders*[4] and, in more modern times, in opera and in the theatre, in historical novels and in Hollywood films. Richard was a legend in his own lifetime; it is small wonder that the legend has been embellished over the years by much literary invention.

The best-known of the legendary tales surrounding Richard concerns his captivity at the hands of Duke Leopold of Austria, whom Richard had grievously offended at the siege of Acre. In October 1192, Richard turned his eyes away from Jerusalem, the prize he had been unable to capture, and began his journey home. This proved to be an adventure fraught with hazards, mishaps and mystery, barely recorded by the chroniclers but lavishly embroidered by the writers of historical fiction.

Much has been made of Richard's choice of homeward route. Why did he not opt for the direct sea-voyage via the Straits of Gibraltar? Why did he choose to risk capture and imprisonment by passing through the lands not only of the aggrieved Leopold, Duke of Austria, but also of the Emperor, Henry VI, who had ordered every town in his realm to seize the king if he came their way? Richard was reckless of his own safety; and, as Saladin himself once remarked, 'he is imprudent, not to say foolishly so, in thrusting himself so frequently into danger'. On this occasion, however, Richard's choice of action was not determined by impulse or natural imprudence. It seems unlikely that he was deterred from taking the sea route via the Straits of Gibraltar because of the certainty of stormy weather in the late autumn – after all, the queen came home that way and, in any case, his ship had a rough passage to Corfu and over the Adriatic. Legend has him escaping from pirates and shipwreck before he eventually made landfall at the port of Dubrovnik whence he continued his journey northwards. It seems highly probable that Richard had a serious purpose in his choice of route, namely to visit King Bela III of Hungary with whom England had diplomatic relations for some years, which included negotiations for a marriage between Bela and Richard's niece.[5] He may also have intended to consolidate the Anglo-Welf alliance against the emperor further north.[6] If these were the king's intentions, then his apparently foolhardy arrival at Erdberg on the outskirts of Vienna, where he was apprehended and taken into custody, has a rational explanation, since this was the most direct route to Budapest. Tales of a poor, benighted hero of the Crusades lost in the wild mountains of Carinthia, forced to flee from his pursuers disguised as a merchant, a Templar or a kitchen turnspit, and finally blundering into a trap set by Duke Leopold, rely more on folklore embellished down the ages than on acceptable historical evidence.

Be that as it may, Richard was indisputably made prisoner by Leopold and whisked away to the castle of Dürnstein, a remote fortress high on an outcrop of rock above the Danube west of Vienna. Shortly afterwards, for a fee of 80,000 marks (£60,000) Leopold handed the king over to the emperor, Henry VI, who secured his prize in his castle at Speyer.

Of the various legends surrounding Richard's imprisonment, none has achieved greater fame or credence than the story of Blondel, the king's minstrel and companion. Even in 1924, so distinguished a historian as Kate Norgate could write that such a fable was 'not in itself impossible'.[7] Significantly, it does not appear in any of the more reliable chronicles of the time. The story first appeared in a thirteenth-century French romance, *Le Récit d'un Ménestrel de Reims*,[8] in the heyday of the troubadours and their imaginative poesy.

According to the *Récit*, the story begins in England where Richard's queen, Berengaria, waited anxiously for news of her missing husband. All that she knew was that he had fallen into the hostile hands of the Duke of Austria and was incarcerated in an unknown castle awaiting an unknown fate. No one in England knew the location of his prison and, as time went by, the queen and those who were ordering the affairs of the kingdom became increasingly desperate. Eventually the king's minstrel, Blondel, devised a plan to discover where Richard was held. In happier days he and the king had spent many leisure hours composing and singing the songs of love that were so much a part of the culture of the age of chivalry. Blondel proposed to wander from castle to castle through the vast extent of the Holy Roman Empire, and under the walls of each he would play his lute and sing Richard's favourite song until, one day, he would hear the king respond. For a year and a half he pursued this quest without success and then he was told by a widow with whom he lodged that a mysterious prisoner had been kept in a nearby castle for the past four years. But Blondel could discover nothing more about such a prisoner 'until', as the *Récit* tells us,

> he went out one day on the Easter festival alone in a garden by a tower and hoped that perhaps he might see the prisoner … The King was looking through a loophole and saw Blondel and wondered how he could make himself known to him. He remembered a song which they had composed together … so he began to sing the first phrase loud and clear, for he could sing very well; and when Blondel heard him he knew for certain that this was his lord.

Blondel's discovery of Richard's prison led to the negotiations that soon afterwards secured the king's release.

The legend then disappeared for more than 300 years when it resurfaced in a scholarly collection illustrating the origins of the French language and its poetry.[9] Here, Blondel's adventures are given the form that, with a few romantic additions, has remained familiar ever since. Blondel sings the first few lines of the song and waits for Richard to respond with the next. Having discovered the location of the king's 'prison', he hurries home with the good news and two delegates are sent from England to negotiate terms for his release. Richard regained his freedom but at a cost to the English taxpayer of 150,000 marks (£100,000).

Contemporary chronicles and various State papers reveal a number of factual errors in this attractive tale: Richard was certainly not in captivity for 'four years' – he was seized by Duke Leopold's men in December 1192 and set free on 4 February 1194, a period of little more than thirteen months. Consequently, Blondel's 'tour' of the castles of Germany could not have extended to 'a year and a half', especially since the king was missing for no more than a few weeks before he was handed over on 14 February 1193 to the custody of the emperor and taken to the castle at Speyer. Here, he was certainly not 'lost', for, as Roger of Hoveden tells us, the abbots of Boxley and Robertsbridge went there to open diplomatic talks for his release. A steady stream of correspondence flowed between Speyer and England as details of the ransom were negotiated, and Richard himself was in constant touch with the administration in London as he was free to receive visitors and to issue orders for the government of his realm and to deal with the treacherous activities of his brother, John. Meanwhile, prisoner and gaoler struck up a cordial friendship and Richard attended imperial court functions on almost equal terms with Henry. The king's letters to his mother, Queen Eleanor, suggest that he was positively enjoying his stay as the emperor's 'guest', stating coolly that he was content to prolong his stay until their 'business' was concluded, that is, 'until we have paid him seventy thousand marks of silver'. There is no sign of a forlorn monarch languishing in some dark foreign dungeon; he even had his own hawks sent from England for hunting expeditions.

Finally, it is a distortion of contemporary events to portray the emperor as anxious to keep Richard in strict confinement. On the contrary, he was deeply concerned that, in his absence from his kingdom, Richard's arch-enemy Philip Augustus, King of France, should exploit the situation by supporting John's attempt to seize the English throne in return for surrendering England's extensive

Angevin possessions in France, thus greatly strengthening Philip's power in his struggle for supremacy over the empire. Henry would extort as much as he could from England by way of ransom for Richard, but he was a ruthless diplomat rather than a wicked gaoler.

Richard returned to England in March 1194, secured the surrender of the various castles that had supported his brother John, and established order and sound government, before, just sixty days later, he set sail for France to renew his war with Philip. He never returned.

The legend of Blondel was lost until the 1620s when it was referred to in an English translation of a French work entitled *The Theatre of Honour and Knighthood*. But it achieved a wider audience in a romantic novel, again from France, with the gothic title *La Tour Ténébreuse*, published in 1705. This may have been the source used by Oliver Goldsmith when he gave the Blondel story his blessing in his widely read *History of England* (1771).

Neither of these would have been enough to assure Blondel of the firm place in popular historical anecdote that he achieved in the nineteenth century. This was achieved in 1784 when the French composer Grétry produced his opera *Richard Coeur de Lion* with a libretto based on the traditional Blondel story, with the addition of much romantic invention. Grove's *Dictionary of Opera* notes that this opera was staged 'throughout the nineteenth century and became perhaps the most universally familiar eighteenth century opera comique'.[11] In the course of the opera, Blondel sings beneath the walls of Linz Castle the first lines of romantic songs that he and Richard had composed together. These airs enjoyed immense popularity for many years, and did more than any historian or novelist could hope to do to perpetuate and give credibility to the whole legend: 'O! Richard! O! Mon Roi! l'univers t'abandonne' and 'Une fièvre brûlante un jour me terrassait', ensured that Blondel's story found a place in almost every history of England written in the nineteenth century. Grétry's songs were sung by the Flanders Regiment at the famous banquet at Versailles on 1 October 1789; and there is a reference in Charles Dickens's *A Child's History of England* when Blondel, having sung his song 'outside the walls of many fortresses and prisons ... at last heard it echoed from within a dungeon, and knew the voice and cried out in ecstasy, "O! Richard! O! my King! Thou art by all forgot!"'

Dickens added bluntly, 'You may believe it if you like'; Mrs Markham was more gently dismissive: when her son Richard, perhaps curious about his famous namesake, asked 'Is that pretty story true about Richard's page finding out where he was by singing a song under his prison windows?', he received the admirable reply 'I believe there is no other authority for the story but an old French romance'.[12]

The verdict of the most recent authoritative biographer of Richard states conclusively, 'There is not a shred of evidence to indicate that there is any truth in the story – but it was good publicity for the minstrels.'[13]

Blondel himself we cannot dismiss. He was a flesh-and-blood troubadour of some renown. He was chosen to sing at the magnificent coronation festivities of Philip of France in 1179, and he was a bosom friend of young Prince Richard at the court of Eleanor of Aquitaine. He helped nurse Richard when he was struck down by a disease during the Crusade. As Blondel de Nesle (a small town near Amiens), he achieved widespread fame as a troubadour; many of his compositions have survived and were collected and published in the nineteenth century.[14] But it was Gretry's 'fièvre brûlante' rather than Blondel's 'coeur désireux' that secured his place in popular culture and in the history books.

A recent study of this anecdote and the events that surround it has much interesting detail to supplement the analysis given here: David Boyle, *Blondel's Song: the Capture, Imprisonment and Ransom of Richard the Lionheart* (Viking (Penguin imprint): 2005).

14

Prince Arthur of Brittany:
Murdered by King John? 1203

You cannot wonder that John was disliked; but when I have told you how he treated a nephew of his, called Prince Arthur, you will, I am sure, dislike him as much as I do. Some people thought that this Prince Arthur ought to have been King of England because he was the son of John's elder brother Geoffrey. And John was afraid that the barons and other great men would choose Arthur to be king, so he contrived to get Arthur into his power.

He wished very much to kill him at once ... Then he thought that, if he put out his eyes, he would be so unfit for a king, that he should be allowed to keep him prisoner all his life, and he actually gave orders to a man named Hubert de Burgh to put his eyes out, and Hubert hired two wicked men to do it.

But when they came with hot irons to burn his eyes out, Arthur knelt down and begged hard that they would do anything but blind him; ... neither Hubert nor the men hired to do it could think any more of putting out his eyes, and so they left him ...

One night afterwards, it is said that Arthur heard a knocking on the gate; and when it was opened, you may think how frightened he was to see his cruel uncle standing there, with a servant as bad as himself, whose name was Maluc; and he was frightened with reason; for the wicked Maluc seized him by the arm, and stabbed him in the breast with his dagger, and then threw his body into the River Seine, which was close to the tower, while King John stood by to see it done.

Maria Callcott, *Little Arthur's History of England*

In 1182 Henry II had a vast territorial empire extending from the Cheviots to the Pyrenees. He also had four sons, all expecting a share of the family lands, and a formidable estranged wife, Queen

Eleanor of Aquitaine, adamant that she and not Henry should dispose of provinces that were hers by rightful inheritance. Years of family strife, exacerbated by much diplomatic and military meddling by the King of France, had left Henry weary of the whole problem, and at the age of forty-nine, when it seemed that at last he had succeeded in imposing his authority throughout his possessions, he decided to make an attempt to resolve it once and for all. Henry, the oldest son, would receive the Kingdom of England, the Duchy of Normandy and the county of Anjou; Richard was to have Aquitaine but with the King of France as his overlord; Geoffrey would hold the Duchy of Brittany but as a vassal of his older brother, Henry; John, the youngest, hitherto unprovided for and so dubbed 'John Lackland', was to become ruler of a new Kingdom of Ireland.

Henry was quickly to discover that the best-laid schemes 'gang aft a-gley'. None of his sons accepted the terms of this disposition of their father's estates, while Eleanor insisted that Aquitaine was hers and not Henry's to dispose of; the strife continued, even as far as open warfare between the brothers. Then in 1183, Henry, the heir to England and Normandy, caught dysentery and died; three years later Geoffrey was killed in a tournament; in 1187 Geoffrey's posthumous son, Arthur, was born, thus adding a further complicating factor to the problem.

Shortly before Henry II died in 1189 he had reluctantly agreed, under duress, that Richard should succeed him as King of England and as lawful heir to all his father's lands. Richard was unmarried at that time, and had no plans to marry before his return from a Crusade to Jerusalem.

Who would now be the rightful heir to Richard's kingdom if he should have no legitimate son or fail to survive his hazardous adventures in the Holy Land?

Later generations would establish guidelines on the rules of succession, but in the twelfth century there was no such constitutional guidance. Legitimate kinship with the royal house was an essential requirement for any claimant, but there was no generally accepted order of precedence. Of the six kings who followed William the Conqueror, only Richard I succeeded according to what was to become the rule of hereditary succession.[1]

If this rule had prevailed in the late twelfth century, then the right of the young Prince Arthur of Brittany to take the throne in 1199 on the death of the childless Richard I would have been beyond legal challenge, for he was the legitimate son and heir of John's older brother, Geoffrey. But the rules were still far from certain, as is made clear in the account of *English Laws and Customs*, usually attributed to Henry II's Chief Justiciar, Ranulf Glanville, who indicates that there was considerable doubt whether a younger brother of a previous king or the son of an older brother has a stronger legal claim; on balance he appears to favour the nephew.[2] If there was even a possibility that this could be upheld in law it is small wonder that, during Richard's reign, John became involved in various wild schemes to try to secure his own succession, for all through these years the young Prince Arthur was becoming the focus of baronial conspiracies in Brittany, Anjou, Maine and Touraine to declare Arthur the rightful successor to these provinces on the death of Richard (Richard had unexpectedly married, at his mother's behest, on his way to the Holy Land. Queen Eleanor had arrived in Cyprus accompanied by the bride she had chosen for her son, Berengaria of Navarre, and supervised the marriage. There were no children to succeed).

When that time arrived in 1199 there were, indeed, several years of warlike hostility to John, (with the King of France intervening in his own interests), but by 1201 John had established his authority and also achieved an apparently satisfactory feudal relationship with Philip of France. He hoped (mistakenly) that his marriage to Isabelle of Angoulême would resolve his problems with the troublesome feudal sensitivities of the baronial families of Poitou in the heart of Aquitaine. Arthur's most active protagonist, his mother, Constance of Brittany, had just died. In his Kingdom of England a leisurely and extensive royal progress had made it clear that there was no enthusiasm for Arthur among his English subjects. For the first time in his life, John Lackland could feel secure in his inheritance.

The flaws in John's character now revealed themselves. He was unable to show generosity or restraint in his moment of victory and he determined to teach a needless lesson to the restless barons of Poitou, issuing against them a gratuitous charge of treason. At the same time he deliberately and provocatively flouted the authority of his feudal overlord, Philip of France, who seized the occasion to invade Normandy and lend support to the discontented Poitevins and to a force, led by Prince Arthur of Brittany, that had invaded Aquitaine. Suddenly John's Angevin empire was collapsing about him, and his nephew, Arthur, had returned to haunt him once more. In the end this conflict was to lead to the loss of Normandy and effective control of all Angevin provinces in France – and to a humiliating invasion of England by the French.

But first John had a remarkable success brought about by a characteristic Angevin *coup d'éclat*. His mother, Queen Eleanor, now in her eightieth year, was a determined opponent of the attempts of her grandson, Arthur, to seize John's lands in Anjou and Poitou, and in 1202 she emerged from her retirement at the Abbey of Fontevrault to confront yet another invasion from Brittany. This time, however, Arthur's forces succeeded in trapping her in the castle of Mirebeau, 20 miles north of Poitiers; John and his army were over 80 miles away near Le Mans, but by an impressive forced march within two days they surprised Arthur's besieging camp with a dawn attack. Eleanor was released, Arthur and his chief supporters were captured together with 'all our other Poitevin enemies who were there, being upwards of two hundred knights, and none escaped'.[3]

The two most important prisoners, Prince Arthur and Geoffrey de Lusignan, were closely confined in the castle at Falaise in Normandy; others were securely held at Caen; some of the others were taken to Corfe Castle in Dorset. At a stroke John had eliminated any internal threat to his Angevin provinces and had secured his most serious potential rival, Arthur of Brittany. Once again his impulsive folly threw it all away.

William des Roches, the most powerful baron in Anjou, had initially supported Arthur's claims but had later recognised John's overlordship and had played the key part in the relief of Mirebeau Castle on condition that he should have custody of Arthur. John now broke his word and ignored des Roches in all his counsels, with the result that he deserted and once more joined John's opponents. These were soon reinforced by John's astounding decision to release his Lusignan prisoners who immediately broke their oath of loyalty and returned to their customary harassment of their Angevin rulers.

As one horrified chronicler put it, 'John had put the head back on the trunk of Poitevin disaffection.'[4] More damaging to John's reputation was the mysterious disappearance of Prince Arthur and the spread of rumours that he had been murdered.

Arthur had once more become a serious rival to John when Philip of France, in 1202, declared John disinherited of all his French fiefdoms and acknowledged Arthur as his successor. Rumours soon reached Ralph Coggeshall that John had ordered Hubert de Burgh, Arthur's custodian at Falaise, to have Arthur blinded and castrated to make him unfit as a possible rival. De Burgh refused to commit this barbarity and, on his own initiative, announced that Arthur was dead. The Bretons swore vengeance on John, whom they held responsible for his death, and de Burgh had to admit that his prisoner was, in fact, still alive. John now transferred Arthur to the castle at Rouen where, shortly afterwards, he was put to death.

Shakespeare made Arthur's death an important feature in his play *The Life and Death of King John*, but following Holinshed's chronicle he created a scene where Arthur leapt to his death from the castle walls in an attempt to escape his captors.[5] The chroniclers appear to be unusually uninformed of the actual circumstances, and all later versions seem to owe much to an account given in the Annals of Margam Abbey, which had a close relationship with the Briouze family, who were patrons of the abbey. William de Briouze was a constant companion of King John and it was he who had personally captured Arthur at Mirebeau; he may well have provided the Margam chronicler with what is probably the true account of Arthur's death:

> After King John had captured Arthur and kept him alive in prison for some time, at length, in the castle of Rouen, after dinner on the Thursday before Easter, when he was drunk and possessed by the devil, he slew him with his own hand, and tying a heavy stone to the body cast it into the Seine. It was discovered by a fisherman in his net, and being dragged to the bank and recognised, was taken for secret burial, in fear of the tyrant, to the priory of Bec called Notre Dame des Près.[6]

J. R. Green, in his popular *Short History of the English People*, confirmed for the modern reader the image of John as an irredeemable villain, and ensured, as Green himself put it, that 'the terrible verdict of the king's contemporaries … passed into the sober judgement of history', quoting in support the thirteenth-century chronicler Matthew Paris in his most colourful style: 'Foul as it is, Hell itself is defiled by the fouler presence of King John.'[7] More recent studies have treated such assessments with scepticism and attempted to present a more balanced view of the man and his achievements, notably as an administrator and as upholder of the law, together with a more sympathetic understanding of his complex character, which was fraught with inconsistencies so that 'almost any epithet might be applied to him in one or other of his many and versatile moods'.[8]

Above all he had inherited the violent temper and blind rages of the Angevin family. He also had an almost pathological suspicion of those who held power and influence in his counsels, even of those who had demonstrated outstanding ability and loyalty in his service: thus, in his fury, he alienated such men as William Longchamp, William des Roches, William de Briouze and William Marshal, Earl of Pembroke and elder statesman. In these frenzied outbursts, John, like his Angevin father and brothers, could vent his anger on his victims with ruthless cruelty, of which perhaps the best-known example is his vindictive prosecution of Matilda, wife of William de Briouze, who refused to hand over her sons to the king as hostages with the defiant reply that she would not deliver her sons to the man who had murdered his nephew, Arthur. When she was eventually captured, Matilda and her son were locked in a dungeon in Windsor Castle and starved to death. Matilda's sharp response to the king had clearly touched a sensitive nerve; John's vicious reaction must be held against him in any assessment of his responsibility for the murder of Prince Arthur.

It is difficult to believe, however, that even King John would not have realised the personal and political consequences of so direct an involvement in the murder of his own nephew. John's arch enemy, Philip of France, and Arthur's sister, Eleanor, failed to show any significant reaction to Arthur's sudden death. The balance of probabilities would seem to be, as Matthew Paris wrote within living memory of the event, that Arthur died trying to escape from his prison and fell from a great height into the river below where his body was subsequently found.

15

King John:
Loss of Treasure in the Wash, 1216

Crossing dangerous quicksands called the Wash ... the tide came up
and nearly drowned his army. He and his soldiers escaped; but looking
back from the shore when he was safe, he saw the roaring water sweep
down in a torrent, overturn the waggons, horses and men that carried
his treasure, and engulf them in a raging whirlpool from which nothing
could be delivered.

Cursing and swearing, and gnawing his fingers, he went on to
Swineshead Abbey, where monks set before him quantities of pears
and peaches and new cider – some say poison too, but there is very little
reason to suppose so – of which he ate and drank in an immoderate and
beastly way. All night he lay ill of a burning fever, and haunted with
horrible fears. Next day they put him in a horse litter, and carried him
to Sleaford Castle, where he passed another night of pain and horror.
Next day, they carried him with greater difficulty than the day before to
the castle of Newark upon Trent; and there on the eighteenth of October,
in the forty-ninth year of his age, and seventeenth of his vile reign, was
an end of this miserable brute.

Charles Dickens, *A Child's History of England*

'Given by our hand in the meadow which is called Runnymede
between Windsor and Staines on the fifteenth day of June, in the
seventeenth year of our reign.' Thus did King John allow his Great
Seal to be affixed to the document known to history as Magna
Carta and hailed as a 'Charter of Liberty'. It was, in fact, little more
than a draft schedule setting out 'The Articles of the Barons', a
complex feudal document designed to remedy immediate baronial
grievances and to secure the interests of the upper echelons of
medieval society against an unscrupulous monarch. For the future

it was rightly seen as a code of law and custom established by royal charter, and as a statement (even if implied only) that government should not be conducted contrary to the interests of the governed; but in 1215 there were many on both sides who were determined to ensure that it did not survive: some even slipped away from the ceremony at Runnymede to prepare to renew hostilities, and Pope Innocent III had declared the charter 'to be null and void of all validity for ever'.

On 24 June 1215, just nine days after Runnymede, John issued twenty writs to eighteen religious houses, to the Bishop of Tipperary and to Hugh de Neville, his treasurer at Marlborough, as follows:

> We command you that, immediately on view of these letters, with all haste you send to us by two of your monks and by others of your people in whom you have confidence, all that you have of ours in your custody, both of recent and ancient commending, such as vessels, jewels, golden and silver and other.

The king was securing personal possession of his immense collection of valuables before the storm of civil war once more broke over him. The last delivery of his treasure had been made by 25 July; in September the rebel barons seized Rochester Castle and open warfare began.

For the twelve months that remained of his reign, John was engaged in almost continuous campaigning against rebel forces, campaigns which took him from Dover to Berwick-on-Tweed. Circumstantial evidence suggests that the gathered treasure was delivered to Corfe Castle, which was John's headquarters at that time and from where he set out in August 1215 on his campaign. It seems probable that his garnered treasure went with him: the shires of eastern England were in too volatile a state for such accumulated wealth to be dispersed again or to be removed from the king's immediate and closely guarded entourage. Significantly, there is no further reference to it in the official records.

So when, in the autumn of 1216, John began his offensive to subdue the rebels who held much of the eastern counties (aided now by the King of Scots), he almost certainly had an impressive quantity of gold, silver and jewellery with him. We are fortunate that the Patent Rolls have preserved a detailed inventory of John's hoard, and it is easy to understand the 'great grief' that the chroniclers say he suffered when he heard the news of his loss. Scheherazade herself might well have been hard pressed to conjure up so dazzling a collection of gold, silver and precious stones. The principal items in the inventory included over 150 cups and goblets; many dishes and flagons and basins; forty leather belts set with green jasper, sapphires and turquoise, and with gold and silver ornamentation; over fifty rings set with rubies, sapphires, pearls and garnets; several resplendent staffs studded with rubies, sapphires, diamonds, garnets, topaz, emeralds and bloodstone; gold crosses, candelabra, pendants, clasps, phylacteries; four gold and silver shrines elaborately ornamented with many precious stones; and a number of silver vessels, gold coins, and four large drinking bowls with gilded feet and bands. In addition, John had reclaimed the English Crown Jewels and also the Imperial Regalia, which had belonged to his grandmother, the Empress Matilda – an assemblage of crowns, sceptres, swords, crosses, brooches, necklaces and spurs, various robes, tunics, belts, shoes and gloves, all embroidered with precious stones of all kinds.[1]

It is not possible to prove that John had all of this treasure accompanying him in his march to Lincolnshire but, in addition to Roger of Wendover's statement that the king 'lost all the wagons, carts and packhorses with the treasures, precious vessels and all the other things which he cherished', there are the significant facts that the Empress Matilda's Imperial Regalia was never heard of again, and that the inventory for the regalia used at the Coronation of Henry III in 1220 bears little relationship to that which John is known to have possessed in 1216. It would seem that King John did, indeed, lose much of his treasure in the Wash on 12 October 1216.[2]

It is not surprising that several attempts have been made to try to discover such a treasure trove; it is less surprising that all such enterprises have been futile. There are historical and geographical problems that create immense uncertainties in locating even an approximate site for the disaster: neither the chronicles nor the known details of John's itinerary are helpful in indicating the exact route taken by the baggage train as it attempted to cross the Wellstream, although several possibilities have been suggested. There have been important changes in the actual coastline in that area since the thirteenth century and, therefore, in the pattern of currents and quicksands.

Each successive analysis of all the known factors and each impeccably argued theory has been countered within a generation by a new, imaginative reconstruction of the events of those few October days.[3]

The undisputed facts are that, during the autumn and winter of 1215/16, John had conducted an aggressively punitive military operation to subjugate rebel barons in the eastern half of his kingdom, and within three months only London held out against him. At this point Louis of France decided to send an army to overthrow John and seize the English throne for himself. Foreign invasion did not rally the barons to John's side; on the contrary, the country was in turmoil as the disgruntled barons, who had so recently bowed to the king's will, now defected to the invader. Within weeks, however, the French had made it clear that they had come not to assist fellow feudal magnates in their struggle with a heavy-handed monarch but to seize land for themselves. Disillusioned, the rebels hastened to make their peace with John who, spurred to action by this turn of events, once more set out to subdue the eastern counties and to bring relief to the gallant Dame Nicola de la Hay, Castellan of Lincoln, who was holding the castle against the rebel earl of that county. This was achieved with speed and success and, on 11 October, John returned to Lynn (then one of the most important seaports in the kingdom) to arrange for ships to take supplies to his northern strongholds. Here he was warmly received and the prosperous citizens held a special feast in his honour, a feast at which John appears to have indulged himself somewhat unwisely on ripe peaches and new cider. A severe attack of dysentery ensued, and on the next day (12 October) he had difficulty riding his horse as a developing fever steadily drained his strength. The report of the disaster in the Wash added to his woes.

His intended destination that day was the Abbey of Swineshead, some 10 miles north of Spalding, and as the king had business to transact in Wisbech it was apparently decided that the cumbersome baggage train should take the shorter route across the estuary of the Wellstream, notorious for its quicksands and its sudden tidal surges. Low water on that day would have been at noon, and Ralph of Coggeshall states quite clearly that they ran into trouble 'because they had set out incautiously and hastily before the tide had receded' and so 'were submerged in the waters of the sea, and sucked into the quicksand there'.[4] He also implies that only the vanguard actually perished. Precise information on what actually happened at the Wash on 12 October 1216 may never be known. The extent of the loss of the king's treasure, the exact nature of the accident out in the estuary, the precise location where it occurred may always be a matter of fascinating speculation – unless some massive movement of sand and silt one day reveals all.

Within a week the king was dead. He was too ill to ride for the final part of his journey and had to be carried in a litter. He arrived at Newark Castle on 16 October but was too weak to go further. The Abbot of Croxton, renowned for his medical skills, was sent for but to no avail.

It was not long before the thirteenth-century chroniclers began to repeat rumours that John was poisoned by a monk at Swinehead Abbey, who gave him three poisoned pears with his meal. The reason for this desperate act was alleged to be that John had declared his intention of raping one of the nuns, the sister no less of the abbot himself. Given the king's exhausted state after a painful day's journey, the debilitating effects of his illness and the shock of his loss in the quicksands, it seems unlikely that he was contemplating such a venture at that time.[5] John had been on campaign for many weeks before he arrived at Lynn, sometimes riding up to 50 miles a day and then dealing with state affairs each evening; he was already tired and careworn – and not helped by his irascible Angevin temperament. Overindulgence in the peaches and cider of the traditional story would almost certainly bring on the illness and fever that caused his death.

16

The Death of King John: 'A Surfeit of Peaches and New Ale', 1216

King John suffered a prolonged and painful death. The mystery that often surrounds the death of kings and the almost universal belief in John's black-hearted villainy encouraged most chroniclers to follow the lead of Thomas de Wykes, the thirteenth-century chronicler of Osney Abbey, who stated that John had been poisoned by a monk at Swineshead Abbey. A later chronicler, Walter of Gisburn, offered the additional information that the monk had served the king three poisoned pears and had done this because John had declared that he intended to violate a nun at the abbey, none other than the sister of the abbot. An even later version, the best known in modern times, substituted ripe peaches for the pears, omitted the poison and added the effects of excessive indulgence in drinking newly made cider.

The virulent detestation of John displayed by most medieval monastic chroniclers advises a cautious and critical assessment of their writings about him. We may safely discount the tale that John threatened to assault the abbot's sister: he had endured almost three days of agonising and debilitating dysentery on his journey from King's Lynn to Swineshead and rode his horse only with immense discomfort, later having to be carried in a litter. It is difficult to believe that even he was in the frame of mind or physical condition to contemplate an act of rape or any other sexual activity. It is also clear that his illness began two days before he arrived at Swineshead. At King's Lynn – one of the towns that had flourished during John's reign – the citizens feasted the king in great style and it seems that John showed excessive zeal in his appreciation of their hospitality, including an unwise consumption of the new season's cider accompanied by quantities of ripe peaches (it seems more likely that peaches rather than pears would have been served on such a royal occasion; pears were quite widely grown in England by the thirteenth century but peaches were still a luxury – even in the seventeenth century Andrew Marvell wrote of the 'curious peach'). The result for John was an acute attack of painful dysentery, which, combined with exhaustion following many days of hard riding – up to 40 or 50 miles a day, brought on a severe fever, which caused his death two weeks later. Generally reliable thirteenth-century records, such as those compiled by Walter of Coventry and the Annals of Barnwell Priory, provide compelling support for the traditional story that King John did indeed die of 'a surfeit of peaches and new cider', a story so hallowed by time that it appeared as assumed knowledge in G. M. Trevelyan's *History of England*, the most popular general history written in the twentieth century.

King John received little sympathy or understanding from the chroniclers of his time. His aggressive policies towards the Church resulted in almost universal hostility from these monkish accounts, on which historians of the medieval centuries relied for their studies. The Victorian historians seized on these often quite implausible accounts of John's multiple defects of character, and so set in stone the image most people still have of John as thoroughly 'bad'. J. R. Green considered him to be 'the worst outcome of the Angevins';[1] J. W. Stubbs saw him as 'polluted with every crime … there is no redeeming feature';[2] Kate Norgate found him guilty of 'superhuman wickedness'.[3] Recent historians have attempted to present a more favourable interpretation of the man and his reign, particularly his achievements as an administrator,[4] and have commented on the difficult political problems brought about by the changing relationship between the king and his barons. But even though, as W. L. Warren believed, 'the monster of personal depravity … must be dismissed', and 'his most reprehensible acts of wilful violence' should be seen 'as attempts to still his nagging fear of traitors and rebels', the fact remains that John 'could be mean and nasty' and flawed with 'an ignoble small-mindedness about his suspicion'.[4] All in all it is not surprising that the circumstances surrounding his death should be portrayed by the chroniclers in a manner worthy of modern tabloid journalism. One story that does seem plausible is that John's overindulgence at the feast in King's Lynn (which could well have included the traditional ripe peaches and newly made cider) brought on a severe attack of dysentery, which was exacerbated by too many hours and too many miles in the saddle on the journey to Newark, where he developed a high fever and died.

17

Queen Eleanor of Castile:
On Crusade with Prince Edward, 1272

The Saracens ... found (Edward) a very powerful enemy, (and) employed
an assassin to murder him. Edward wrenched the dagger from the man's
hand, and killed him in the attempt, not however before he himself had
been wounded in the arm with the poisoned weapon. The wound, we
are told, might have proved fatal, had not his affectionate wife, Eleanor,
who had accompanied him to Palestine, prevented the effect of the
poison by sucking the wound.

Mrs Markham's *History of England*

Eleanor, daughter of King Ferdinand III of Castile, was married
to Edward, eldest son of King Henry III of England, at Burgos
Cathedral in 1154. Eleanor was twelve years of age and her
husband fifteen. This was a diplomatic arranged marriage to
avoid a threatened Castilian invasion of Gascony and to ensure
that this province remained with the English Crown; but it was
a singularly successful royal marriage with genuine and lasting
affection and devotion. Edward was well above the average height
and was endowed with a strong physique – both useful assets in
the sport of tournaments, of which he was so fond.[1] Eleanor is
described as being 'fair, discreet and devoted',[2] and the little we
know of her certainly bears this out: she accompanied Edward
everywhere, even on the hazardous, crusading expedition to
Palestine; she managed her estates with rigorous (and unpopular)
efficiency; she always upheld the dignity of the Crown of England;
and in 1285 she acted as arbitrator in a long-running dispute
between Edward and the Count of Fronsac. A recent biography
of Edward observes that he was 'fortunate to have Eleanor by
his side during the really constructive years of his reign ... there

can be little doubt that Edward's family was a source of stability and strength'.[3] That family was numerous, too: between 1264 and 1284 Eleanor gave birth to probably fourteen children, of whom five daughters and one son (the future Edward II) survived to adulthood. One of these daughters, Joan of Acre, was born while Eleanor was accompanying Edward on his crusade in 1272.

Edward had distinguished himself in the Baron's Wars of 1264–66, playing a key part in the downfall of Simon de Montfort and the rebellious barons. His father, Henry III, however, refused to award him any official status in the kingdom or to give him any responsible authority, and there was no outlet for the martial skills for which he had recently shown such aptitude. He was, in short, a young man with abundant energy and few outlets for it. This may well have influenced his decision in 1268 to take the Cross, to make a solemn pledge to go crusading against the Saracen in the Holy Land, but it would be unjust to suggest that Edward's motives were entirely self-indulgent. Certainly a Crusade was looked upon as the most exciting adventure of the time for the restless youth of Europe, even if they were, like Edward, no more than conventionally religious. In the 1260s there was a pressing need for a new Crusade: under their powerful and talented sultan, Baibars, the Mamluks of Egypt had swept all before them and, with the fall of Jaffa in 1268, Jerusalem itself was threatened.

Even so, there was no general enthusiasm for another Crusade at the time and Edward soon found that the men and money he would need were not readily forthcoming. Parliament had not been asked to raise money by special taxation for over thirty years and were reluctant to repeat such a grant for Edward's Crusade. Eventually, against the wishes of a complaining clergy, a tax of one twentieth was voted which would yield about £30,000, a totally insufficient financial backing for such an exercise. Recruiting also proved difficult and it is doubtful if Edward's force, which landed at Acre in May 1272, exceeded 1,000 men.

Edward's Crusade, the eighth and last of these military adventures of the European feudal nobility in the Holy Land, was a forlorn enterprise. The forces of the Christian cause were quite inadequate, even when supplemented by knights from the Templars, Hospitallers and Teutonic Order, to operate effectively against the juggernaut of

Baibars' army, which had just successfully stormed the formidable crusader castle of Crac des Chevaliers. Minor sorties against the enemy demonstrated Edward's military prowess but, in the context of the prime objective of the Crusade, were futile. Heat, disease and lack of successful action undermined the already half-hearted commitment of many participants, who began to abandon the campaign and leave for home. When it became clear that the Mongol armies that Edward had hoped would join his crusaders against Baibars had no intention of invading the Holy Land, the Crusade was effectively at an end and a truce was agreed. This was to last for ten years, ten months, ten days and ten hours.

Edward's excursion to Palestine may have done little to secure Jerusalem for the Christians but it enhanced his reputation in the courts of Europe as an able champion of the crusading cause. The last Crusade was made memorable not by military exploits or tales of knightly valour but by the dramatic attempt on Edward's life after it was all over.

Edward delayed his departure from Acre to give his wife time to recover from the birth of their daughter before the long sea journey back to England, and it was during this period of waiting in the oppressive heat of June that the assassin struck. There are many accounts of this incident, with inconsistent versions of what actually occurred, but there is general agreement that the attack took place and that, for a time, Edward's life was in some danger. It seems probable that the assault was carried out by a member of a fanatical Muslim sect, but whether this was the work of the assassins who specialised in the murder of important political figures or was the responsibility of an agent acting at the instigation of Baibars himself remains obscure. Most sources agree that Edward sustained a deep slash in the forearm from his attacker's poisoned dagger, and it is this wound that is at the centre of the famous story of how his distraught but courageous wife sucked the poison from the wound and so saved his life.

This appealing tale first appeared a century after the event in an Ecclesiastical History written by Ptolemy of Lucca, a work not highly regarded by historians. A chronicler from Ypres, also writing in the fourteenth century, states that it was Edward's confidential friend, Otto of Granson, who first suspected poison and sucked the wound.[4] The fullest account is given in the chronicle of Walter of Guisborough, written in the early years of the fourteenth century. It is not necessarily more reliable than any other version of the event, and details of the conversations he records bear the stamp of the novelist rather than the meticulous chronicler. It is Guisborough's account that most directly influenced all those who, in later generations, made this story popular – although the fair Eleanor is not here portrayed as the brave heroine of legend.

Guisborough writes that one evening in June, because of the great heat, Edward was resting on his couch wearing only his shirt and with his head uncovered. A Muslim purporting to be a messenger carrying letters for Edward was admitted to his presence; he suddenly put his hand to his sword-belt as if to take out the letters, but instead produced a poisoned knife and lunged at the prince's stomach. Edward raised his hand to ward off his assailant and suffered a deep wound in his forearm; he then thwarted a second assault by kicking out with such force that he knocked his attacker to the ground; he seized the knife that had wounded him and plunged it into the assassin's stomach and killed him. The Master of the Temple gave Edward a drink containing a precious stone ground up – a not uncommon 'cure' of the time – and encouraged him to 'take comfort and be not afraid for you will not die from this poison'. Doctors applied various medicines to the wound but after a few days the flesh turned black and these doctors held secret discussions among themselves. Edward asked, 'What is it you are muttering about? Am I not going to get better? Tell me. I am not afraid.' One of them, an Englishman by birth, replied, 'You can certainly be cured but it will be necessary for you to suffer pain.' Edward agreed to accept the advice of his brother and a close friend who were nearby. When the discussions were over the doctor ordered that Eleanor should leave the room. 'So,' wrote Guisborough, 'they bore her away weeping and wailing, saying, "Lady, how much better it is that you pour forth your tears than that the whole of England should weep." The blackened flesh was then cut out from Edward's arm and the surgeons assured him that within fifteen days he would be fit enough to mount his horse, a promise that was fulfilled to everyone's admiration.'[5]

This account does nothing to invalidate the traditional story that Eleanor herself sucked the poison from her husband's wound. This she would have done spontaneously immediately after he had been attacked but, according to Guisborough, she was escorted from the room a few days later when it was decided that the rather gruesome surgery was to take place. It is, however, surprising that Guisborough should have omitted such a royal act of courage and wifely devotion if he had knowledge of it. From all the various accounts of this event, despite their apparent contradictions, it would appear that an attempt was made to suck the poison from the wound, that some kind of magic potion was administered and that, in the end, minor but painful surgery was necessary.

Emotional credence in the traditional story is strengthened with the knowledge that, for the remaining twenty-eight years of their marriage, Edward and Eleanor were a devoted, faithful and affectionate couple, a noteworthy exception to the record of most royal marriages. When Eleanor died in 1290 at Harby in Nottinghamshire, Edward ordered a cross to be erected at each one of the places where her coffin rested on its way to Westminster Abbey. These 'Eleanor crosses' stood at Lincoln, Grantham, Stamford, Geddington. Hardingstone, Stony Stratford, Woburn, Dunstable, St Albans, Waltham, Cheapside and Charing Cross. Just three still survive, at Geddington, Hardingstone and Waltham; these and a beautiful effigy on her tomb in Westminster Abbey commemorate, 700 years later, the 'fair, discreet and devoted' Eleanor of Castile.

18

Robert Bruce and the Spider, 1306

Bruce was looking upward at the roof of the cabin in which he lay; and his eye was attracted by a spider, which, hanging at the end of a long thread of its own spinning, was endeavouring, as is the fashion of that creature, to swing itself from one beam in the roof to another, for the purpose of fixing the line on which to stretch its web. The insect made the attempt again and again without success; and at length Bruce counted that it had tried to carry its point six times, and had as often been unable to do so. It came to his head that he himself had fought just six battles against the English and their allies, and the poor persevering spider was exactly in the same situation as himself, having made as many trials, and been as often disappointed in what it aimed at. 'Now', thought Bruce, 'as I have no means of knowing what is best to be done, I will be guided by the luck which has attended this spider. If the insect shall make another effort to fix its thread, and shall be successful, I will venture a seventh time to try my fortune in Scotland...'

Walter Scott, *Tales of a Grandfather*

On 10 February 1306, Robert Bruce and his followers murdered John Comyn, Lord of Badenoch, in the church of the Greyfriars at Dumfries. Comyn was Bruce's last serious rival among the original thirteen claimants to the Scottish throne, left vacant in 1290 without a clear heir on the death, at the age of seven, of Margaret, the Maid of Norway. Of the other main candidates, William Wallace had been crushed by Edward I of England at the Battle of Falkirk in 1298; John Balliol had retired in defeat to a castle in Normandy; John, Baron Hastings, had withdrawn with the grant of an estate in England and the rest were of little account. But Comyn was a formidable opponent; even so, it is unlikely that his murder was premeditated. It was probably the outcome of a heated quarrel over Bruce's plans to campaign against Edward I's 1305 ordinance, which effectively deprived Scotland of its status as an independent kingdom. Symbolic of this was the removal of the Stone of Scone, on which Scottish kings had been crowned since the ninth century, to London, together with the Scottish Crown Jewels. Within a week of Comyn's death, Bruce had himself crowned at Scone and led a patriotic call to arms against the English invader.

Patriotism was not enough. Bruce's ill-armed bands were repeatedly routed by the better-equipped English forces, and Edward decreed brutal and humiliating punishments for any captured 'rebels'. He cast aside all the conventions of chivalry, imprisoning Bruce's sister and the Countess of Buchan in open cages and ordering barbaric executions. Bruce himself succeeded in escaping to a refuge on the island of Rathlin off the coast of County Antrim and, later, on the Isle of Arran.[1]

Within a year, Edward was dead and Bruce resumed his struggle to free his country from English domination and to reaffirm his claim to the throne. His campaign reached its climax with the decisive defeat of the English at Bannockburn in 1314 and the recognition by Edward III in 1328 of the sovereign independence of the Kingdom of Scotland.

Many of the legendary tales that have become attached to the exploits of national heroes do not appear in the chronicles of their own times. The story of Robert Bruce and the spider, perhaps the best known of all the 'moral' tales from our history (if at first you don't succeed, try, try again), first appeared some 500 years after the death of its hero. For it was not until the 1820s that Sir Walter Scott wrote his *Tales of a Grandfather* for his grandson, John Lockhart. As he explained in his preface, they were 'an attempt' at a general view of Scottish history, 'with a selection of its more picturesque and prominent points'. One such point was Robert Bruce's decision to shake off his despondency, emerge from his refuge and embark on another attempt to expel his enemies from the kingdom he claimed was rightfully his. Scott's version of this turning point in Bruce's fortunes has endured with the seal of authenticity derived from Scott's reputation as a scholarly and erudite historian.

Scott did not invent this tale of the spider. A version of it appeared almost 200 years earlier in David Hume's *The History of the House and Race of Douglas and Angus* (David Hume was a historian and poet, 1560–1630. His *History of the House and Race of Douglas and Angus* was published by his daughter, Anna, in the 1640s). Here, Hume related that James Douglas, who was Bruce's close ally and scourge of the English, had one day watched a spider trying to climb a tree. It had fallen to the ground twelve times but had succeeded at the thirteenth attempt. Douglas, seeing Bruce sunk so low in despair, told him of this incident to try to encourage him not to give up hope: 'My advise is to follow the example of the spider, to push forward Your Majestie's fortune once more, and hazard yet our persons the 13 tyme.'[2]

Scott was an assiduous researcher into the archives of Scottish history, and it seems very probable that he discovered this story in David Hume's work and, with his well-tuned literary instincts, saw that it would make a memorable anecdote to anchor Bruce in the mind of his grandson. It was a simple matter to transfer the spider from Douglas to Bruce and from a tree to Bruce's 'cabin'. But it was Douglas rather than the spider who put new resolve into the despondent Bruce.

In most modern versions of the story Bruce is hiding in a cave rather than a 'cabin', and so firmly rooted in tradition and folklore is this tale that on the west coast of the Isle of Arran, an ancient sea-cave has been designated by the Tourist Office and by the Ordnance Survey as 'The King's Cave', a popular tourist attraction but of debatable authenticity.

The earliest account of Bruce's struggle for Scottish independence is in John Barbour's long epic poem 'Bruce', a celebration in verse of the careers of Bruce and his companion-in-arms, James Douglas. The poem dates from 1375, less than seventy years after the events described, and so it conveys much of the immediacy of contemporary history with all the shortcomings of partisan hagiography. Here, the point of interest lies in the absence from the poem of any of the legendary caves or spiders. For these we have to look first to James Douglas and then to Sir Walter Scott. John Barbour, no stranger to legendary tales, knew nothing of spiders.

19

Edward III:
The Order of the Garter, 1348

Mrs Markham: The reign of Edward the Third was the reign of heroes. The martial spirit of the king and of the Black Prince inspired the young nobility with an enthusiastic valour, and it was to encourage this chivalrous spirit that the king instituted the order of the Garter.

Mary: Was it not called so because a lady lost her garter at a ball?

Mrs M: There is a vulgar story that this happened to the countess of Salisbury at a ball at court, and that the king seeing the courtiers smile at the lady's confusion, good-naturedly took up the garter, and bound it round his own leg, saying, 'Honi soit qui mal y pense;' which words have been adopted as the motto of the order. But the story is generally believed to be a mere fabrication.

Mrs Markham's *History of England*

Victorian England had some difficulty with the traditional story that the highest order of knighthood in the kingdom, the Most Noble Order of the Garter, owed its origin to a royal public entanglement – however chivalrous – with so intimate an item as a lady's garter. Many histories of the time choose to make no reference to the legend at all; others – such as, for example, Mrs Markham's – do so only to disparage it as a vulgar fabrication. At the same time professional historians were revising the conventional interpretation of Edward's reign, which was no longer seen as the high point of the Age of Chivalry but as a time of social unrest, economic upheaval, financial extravagance, constitutional misjudgement and irresponsible warfare, thus imposing the values of the nineteenth century on the history of the fourteenth. Edward III understood full well 'how little a policy of peace, retrenchment and reform was likely to appeal to the knightly classes among his subjects'.[1] These privileged men-at-arms, the mainstay of the feudal monarchy, when not engaged in real war demanded a succession of splendid tournaments, colourful pageantry and lavish entertainments as well as all the sexually charged fantasies of courtly love. Edward offered all this in abundance, for, from an early age, he had himself been obsessed with the thrills, the hazards and the rituals of tournaments and joustings – displays of ever-more-dangerous mock battles, all played out to a gallery of noble ladies, whose 'favours' the combatants were pleased to wear. Success on the real battlefield was the ultimate proof of a knight's – and a king's – valour and manhood: Edward could celebrate among his battle honours victories at Sluys, Crécy, Neville's Cross, Calais, Poitiers and the capture of both the King of France and the King of Scotland. The splendour of his court was renowned throughout Europe. To his contemporaries, Edward was the paragon of the Age of Chivalry, and this is the setting against which the tale of the garter is best interpreted.

In 1337, Edward III had vowed to pursue the right he claimed to have, through his mother, to the throne of France, and with a typical flourish of youthful ardour some of the young knights 'made a vow among the ladies that they wolde nat se but with one eye, tyll they had done some dedes of armes in France' and, some nine years later, English knights were still to be seen engaged in battle 'with one of their eyen closedde' with a piece of white silk.[2]

By 1343 these dashing warriors had achieved very little in the preliminary skirmishes of what was to become the Hundred Years' War, and Edward's Christmas feast was preoccupied with plans to rekindle enthusiasm for the fight. On New Year's Day 1344, he proclaimed a series of tournaments to be held at Windsor to commemorate King Arthur, the hero and embodiment of chivalry and knightly valour. A Round Table measuring 200 feet in diameter was built at Windsor Castle, and it was here that Edward announced that he would found a new and prestigious Order of Chivalry. These tournaments were, as John Selden put it, the 'seed-bed' of the order that was to be known as the Order of the Garter.[3] It was to be four more years before this finally came to fruition.

Among the ladies at these royal tournaments would certainly have been seen Queen Philippa's adopted daughter, the young Joan of Kent, aged sixteen years in 1344 and soon to be celebrated as the Fair Maid of Kent, 'the most beautiful woman in the whole realm of England', 'one of the loveliest women in the world', and her contemporary Geoffrey Chaucer confessed that 'to telle yow al hir beautee, it lyth nat in my tonge, n'yn my konnyng'.[4]

At the age of thirteen, Joan had been pressured into a marriage with William Montague, officially the son of the Earl of Salisbury but almost certainly the offspring of a liaison between King Edward and one of the earl's sisters, Catherine. As the queen's adopted daughter and heiress to the Countess of Kent, and from 1344 as Countess of Salisbury, Joan held a prominent position at Edward's court: Froissart confusingly even describes her as 'the quene of England'. In 1346, she was with her father, the Earl of Kent, who in the king's absence in France was in charge of the kingdom and responsible for protecting the North of England against the invasion by David Bruce. This he successfully achieved by the capture of the Scottish king following the Battle of Neville's Cross on 17 October 1346. Eight weeks earlier, Edward's longbow archers had destroyed the French at Crécy.

Edward was well aware that this victory and a triumphal march through Normandy would count for little without possession of the key port of Calais. Anticipating a long siege, the English began the construction of an extensive camp – described by Froissart as 'une bonne ville et grande' – where Edward was soon joined not only by Queen Philippa but also by Joan, Countess of Salisbury, the Fair Maid of Kent, now in her nineteenth year and at the peak of her remarkable beauty. To honour her arrival before Calais 'the kyng made a great feest and dyner to al the lordes and ladyes that were ther', an occasion when, according to the chroniclers of the time, Edward became infatuated with this radiant beauty, 'si noble, si frice, si douce et si belle', and was smitten with 'a sparcle of fyne love that endured longe after'. So ardent and so public did his amorous attentions become that the countess had to reprimand him for his conduct, and the chroniclers took refuge in a deliberate confusion of characters or in embarrassed silence. Enough had been revealed, however, to leave no doubt that, during the many months of the siege of Calais, King Edward became totally enamoured, indulging in gallantries that went far beyond the accepted rituals of courtly love, although there is no evidence or innuendo that their 'affair' was ever more than this.

Calais surrendered on 4 August 1347 and Edward entered the town in triumph. Shortly afterwards there occurred the famous incident when Queen Philippa successfully interceded with her husband to show mercy to six burghers of Calais, whom he proposed to humiliate and then summarily execute. There seems no good reason to doubt the authenticity of this well-known story, which also suggests that, even in the turmoil of his infatuation with the Countess of Salisbury, Edward retained a deep admiration and respect for his wife.

The victorious English now proceeded to celebrate their capture of the town and, at the height of the Age of Chivalry, it seems likely that a grand ball was arranged attended by most of the royal court. It was probably during this revelry that, as Joan was dancing, one of her blue garters slipped from her leg. The king picked it up and put it round his own knee, sharply responding to insinuating remarks from some who watched, 'Honi soit qui mal y pense', adding that before long the blue garter would be honoured by all. This promise was to be fulfilled just a few months later when, at a victory tournament held at Eltham early in 1348, the king appeared wearing a mantle, surcoat and hood decorated with blue garters, while twelve of his knights wore blue garters embroidered with the motto 'Honi soit qui mal y pense'.[5] The new order of chivalry planned by Edward at the Windsor Round Table in 1344 had come into being as the Most Noble Order of the Garter.

Much of the scepticism surrounding this story has been based partly on the confusion arising from contemporary references to Joan, Countess of Kent and Salisbury, as 'the queen', but this term was often used to refer to her in the fourteenth century.[6] The coyness of chroniclers such as Froissart, Jean le Bel and John of Bridlington reveals more than it obscures – Froissart commits himself only to the information that the members of the new Order were to be called 'knyghtes of the blewe garter'; Jean le Bel shies away with the words 'Mais je ne la sçay pas bien deviser, si m'en tairez à tant' (But I do not know how best to explain it, so I'll keep silent about it); John of Bridlington confesses 'Si modo plus dicam, faciam mihi inimicam' (If I say more in this manner I shall make enemies). Chaucerian scholars have pointed out many allusions to Joan and the events in her life, which are to be found in 'The Knight's Tale' and 'The Squire's Tale', stories which are believed to have been written to be read at Garter occasions – Chaucer had been in Edward's service for twenty years and so was well acquainted with the court and the lives of those who surrounded the king.[7] Sceptics have in the past been quick to note that there was no certainty that the lady whose garter is alleged to have slipped off during the dance could positively be identified with Joan of Kent, Countess of Salisbury. Proof that she was indeed the lady involved was established some sixty years ago by Margaret Galway in a study that at last confirms that the traditional story of the origins of the Order of the Garter, as described by John Selden in 1614, is substantially correct: 'The Lady Joan Countess of Kent and Salisbury, her Garter, that falling from her leg in a dance, was taken up by the King, who much affected her.'[8] The 'blewe garter' that fell to the floor at Eltham Palace in 1348 and was immortalised by Edward III undoubtedly belonged to Joan, the Fair Maid of Kent, Countess of Salisbury, later the first English Princess of Wales and the second lady admitted to the Order of the Garter (the first was the king's daughter, Isabella).

There is, it would seem, no good reason to reject the story of the garter and every reason to accept it. Sir Harris Nicolas, the nineteenth-century antiquary, in his astute analysis of the question, commented perceptively that it is 'impossible to believe that a Garter, and so remarkable a Motto, would have been selected unless some incident had given interest to both, more especially as no trace has been found of either having ever before been used as a Badge or Device'.[9]

The New Oxford Dictionary of National Biography (2004) does not accept this interpretation of the story. The garter emblem of the Order it describes as 'enigmatic' and asserts that 'it seems more likely to have been a sword belt exemplifying the martial values of this exclusive band of twenty-knights'. The author claims that 'the story that it represented an item of clothing dropped by the Countess of Salisbury has been discredited'.

The modern emblem of the Order introduced in 1816 may appear to be more like a sword belt than a garter, but it is difficult to believe that there would have been any confusion in the minds of those who first set eyes on the emblem on the mantles of Edward III and his knights in 1348. Jean Froissart, writing at the time, was apparently in no doubt, stating clearly that the members of the Order were known as 'Knyghtes of the blewe garter'.

It is also worth noting that for centuries it was a common folk custom for young men to wear a girl's garter on their hat or round the knee as a mark of affection and esteem. Garters feature prominently in medieval folk traditions.

Addendum

The Countess of Salisbury's loss of her garter in 1348 was not the only historic occasion when such a mishap occurred. In 1580, when Queen Elizabeth was going aboard Francis Drake's ship *The Golden Hind*, her garter slipped off and was gallantly retrieved by her escort. She promptly put it on again in full public view.

20

Dick Whittington and His Cat, *c*. 1375

Nowell: This Sir Richard Whittington, three times mayor
   Sonne to a knight and prentice to a mercer
   Began the Library of Grey-Friars in London,
   And his executors after him did build
   Whittington Colledge, thirteen almshouses for poore men,
   Repaired S. Bartholomewes in Smithfield,
   Glased the Guildhall, and built Newgate.

Hobson: Bones of men, then I have heard lies;
    For I heard he was a scullion,
    And rais'd himself by venture of a cat.

Nowell: They did the more wrong to the gentleman.
                Thomas Heywood, 'If you don't know me,
                       you know nobody', 1606

Thomas Heywood appears to be making two points quite clearly: Richard Whittington was a real historical character but the story of his cat, although well-known in 1606, is fiction. In the 400 years since then, the historical Richard Whittington has been almost entirely forgotten but the legend of Dick Whittington and his cat has become a part of English folklore rivalled in popularity only by Robin Hood and Maid Marian. The innate appeal of the story had made it a popular favourite as early as 1668 when Samuel Pepys went to Southwark Fair and 'saw the puppet show of Whittington', reflecting in his Diary afterwards, 'How that idle thing do work upon people, and even myself too.'[1]

Richard Whittington was born probably sometime in the late 1350s, the third son of Sir William Whittington, who, according to Samuel Lysons,[2] held lands in Pauntley, Gloucestershire, and in Sollers Hope, Herefordshire, manors which had been family estates since the thirteenth century. We know nothing of his childhood, but he was clearly no 'poor, orphan boy' compelled to beg a lift from a passing waggoner to help him get to London to seek his fortune. Nor did he starve there until he managed to find work as a scullion in the home of a rich merchant. He made his way to London, certainly, but he quickly established himself as a mercer, prosperous enough by 1379 to contribute to a loan to the City and with such influential connections that by the 1380s, when he was not yet thirty, he is recorded as supplying velvets and damasks to Henry Bolingbroke, Earl of Derby (later King Henry IV). In the 1390s, he became successively Councillor, Alderman, Sheriff and finally Mayor of London, an office he held in 1397/8, 1406/7 and 1419/21.[3]

His importance in the life of the City is reflected in his presence at a meeting of Henry IV's Privy Council in 1400, probably in relation to the new king's request for substantial loans. For Whittington was by this time one of the richest men in London, and between 1400 and 1421 he was prominent among those who had made a number of substantial loans to both Henry IV and Henry V. E. F. Jacob in the *Oxford History of England* notes that in 1402 he contributed two-thirds of the entire City loan to Henry IV, and states unequivocally that 'with the possible exception of John Hende (another mercer) he was the wealthiest citizen in London'.[4] Only one estimate has ever been put on the amount of Whittington's fortune; a letter to *The Tatler* in 1709 (No. 78) claimed that 'he who began the world with a cat died worth three hundred and fifty thousand pounds sterling'. These loans were not primarily agreed to out of personal loyalty to the monarch nor were they inspired by philanthropic patriotism; they were calculated capitalist ventures with tough contracts and severe penalties for non-payment; lenders expected to double their capital from such financial arrangements.[5] Whittington's dramatic burning of the bonds to cancel the king's debts to him is pure fantasy. Nor did these kings show gratitude to their financial saviours: Whittington never received a knighthood – Sir Richard belongs only in the folktale.

Whittington did marry Alice, the daughter of Sir Ivo Fitzwaryn, also a wealthy merchant who owned extensive estates in the south-western counties. They had no children and Whittington's will records a number of generous benefactions to several institutions in London. These are, perhaps, his chief claim to a place in history: the *Dictionary of National Biography* considers him to have been 'the last of the great medieval mayors'.

Whittington's principal benefactions included the new library at Greyfriars (now the north side of Christ's Hospital); the extension, glazing, and paving with Purbeck stone of the Guildhall; the foundation of Whittington College with almshouses for thirteen poor men and an endowment for divinity lectures to be read there in perpetuity; the rebuilding of Newgate; the renovation of St Bartholomew's Hospital; the foundation of St Mary's College for the education of young clerks and scholars; the establishment of a fish and meat market; the engineering of a water conduit and the building of the church of St Michael de Paternoster, where he was buried.

Whittington died in 1423, and according to Stow's *Survey of London* the Latin epitaph on his tomb referred to him as 'flos mercatorum' (the flower of all the company of merchants). The tomb was rifled for treasure during the Wars of the Roses and entirely destroyed in the Great Fire of London in 1666.

There are various sites in London that claim to be the spot on which Whittington's house stood. J. T. Smith's *Topography of London* of the 1790s featured a large house in Sweedon's Passage, Grub Street; and a house in Crutched Friars was popularly known as Whittington's Palace; but there is no evidence to show that Whittington lived in either. Both were destroyed early in the nineteenth century. Whittington's will states that his house was close to his church of St Michael and this may be taken as a more reliable guide.

An illumination in a copy of the ordinances for Whittington's Hospital is the only probable likeness of Whittington to have survived. The portrait by Renold Elstracke cannot be regarded as authentic since it was painted in the early seventeenth century and shows its subject in a costume characteristic of the reign of Henry VIII. It is of interest only for an alteration made after the painting was finished. James Granger, the eighteenth-century biographer and print collector, points out that the original print had been changed in response to popular demand. In the original version, Whittington's hand rested on a skull but in the popular print this had been replaced by a cat because 'the cat has been inserted as the common people did not care to buy the print without it'.[6]

As Thomas Heywood appeared to suggest in his play, the legend of the cat was apparently well-known by the early years of the seventeenth century, and some years later he wrote *The Famous and Remarkable History of Sir Richard Whittington*, which included the details of the folk tale as it has been told to every generation since in storybooks, puppet shows and pantomimes. In 1885 this was edited by Henry Wheatley, who began his introduction with the words, 'The popular story of Whittington and his Cat is one in which a version of a widespread folk tale has been grafted upon the history of the life of a historical character, and in the later versions the historical incidents have been more and more eliminated.'[7]

Cats were important throughout medieval and early modern times and were found in every household, not usually as domestic pets but as the most effective form of protection against the ubiquitous population of rats and mice. Rarely were they regarded as objects of affection or companionship, but by the reign of Elizabeth I attitudes were slowly changing and within the next hundred years the cat had become a domestic pet 'cosseted and cherished for its companionship'.[8] Samuel Lysons noted that it was in the late sixteenth century that Richard Whittington first acquired his cat[9] and it was in 1605 that it first appeared in literature. This was in the play *Eastward Ho* by Ben Jonson, George Chapman and John Marston, when one character assures another he will be remembered 'when the famous fable of Whittington and his puss shall be forgotten'. A few years later in 1612 the first full version of the story was in the form of a ballad by Richard Johnson, on which many subsequent accounts were based, although each may have added its own embroidery to the detail.[10]

By the early eighteenth century, Whittington and his cat were as firmly entrenched in English folklore as the companionable cat was in the English household (Daniel Defoe noted that few families were without a domestic cat 'some having several, sometimes five or six in a house').[11] In 1711 it was even proposed to produce an opera of Whittington and his cat, but the idea came to nothing because the proprietor refused to allow such 'a great quantity of mice' to be let loose in his theatre. Between 1841 and 1881 there were at least ten publications presenting this now immensely popular folk tale, three of which reflect the evolution of the legend: in 1841 there appeared *The Life and Times of Dick Whittington: A Historical Romance* and in 1881 *Whittington and His Cat: An Entertainment for Young People*, which was soon followed by *The Remarkable History of Richard Whittington and His Cat* by Aunt Busy Bee.

The legend of Whittington and the cat did not spring from the inspired imagination of some unknown Elizabethan, although it was perhaps a touch of genius that brought them together. Folk tales very similar to this were told in many parts of Europe in the Middle Ages. Thomas Keightley in his *Tales and Popular Fictions* (1828) refers especially to the many features that the Whittington story has in common with folk tales from other countries, and especially with an Italian story – *Novella delle Gatte* – first printed in 1483, concerning a merchant from Genoa whose alleged experiences were similar to those attributed to Whittington. Similar stories were also well-known in Portugal, Germany and the Scandinavian countries. All may owe their origin to a tenth-century tale from Persia, which relates how 'one Keis, the son of a poor widow in Siraf, embarked for India with a cat, his only property. There he fortunately arrived at a time when the palace was so infested by mice and rats that they invaded the king's food, and persons were employed to drive them from the royal banquet. Keis produced his cat; the noxious animals soon disappeared, and magnificent rewards were bestowed on the adventurer from Siraf.'[12] Keis returned to Persia a rich man and had an island in the Persian Gulf named after him. Alfonso, the merchant from Portugal, became the third-most-important man in the kingdom; German, Italian and Danish cats brought their owners similar fame and fortune; the cat foisted on to Dick Whittington joined an honourable line of European folk-tale felines. Not least among these was the puss that came to England via France in the later period of Elizabeth's reign, just a few years before the appearance of Johnson's ballad, which gave literary form to the tale of Whittington and his cat. *Le Chat Botté* tells the story of the young penniless son of a miller, whose cat secures him a fortune and the hand of a rich heiress, a felicitous nursery tale soon adopted by the English as *Puss in Boots*.

Richard Whittington, thrice Lord Mayor and distinguished public benefactor, achieved temporary fame in the London of his day; Dick Whittington, legendary owner of a legendary cat, achieved lasting fame in the nursery and in pantomime.

Acknowledgement

H. B. Wheatley's edition of T. H.'s *Life of Sir Richard Whittington* was printed for the Villon Society in 1885 and is the most useful guide to the literature of the Whittington story.

21

The Wars of the Roses: Origin of the Name

Richard Plantagenet (later Duke of York):

> Let him that is a true-born gentleman
> And stands upon the honour of his birth,
> If he supposes that I have pleaded truth,
> From off this briar pluck a white rose with me.

Duke of Somerset (House of Lancaster):

> Let him that is no coward or flatterer,
> But dare maintain the party of the truth,
> Pluck a red rose from off this thorn with me.
>
> Shakespeare, *Henry VI, Part I*, Act 2, Scene IV

Shakespeare's dramatic scene in the Temple Garden is a literary invention but such a powerful one that for generations it was accepted as the true origin of the term 'The Wars of the Roses'. It is true that the red rose had been chosen as his emblem by Edmund Crouchback, 1st Earl of Lancaster, in the thirteenth century, and also by John of Gaunt, 1st Duke of Lancaster, in the following century; it is also true that Edward III's son, Edmund Langley, 1st Duke of York, had adopted the white rose at about the same time and that, in the initial stages of the wars, the protagonists were John of Gaunt's descendant, Henry VI, and Edmund Langley's descendant, Richard Plantagenet. However, Henry VI never used the red rose as his badge; and the white rose was just one of the many badges of Edward IV, while Richard III was always known by his badge of the white boar. It was only when the wars had ended that, for obvious political reasons, the Tudors put deliberate emphasis on the identification of the two rival houses with the two roses, and on the union that the accession of Henry Tudor, heir to Lancaster, and Elizabeth of York had achieved as husband and wife – and on the strength that this had brought to the monarchy and the stability it promised to the countryside after thirty years of warring factions and sporadic lawlessness.

The united roses first appeared in a pageant held to receive Henry and Elizabeth as they entered the city of York in 1486, but it was the birth of Prince Arthur on 19 September a few months later that the chroniclers hailed as the final reconciliation of the white rose with the red.[1] The device of the Tudor Rose soon began to appear as an emblem in art and architecture and as a theme in music and literature. Stephen Hawes, court poet to Henry VII, assisted the propaganda in an address to the king:

Two tytles in one thou didest unyfye
When the red rose toke the white rose in maryage

and Henry VIII's poet laureate, John Skelton, used the occasion of Henry's Coronation to continue the theme:

The rose both white and rede
In one rose now doth growe.

By 1592, when Shakespeare devised the scene in the Temple Garden, the concept of the conflict between Lancaster and York as a war between the red and the white rose had become a familiar part of the Tudor interpretation of history. In his important study of the Tudor Constitution (1583), Sir Thomas Smith wrote of 'the striving of the two roses', a phrase which was echoed by Sir John Oglander who, in the 1640s, during another civil conflict, wrote a tract entitled *The Quarrel of the Two Roses*.

The dramatic constitutional upheavals of the seventeenth century overshadowed these earlier dynastic rivalries and it was not until David Hume wrote his immensely popular *History of England* in the mid-eighteenth century (with two volumes on the events leading to the accession of the Tudors) that these earlier years of the country's history became more widely known.[2] Hume used the term 'The Wars of the Two Roses' as a formal description of the conflict between Lancaster and York, and when in 1880 J. S. Brewer made Hume's five tomes more accessible to the general reader with the publication of his abbreviated version known as *The Student's Hume*, generations of readers learned that 'the supporters of the house of Lancaster chose a red rose as a party distinction, the Yorkists chose a white one; and the civil wars were thus known as the "Wars of the Roses"'.[3]

For those hundreds of thousands of voracious readers in Victorian England, whose choice of reading was likely to be the latest novel rather than the latest history book, the concept of a 'war of the roses' became familiar with the publication, in 1829, of Sir Walter Scott's twenty-third Waverley novel, *Anne of Geierstein*, in which Scott refers to 'the civil discords so dreadfully prosecuted in the wars of the White and Red Roses'.[4] This phrase was to appear again a few years later in Charles Dickens's *A Child's History of England*, where his readers learned of 'those terrible civil wars long known as the Wars of the Red and White Roses because the red rose was the badge of the House of Lancaster and the white rose was the badge of the House of York'.

Maria Callcott appears to have derived her anecdote on this subject directly from Shakespeare. Having given Little Arthur a simplified version of the scene in the Temple Garden she then concludes 'and for thirty years afterwards the civil wars in England were called the Wars of the Roses'.[5]

It would seem then that the concept of the strife between Lancaster and York as a 'War of the Roses' owes its origin to astute political propaganda on the part of Henry VII, who wished urgently to convince the populace that the Tudors would bring an end to the conflict by uniting the two rival houses by his marriage with Elizabeth of York and by the birth of an heir who promised a secure future for the dynasty. But if we seek the origin of the term 'The Wars of the Roses' as a formal title for these thirty years of civil carnage, then either Sir John Oglander or David Hume may claim the honour of the first impress, even if, like Scott and Dickens, they did not use the precise five words of the conventional name by which this episode of our history is now known. Chronology must award that achievement to Lady Maria Callcott, thus offering a neat symmetry of a child called Arthur at each end of the story.

Modern historians show no marked enthusiasm for this description of the conflict between the supporters of Lancaster and York but have provided no better alternative. Referring to the clash of armed men in the streets of St Albans in 1455, Bertram Wolffe in his biographical study of Henry VI makes the comment 'This marked the beginning of the longest period of intermittent civil war in English history, which for want of a better title and by long-established convention, we call the Wars of the Roses.'[6]

1. Caratacus in Rome.
(Library of Birmingham)

2. Gregory and the Anglian children. (Library of Birmingham)

3. The martyrdom of King Edmund. (Library of Birmingham)

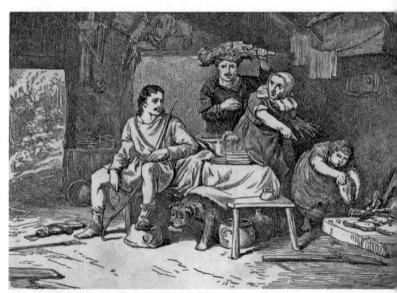

4. King Alfred in the herdsman's cottage. (Library of Birmingham)

5. King Cnut. (Amberley Archive)

6. King Edgar on the barge manned by the eight kings. (Library of Birmingham)

7. Lady Godiva. (Amberley Archive)

8. The death of William Rufus. (Library of Birmingham)

9. The sinking of the *White Ship*. (Library of Birmingham)

10. The murder of Thomas Becket. (Library of Birmingham)

11. Fair Rosamund and Queen Eleanor. (Yale Center for British Art)

12. King John. (Amberley Archive)

13. The Eleanor Cross at Geddington, Northamptonshire. (Author's Collection)

14. Robert Bruce, whose perseverance was said to have been inspired by a spider. (Amberley Archive)

15. Edward III, founder of the Order of the Garter. (Amberley Archive)

16. Henry VI, Lancastrian protagonist of the Wars of the Roses. (Amberley Archive)

17. Edward IV, Yorkist king. (Yale Center for British Art)

18. Henry VII, who emphasised the identification of the two rival families with the two roses. (Yale Center for British Art)

Escape of Queen Margaret.

19. Queen Margaret escaping with her son. (Library of Birmingham)

20. Richard III. (Amberley Archive)

21. Sir Walter Raleigh.
(Amberley Archive)

22. Sir Francis Drake.
(Amberley Archive)

23. Oliver Cromwell.
(Amberley Archive)

SIR ISAAC NEWTON.

24. Sir Isaac Newton.
(Amberley Archive)

25. General James Wolfe. (Amberley Archive)

26. George Washington. (Yale Center for British Art)

27. Admiral Horatio Nelson.
(Amberley Archive)

THE LADY WITH THE LAMP.
(MISS NIGHTINGALE AT SCUTARI, 1854.)

28. Florence Nightingale:
the 'Lady with the Lamp'.
(Amberley Archive)

29. Queen Victoria throwing a rocking horse out of a window: 'we are not amused.' (Amberley Archive)

30. Queen Victoria. (Amberley Archive)

22

Queen Margaret of Anjou:
The Robbers in the Forest, 1462

Queen Margaret and the young prince escaped into a wild forest, where
they were met by some robbers, who took away the Queen's necklace
and her rings, and then began to quarrel about who should have the
most. Queen Margaret took the opportunity of their quarrelling, and,
holding her little son by the hand, she began running through the forest,
in hopes of meeting some of her friends; but she only met with another
robber. She was afraid he would kill her and the little prince, because
they had nothing to give him. Margaret then fell upon her knees, and
owned she was the queen, and begged the robber to protect the king's
son. The robber was surprised, indeed, to see the queen and prince by
themselves, half-starved and weary with running in that wild place. But
he was a good-natured man, and took them under his care; he got them
some food, and took them to a cottage to rest; after which he contrived
to take them safely to the seaside, where they got on board ship and
went to Flanders.

Maria Callcott, *Little Arthur's History of England*

Margaret, daughter of Réné of Anjou, arrived in England in 1443
as the newly-wedded queen of King Henry VI. She was aged fifteen.
Her childhood years had been spent largely in the company of two
remarkable and resolute women: her mother, Isabelle of Lorraine,
and her grandmother, Yolande of Aragon. Both had been deeply
involved in defending the rights and domains of their families in
the complex dynastic feuding of the time when their husbands had
been unable to do so. 'Politics, war and administration seemed to
be the natural vocations of women in her family',[1] and so when
she arrived in England she found the preliminary sparrings, which
were to lead to the Wars of the Roses, a familiar political scene,

and one in which she, like her mother and grandmother, would naturally play an active role. Before many years had passed, she also had to defend the rights of a husband who could no longer take that responsibility himself. In 1453, the birth of her son and heir to the throne of England, Edward, gave her a dedicated mission in life – to protect his safety and to uphold his right to succeed to his father's throne against all those who would deny him amid all the devious conspiracies and treacherous alliances of the conflict between Lancaster and York.

Margaret of Anjou has been criticised for meddling in the politics of her time and she certainly became an unpopular figure in England following some of her actions. She had been schooled in the pragmatic arena of Continental feudalism, where diplomatic agreements were between sovereigns supported by a few powerful noble retainers. Margaret failed to understand that England was a national entity, not a mere family domain where bits and pieces of territory were bargaining counters and where towns and countryside could be pillaged by hired armies with impunity. In defence of her mentally ill husband's right to the English throne and of her young son's right to succeed him, she saw nothing wrong in surrendering Berwick to the Scots in return for Scottish armed assistance, or, in her secret treaty with Louis of France, in handing over Calais in return for similar aid, or in presenting Jersey and Guernsey to her faithful and invaluable retainer, Pierre de Brézé, Grand Seneschal of Normandy. Nor, in the traditions she had inherited, was there anything to warn her that, in England, for the Crown to ally itself with any particular faction of warring nobles was ultimately to invite disaster. That disaster came in 1461 at Towton and again ten years later at Tewkesbury, battles in which thousands of Lancastrian supporters were slaughtered, the power of the great northern barons was shattered and almost all the most eminent Lancastrian nobility were either killed or subsequently executed. Prince Edward himself was found dead on the field of battle, and Margaret was taken prisoner.

Whatever her failings as a politician and military strategist, Margaret of Anjou deserves a certain admiration for the courage and dedication with which, for almost twenty years, she strove to uphold what she believed to be the lawful inheritance of her only son, Edward, Prince of Wales, whom she sought to protect throughout these turbulent years from capture by his ruthless Yorkist enemies. He accompanied her on all her endless campaigns of war and diplomacy, even among the hazards of military engagement. It was the culminating tragedy of her life that Edward was killed in the final disaster at the Battle of Tewkesbury in 1471 and Henry, her pusillanimous husband, for whose rights she had fought, was murdered less than three weeks later. This was truly the end for the House of Lancaster; Margaret was paraded through the streets of London, the humiliated captive of her Yorkist enemy. She was eventually ransomed by the King of France for 50,000 crowns and compelled to give up all claim to the throne of England and also to all the domains of her father, Réné of Anjou, and of her mother, Isabelle of Lorraine. She lived out the rest of her life in regal poverty in her native province of Anjou.

Margaret of Anjou has received scant attention from modern historians – and that largely unsympathetic and censorious. Indeed, as with other prominent figures of her time, her historical reputation owes much to her appearance in Shakespeare's plays, where she is unforgettably portrayed[2] as the 'she-wolf of France ... whose tongue more poisons than the adder's tooth', the virago who vengefully condemned Richard, Duke of York, to summary execution, and cruelly taunted him by waving a blood-soaked handkerchief before his eyes:

Look, York, I stained this napkin with the blood
That valiant Clifford with his rapier's point
Made issue from the bosom of thy boy.

York, in return, in a few memorable phrases, leaves us with the enduring impression of a thoroughly unpleasant harridan:

How ill-becoming is it in thy sex
To triumph like an Amazonian trull;

'Tis beauty that doth oft make women proud -
But, God he knows, thy share of it is small;

Thou art as opposite to every good
As the antipodes are unto us.

This 'tiger's heart wrapped in a woman's hide' was, in fact, an attractive woman in the prime of life (she was still under fifty when, in 1475, she left England for the last time), endowed with a forceful, dominant – even arrogant – personality, deeply aware of the dignity due to royalty and unwavering in her dedication to upholding the legal right of her son to succeed to his father's throne.

It is perhaps regrettable that this indomitable, if misguided, Queen of England – who, because of Henry VI's deficiencies as king, played a more active role in the nation's affairs than any other Queen Consort – should be remembered in almost every popular history of the period only by the story of her encounter with robbers in a forest. The incident is recorded in several contemporary chronicles and, with invented embellishments, by later histories such as those of Paul de Rapin and the Abbé Prévost in the eighteenth century. With such a wealth of contemporary record it seems very likely that such an encounter did take place, but it is curious that from all these sources it is difficult to establish just where and when it took place. The location of the forest is itself left unclear in the early French Chronicles: 'une forest en Angleterre' is not a helpful description although certainly a more probable location than 'a forest in Hainault', a Burgundian province Margaret is unlikely ever to have visited.[3]

Inaccurate narrative of the history of these years has also added to the confusion concerning the date and place of the event. David Hume's *History of England* (1761) established a tradition that Margaret's adventure took place in the forests of Northumberland during her flight to Scotland following the Battle of Hexham in 1464; James Ramsey's *Lancaster and York* (1892) put the story in 1460 after the Battle of Northampton when Margaret and her son escaped through the forests of Cheshire to take refuge in one of her castles in North Wales. A detailed study in the journal *Archaeologia* suggests that Margaret did not return to England between 1463 and 1471, thus invalidating the theory that the meeting with the robbers occurred after Hexham. On Palm Sunday

1461, a Lancastrian force had been defeated in the bloody Battle of Towton, and Margaret found herself deserted by her Scottish ally, her support from Louis XI rapidly wilting under Yorkist pressure, her Northumbrian castles again in Yorkist hands and Lancastrian loyalty there apathetic. Burgundy was overtly hostile, the Hanseatic League more interested in winners than losers, her money at an end. Impulsively, she decided to intervene personally and directly in the complex politics of Europe to try to convince a slippery Louis XI that he would enjoy greater security in his dominions with a friendly Lancastrian monarch on the throne of England than an untrustworthy Yorkist. She left a relieved Scottish capital with her son in April 1462 to join her staunch ally, Pierre de Brézé, at Bamburgh Castle, from where they sailed on their desperate mission, arriving at Sluys in the Netherlands with the un-regal sum of ten florins in their treasury.[4]

Some historians believe that it was on the journey from Edinburgh to Bamburgh that Margaret had her encounter with the robbers in the forest, as this appears to accommodate most readily the main features of the accounts given by the chroniclers and the known historical facts.

The version of the story that became best known and influenced all subsequent popular interpretations was written in the 1840s by Agnes Strickland for her *Lives of the Queens of England*, twelve volumes of well-researched but romantically presented historical literature, which, as Charlotte Yonge informed us, were read as a group activity in Ladies' Circles in late Victorian times. Miss Strickland's version was based on a lengthy twenty-six page account compiled by the Abbé Prévost and published in 1784, and on a curious fifteenth-century collection known as Monstrelet's Chronicles, in which, so Miss Strickland believed, the story was related to Monstrelet by Queen Margaret herself. The author had clearly failed to note that Monstrelet died some years earlier in 1453. Not to be outdone by the lively imagination of the Abbé Prévost, Miss Strickland introduced a few romantic embellishments of her own to create a very readable adventure story, flawed in its historical accuracy but astutely designed to delight, with a frisson of danger and melodrama, the literary ladies of her time. A brief abstract may serve to give the flavour of her tale:[5]

Setting the scene at the defeat suffered by the Lancastrian forces at the Battle of Hexham (a) the author relates that 'Margaret ... fled with her son on foot into an adjacent forest, where ... she unfortunately fell in with a gang of robbers, who ... surrounded and despoiled her and her son of their jewels and costly robes of estate.' While they were quarrelling about the division of the plunder, 'Margaret snatched up her son in her arms, (b) and fled to a distant thicket, unobserved by the pitiless ruffians ... When the shades of evening closed round, the fugitive Queen and her son ... began to thread the tangled mazes of the forest ... While Margaret ... was considering what course to pursue, she perceived, by the light of the moon, another robber of gigantic stature advancing towards her with a drawn sword. (c) Gathering courage ... she took her son by the hand, and presenting him to the freebooter ... said, "Here, my friend, save the son of your king." Struck with astonishment at the majestic beauty of the mother ... the robber dropped his weapon and offered to conduct them to a place of safety. A few words explained to the Queen that the outlaw was a Lancashire gentleman, who had been ruined in King Henry's service. He led the Queen to his own retreat, a cave in Hexham Forest, (d) where the royal fugitives were refreshed.' Queen Margaret then gives a thoroughly regal but totally improbable speech of thanks for the hospitality and decides to seek help and safety in Scotland, a journey which she chose to make via a crossing of the Solway Firth and an undignified landfall from a sandbank from which Pierre de Brézé (who suddenly reappears on the scene) had to carry the queen ashore 'piggy back', with a hitherto unknown squire called Barville assisting Prince Edward in the same way. Eventually all arrive in Edinburgh and thence proceed to Bamburgh and Sluys, as their verifiable history records.

(a) The Battle of Hexham took place in May 1464 (when Margaret was not in England), not in 1463 as Miss Strickland seemed to believe.

(b) Prince Edward was almost ten years old at the time.

(c) The robber's large stature is a Strickland invention.

(d) The cave at Hexham has never been located nor is there any local knowledge of the 'legend' Miss Strickland refers to.

Other details described in this largely fictitious account of 'The Queen and the Robbers' are likewise unknown to history and include 'Milady Nevill', a lady of easy virtue and allegedly a sister of the Earl of Warwick, and also a character more often met with in children's pantomime than among the ranks of fifteenth-century nobility – Dame Trott. All other details seem to be derived from the account given by the Abbé Prévost or the Monstrelet Chronicles.

Clearly Margaret's adventure with the robbers has been heavily overlaid with literary invention and historical romance. That she had some such encounter seems very likely and it probably occurred in the summer of 1462 on her journey from Edinburgh to Bamburgh en route to Sluys and King Louis XI. Even so, James Ramsey's view that it all happened during Margaret's flight to North Wales after the Battle of Northampton in 1460 is not without support: the contemporary chroniclers William of Worcester and William Gregory both describe how, following this defeat, Margaret and Edward fled towards North Wales and on the way were robbed of their jewels and other possessions by her own servants 'besyde the Castelle of Malepas' in Cheshire, then a heavily forested area. Here, says Gregory, a servant of her own that she had made both yeoman and gentleman, 'spoylyde hyr and robbyde hyr, and put hyr soo in dowt of hyr lyffe and sonys lyffe also. And thenn she com to the Castelle of Hardelowe (Harlech) in Walys'.[6] Either version may, in the end, be true; it does seem improbable, however, that even Margaret of Anjou would have experienced two such adventures in the space of two years.

23

George, Duke of Clarence:
Death in a Butt of Malmsey, 1478

He was found guilty, and sentenced to be publicly executed. He never was publicly executed, but he met his death somehow in the Tower, and, no doubt, through the agency of the King or his brother, Gloucester, or both. It was supposed at the time that he was told to choose the manner of his death, and that he chose to be drowned in a butt of malmsey wine. I hope the story may be true, for it would have been a becoming death for such a miserable creature.

Charles Dickens, *A Child's History of England*

George, Duke of Clarence, was one of a trio of brothers born to Richard of York, the principal Yorkist claimant to the throne of England in the first stages of the Wars of the Roses. Edward, the eldest, reigned as Edward IV from 1460–83 (with a six-month interlude during the temporary restoration of Henry VI); Richard, Duke of Gloucester, the youngest, seized the throne as Richard III in 1483; George, heir presumptive until 1466, was, like his brothers, good-looking, superficially witty and intelligent, plausibly eloquent and gifted with a dangerous charm. He was also lacking in common sense, political perception or judgement and family loyalty, and even at the age of twenty-nine when he met his end, he was continuing to display the petty jealousy, unreal ambitions and self-centred acquisitiveness of a spoilt adolescent. He had tried Edward's patience to breaking point; for eight years 'he had been a public nuisance and a danger to a dynasty only precariously established. Fratricide may be a horrible spectacle but Clarence thoroughly deserved his fate.'[1]

The government of England in the fifteenth century was essentially vested in the person of the monarch and, in an age when baronial strife and inherited family rivalries within the feudal aristocracy were always simmering beneath the surface, a firm hand on the reins of kingship was the bond of society. Edward II, Richard II and Henry VI had all lost sight of this fundamental tenet of medieval government and had paid the price. Edward IV had briefly relaxed his hold in 1470 and allowed an 'overmighty subject' to seize the moment to replace him in a brief 'readeption' (a term used at that time to mean 'restoration') of the feeble and incompetent Henry VI. With the crown once more in his possession, in 1471 Edward saw to it that the same mistake would not be made again – and anyone, even his own brother, who attempted to defy, circumvent or in any way weaken the authority of the king would be summarily dealt with.

Edward had been unusually generous to his younger brother in the years following his accession to the throne in 1461. He was immediately created Duke of Clarence and awarded vast estates in Northumberland, Yorkshire, Kent, Surrey, the Forest of Dean and the West Country. He was subsequently put in charge of Commissions of the Peace in eighteen counties. The indictment against him in 1478 commented that 'so large portion of possessions that no memory is of ... that any king of England gave so largely to any of his brothers'.[2]

Even so, Clarence continued to display childish hostility and jealousy towards Richard, who had in fact been treated much less generously, and towards the Woodville relatives of the queen, who dominated Edward's court and were making the most of their newfound power and influence. This immaturity in Clarence's character was seized upon by the Earl of Warwick, who was conspiring to exploit the rumbling discontent in the countryside over Edward's failure to control the activities of lawless magnates.[3] By 1468 Warwick appears to have seduced Clarence into his conspiracy to mount a rebellion against Edward by vague promises that Clarence would be put on the throne in his brother's place. Clarence now married Warwick's daughter, Isabel, in defiance of Edward's firm and understandable direction that he should not do so. Warwick's temporary success and capture of Edward had no political power base. An outbreak of local discontent in Lincolnshire in 1470, which was fomented by Warwick and

Clarence, ended in the so-called Battle of Lose-Cote Field where the rebels fled in panic before the force rapidly assembled in the king's name. Clarence had gained nothing from Warwick's moment of victory but this did not prevent him from joining Warwick in France, where he was humiliated by having to accept Warwick's arrangement with Margaret of Anjou for an invasion of England to depose Edward and replace him, not with Clarence, but with a Lancastrian restoration of Henry VI, whose son, Edward 'Prince of Wales', was promptly married to Warwick's daughter, Anne, thus virtually ending any remote dream Clarence may have had of succeeding to a Yorkist throne.

At the court of the briefly restored Henry, Clarence was deprived of almost all his estates, contrary to the agreement reached with Margaret of Anjou, and, according to contemporary records, he was 'held in great suspicion, despite, disdain, and hatred, with all the lords, noblemen, and other, that were adherents ... with Henry the usurper'.[4] It is small wonder that when, in 1471, Edward mounted an invasion to recover his throne, Clarence, having joined Warwick in the invasion, defected with 4,000 retainers to his brother's side. At the battles of Barnet and Tewkesbury, the invaders were decisively defeated and, with the death in battle of Prince Edward, the capture of Margaret of Anjou and the subsequent murder of Henry VI, the Lancastrian cause was, for the time being, in ruins; Clarence was again accepted at Edward's court.

Clarence's pathetic greed and unscrupulous ambition had led him into naive and irresponsible political misjudgements but the next few years were to show that he had learned nothing. Despite his treachery to Edward in joining Warwick's invasion and embracing the possibility that he would replace his brother as king, Clarence did not return to court with appropriate grace and humility. On the contrary, he began an open and bitter rivalry with Richard, Duke of Gloucester, the brother who had stood loyally by Edward throughout the crisis of 1469–71 and who was duly rewarded with virtual control of England north of the Trent, except for those lands held by the Percies, earls of Northumberland. Clarence could not contain his resentment and when Richard married Anne Nevill, daughter of the Earl of Warwick and heiress to the vast Nevill estates on which Clarence had designs of his own, he childishly tried to prevent the marriage by hiding Anne disguised as a kitchen-maid. A more prudent man would, in the circumstances, have acquiesced gratefully in the restoration of the lands and the position of real influence to which Edward restored him by reinstating him in his former estates in the West Country with the addition of the lands in Devon and Cornwall forfeited by the rebellious Courtenays. Instead, Clarence demanded that the Nevill estates be shared between himself and Richard even though, according to the Laws of Inheritance, neither had a legal right to them. A bitter conflict ensued that disrupted the life of the court and the efficient government of the realm. For three years the strife continued, and eventually it required two Acts of Parliament to effect an agreed settlement by which Clarence and Gloucester were to succeed to the Warwick estates in the right of their wives (Warwick's daughters): Warwick's widow was barred from any claim and was treated as if she 'were now naturally dead'. The whole episode was dishonourable and sordid and serves to emphasise the extent to which Clarence's deplorable conduct had exhausted the patience of the king: it is no surprise that one of the charges made against Clarence was that he had shown himself to be incorrigible.

Indeed, Clarence was to demonstrate this yet again almost immediately. Isabel, his duchess, died in 1476, shortly after giving birth to her second son, Richard. Clarence accused one of her servants, Ankarette Twynho, of poisoning her; she was forcibly carried off to Warwick for trial, found guilty and promptly hanged. The jury alleged that they 'gave the verdict contrary to their conscience' for fear of the Duke of Clarence who, they declared, had acted 'as though he had used a king's power' compelling them to an 'inordinate hasty process and judgement'. At the same time, Clarence was engaged in suspicious dealings with Louis XI of France and Margaret of Burgundy, involving plans for his marriage to Mary, daughter of Charles, Duke of Burgundy, and 'the greatest heiress of her time', an arrangement obviously fraught with immense danger for Edward IV, already alerted by reports that Clarence was spreading stories that Edward was a bastard and so had no right to the throne. Not surprisingly Edward forbade the Burgundian marriage, and relations between the brothers became openly hostile. Edward's patience eventually snapped and he ordered the arrest and trial of three of Clarence's associates – John Stacey and Thomas Blake, astronomers of Merton College, Oxford, and Thomas Burdett, a gentleman of Clarence's household. All were charged with having used magic arts to 'imagine and compass' the death of the king and the Prince of Wales; all were found guilty. Stacey and Burdett were hanged but an intervention by a royal councillor saved Blake from the same fate. Clarence tactlessly chose to appeal to the council over the king's head, thus increasing Edward's irritation with him. The final straw came when Louis XI cynically revealed to Edward all that Clarence had been boasting he would do in England once he had acquired control of Mary of Burgundy's inheritance. In June 1477, Clarence was arrested and committed to the Tower.

Six months later the king summoned Parliament and introduced a personal Bill of Attainder charging Clarence with high treason, outlining details of Edward's patience, clemency and generosity towards him and listing Clarence's numerous offences and treasonable activities over many years. He had proved himself to be 'incorrigible' and the safety of the kingdom demanded that he be sentenced and all his titles and lands forfeited to the Crown. No one spoke in his defence, but Clarence denied all charges and, melodramatically, insisted on his right to prove his innocence by the ancient Ordeal by Battle. Parliament obediently accepted Edward's indictment of his brother – legal tradition held that the word of the king was 'the most perfect of records' – and Clarence was duly sentenced to death. Reluctant, no doubt, to set a dangerous precedent, Edward hesitated but the matter was resolved when the Speaker of the Commons requested that the verdict of Parliament be carried out forthwith. To avoid family shame and the undesirable spectacle of a public execution Clarence was secretly put to death in the Tower on 18 February 1478.

The manner of his death has become the subject of much debate and it now seems improbable that the exact details will ever be known. The contemporary and usually reliable Croyland Chronicle makes only a vague comment on the event, referring only to 'the execution, whatever its manner may have been'.[5] But the author was a member of Edward IV's entourage and he had to be circumspect. The Chronicle of London, also contemporary, records that Clarence met his end in 'a barell of Malmsey wine', and this is the story that has come down the centuries.[6] It appears in Dominic Mancini's *Usurpation of Richard III*, compiled in 1483, where the 'barell' is translated as a 'butt' and it was repeated by Tudor historians such as Polydore Vergil, Thomas More, Edward Hall[7] and Robert Fabyan, who stated unequivocally that 'the Duke of Clarence ... then being a prisoner in the Tower, was secretly put to death and drowned in a barrel of Malmsey wine within the said Tower'.[8] Shakespeare adopted a similar version, but the murderers stabbed their victim before dumping the body in the barrel of malmsey.[9] The French chronicler Jean Molinet maintained that Clarence was allowed to choose the manner of his death, and drowning in malmsey was his preferred choice.[10] Some historians have had difficulty in accepting this bizarre departure from life and give greater credence to the version given by the Burgundian chronicler, Olivier de la Marche, who claimed that Clarence was drowned in a bath, perhaps a more easily credible, if more mundane, end but infinitely less colourful and less in keeping with Clarence's maverick character.[11] Since the tale of the barrel of malmsey appeared so soon after 1478 in two largely trustworthy chronicles, the balance of probability would seem to lie in favour of the traditional story. It may perhaps be relevant to note that a fifteenth-century barrel or butt of malmsey was large enough to hold 140 gallons.

There is no evidence to suggest that Richard, Duke of Gloucester, took an active part in the murder of his brother as Shakespeare and many others believed. This accusation does not appear in any contemporary source and surfaces for the first time in Thomas More's *History of King Richard III*, but More is careful to add 'but of this point there is no certainty, and whoso divineth upon conjectures, may well shoot too far as too short'.[12] Richard may have been well pleased to look upon the demise of Clarence as the convenient removal of a rival to the crown he was scheming to usurp; he was certainly present at the council meeting where it was decided to proceed against Clarence and he unquestionably made significant gains in lands, title and influence as a direct consequence of Clarence's death. It would seem that he actively condoned the execution but it was left to Shakespeare to make him a direct accomplice: in Scene I of *The Tragedy of Richard III* Richard is given the damning lines:

> Go tread the path that thou shalt ne'er return.
> Simple plain Clarence, I do love thee so
> That I will shortly send thy soul to heaven,
> If heaven will take the present at our hands.

Whatever other crimes Richard may have been guilty of – and they were many – it seems improbable that the murder of Clarence was one of them. Ultimately, Edward must bear the responsibility, but for him it had become a political necessity.

24

Richard III:
'Misshapen Dick'?

Thy mother felt more than a mother's pain,
And yet brought forth less than a mother's hope -
To wit, an indigested and deformed lump
... misshapen Dick ... scolding crookback
> Shakespeare, *Henry VI, Part III*, Act 5, Scenes V and VI

Deformed, unfinished, sent before my time
Into this breathing world, scarce half made up
... thou lump of foul deformity
This poisonous bunch-backed toad
Thou elvish-marked, abortive, rooting hog
That bottled spider, that foul bunch-backed toad
> Shakespeare, *Richard III*, Act 1, Scenes I, II and III

Richard III reigned as King of England for just twenty-six months from 26 June 1483 to 22 August 1485, the shortest reign in post-Conquest history (this excludes the nine-day reign of Lady Jane Grey in 1553, which rarely receives official recognition). Yet he has been the subject of more historical controversy than any other English monarch and the flood of literature relating to his life or aspects of his reign has not ceased for five centuries and is today as vigorous as ever. Richard was already widely unpopular in his own time and Tudor historians exploited this to the full, emphasising the image of a tyrant, usurper and murderer. Shakespeare, in a blistering and dramatic tour de force, portrayed him as a monster, murderer and archetypal villain; and despite the attempts of modern historians (helped and sometimes hindered by the zealots of the Richard III Society) to present a more balanced picture, it is Shakespeare's compelling portrait that remains firmly fixed in the popular mind, an image powerfully reinforced by recent stage and film interpretations.

Shakespeare did not create the 'black legend' of Richard III. His main sources were the Tudor chronicles and histories, which cleverly built upon the hostile tales of Richard's tyranny and villainy already in circulation before the end of his reign. Even the non-judgemental recorder who compiled the Great Chronicle of London for these years is considered by modern editors to be reliably representative of 'the adverse opinion of Richard III already current in the early years of Henry VII'.[1] However, there is no mention in this chronicle of the alleged unnatural birth features or physical deformity that Tudor writers made so much of and that Shakespeare so damningly dramatised.

It was John Rous, who died in 1491, who claimed to know that Richard was born with teeth already grown and hair down to his shoulders – neither, it seems, medically unknown phenomena but both permitting the denigrating description 'unnatural' – a slur apparently justified by the further preposterous assertion that he had spent two years gestating in his mother's womb. These and many other tales concerning Richard's 'monstrosity' were current in London even before his death at the Battle of Bosworth and gained rapidly in circulation and credibility in the years immediately following.[2]

But neither in Rous nor in the Great Chronicle is there any suggestion that Richard had a crookback – Rous says only that his right shoulder was higher than his left. The first direct reference to a more marked deformity appears obscurely in the archives of the City of York where the Civic Records for 1491 note that a certain John Payntour is alleged to have accused Richard of being 'an hypocrite, a crookback and buried in a ditch like a dog'.[3] This northern hot-tempered outburst might have had little historical significance but it was taken up and developed by Sir Thomas More in his *History of King Richard III* (*c.* 1514) and subsequently by later Tudor writers, notably Edward Hall, whose chronicle, The Union of the Two Illustre Families of Lancaster and York, was much used by Shakespeare. More's history was the first not only to draw special attention to Richard's appearance but to inflict permanent damage on his historical reputation by a direct association of his alleged physical defects with his wicked conduct and the flaws in his character: 'Little of stature, ill-featured of limbs, crook-backed ... hard-favoured of visage ... he was close and secret, a deep dissimuler, lowly of countenance, arrogant of heart, outwardly companionable where he inwardly hated, dispitious and cruel.'[4] Polydore Vergil, perhaps a more accomplished historian than More, used the same technique to blacken Richard's character: 'Little of stature, deformed of body, one shoulder higher than the other ... a short and sour countenance, which seemed to savour of mischief and utter craft and deceit.'[5] Edward Hall colourfully embellished what More and Polydore Vergil had begun and presented Shakespeare with a monster whose 'tyrannous reign' marked the 'culmination of savagery', specifically in the murder of Edward V 'who was never king crowned but shamefullie by his uncle slaine'. Shakespeare set in stone this image of Richard Crookback, the archetypal villain, and it is now set in glass in John Hutton's striking etched-glass portrait of Richard at Stratford-upon-Avon.

Modern historical studies have, quite rightly, attempted to break away from the 500-year-old obsession with Richard III's responsibility for the various crimes he has stood accused of, and from the historically peripheral issues of his moral and physical shortcomings. His life and reign are now more appropriately assessed in the social and political context of his time and, while he cannot be exonerated from some of the charges against him – notably his treasonable act of usurpation of the throne, some of them are now seen more as errors of political judgement than acts of moral turpitude.

It does seem possible, however, that we can now try to dispose of the legend of Richard Crookback or 'misshapen Dick'. This was a Tudor fabrication intended to create an association between a man's 'monstrous' appearance and the villainy he was accused of. It was developed by most Tudor writers and finally sanctified by Shakespeare in the most compelling and devastating character assassination in all literature, so compelling that a historian of such distinction as James Gairdner could write at the end of the nineteenth century, 'a minute study of the facts of Richard's life has tended more and more to convince me of the general fidelity of the portrait with which we have been made familiar by Shakespeare and Thomas More'.[6]

New light was shed on this problem when the two earliest surviving portraits of Richard were placed under scientific scrutiny: that in the Royal Collection, probably painted in the early 1480s, which now clearly suggests a raised right shoulder, reveals under X-ray examination that this is a later overpainting and that the original showed a straight shoulder. The portrait in the London Society of Antiquaries, which has been dated to 1505, also shows Richard with a straight shoulder-line.[7] It is, of course, well known that portrait painters presented their subjects in the best possible light, glossing over any defects and creating whatever degree of beauty or dignity seemed necessary to please their patrons – only Oliver Cromwell famously insisted that the artist must include 'all these roughness, pimples, warts and everything as you see me'. Even so there is a significant difference between a raised shoulder and a crookback.

Modern medical science has also investigated the problem. In 1977 a study in the *British Medical Journal* examined the available evidence concerning Richard's birth and physical condition, giving full consideration to the tradition that his mother had a long and painful labour before a breech delivery, a circumstance which could have involved forcible traction resulting in some form of injury to the scapula and the upper arm muscles. Any suggestion of a hunchback is rejected, as is the likelihood of any paralysis. In his youth Richard exercised constantly to become more than proficient in the martial arts; he was certainly in the thick of the fight at the battles of Barnet and Tewkesbury, a situation which would demand the ability to wield a heavy battleaxe, indicating no serious muscular weakness, especially for a man of small stature. The medical analysis concludes that if Richard suffered from any 'deformity' at all it was either no more than an exaggeration of the normal inequality in the height of the shoulders or a minor form of Sprengel's deformity, an underdevelopment of the scapula affecting the muscles so that, with growth, one shoulder would not descend as far as the other. There is no historical evidence from Richard's own lifetime of almost thirty-three years referring to any deformity; this was an invention of Tudor writers who aimed to portray the last usurping Yorkist king as a monster and 'a monstrous body was the natural casing for a monstrous mind ... so the image of Richard the Monster was magnified by his unnatural birth, his deformity and his dishonourable death'.[9]

The discovery of the remains of Richard III in Leicester in 2013 revealed that the king did have a slight curvature of the spine but this would hardly have resulted in the hunchback appearance of historical legend.

The identification of Richard's remains in the foundations of the church of the Grey Friars also disposes of the traditional story that when the convent was dissolved Richard's body was thrown into a river.

25

The Battle of Bosworth:
The Crown in a Hawthorn Bush, 1485

> After the battle the crown was found hanging up in a hawthorn tree on top of a hill. This is memorable as being the only occasion on which the crown has been found after a battle hanging up in a hawthorn tree on top of a hill.
>
> W. C. Sellar and R. J. Yeatman, *1066 and All That*

In his authoritative biography of Richard III, Professor Charles Ross commented that 'there have been almost as many different accounts of the battle of Bosworth as there have been historians. The main problem arises from the fact that no reliable and first-hand account of the engagement was ever written, or, at any rate, has survived', a circumstance guaranteed to produce a profusion of studies all claiming to shed more accurate light on the events of that August day when the Plantagenet monarchy came to an end and the Tudors seized the throne.[1] The numerous volumes of monastic chronicles, which provide so much of our historical information about the Middle Ages, were almost a thing of the past in the late fifteenth century and the chronicles and accounts of events that replaced them were often strongly laced with Tudor propaganda. The only contemporary account of the final days of Richard III – the Croyland Chronical Continuation – has little to say about the Battle of Bosworth, showing interest only in the list of casualties, while the contemporary ballads known as 'The Ballad of Bosworth Field' and 'The Ballad of Lady Bessy' give few details of the actual course of the battle.[2] For much of our knowledge of the battle we must rely on the full description given by Polydore Vergil (a naturalised Italian) in his *English History*, written some twenty years after the event at the behest of Henry VIII. Later chronicles were largely based on Vergil – neither Edward Hall nor Holinshed was able to add much of significance, nor was Francis Bacon's *History of the Reign of Henry VII* able to do more than make a few speculative suggestions.[3]

Shakespeare's *Richard III* was a powerful instrument in consolidating Richard's historical reputation as the epitome of villainy but, as a dramatist, his only interest in the actual battle was in the final clash of arms between Henry and Richard, memorable in literature for Richard's alleged cry, 'A horse! A horse! My kingdom for a horse!' and for Henry's curt pronouncement, 'The bloody dog is dead.'

Whatever may have been the actual sequence of events on this field of battle, there seems to be no doubt that immediately after the melee was over Henry of Richmond was proclaimed king, and the 'crown' – in the form of the golden circlet that Richard, like Henry V at Agincourt, had worn throughout the battle – was ceremoniously placed upon his head to the acclamation of all those still on the scene. This 'Coronation' confirmed the right of kingship that God had granted to Henry 'by manifest, certain and authentic revelation' in the defeat and death in battle of his rival.[4] Who precisely performed the act of coronation has been one of the minor mysteries of this momentous occasion: Polydore states clearly that it was Lord Stanley, now unhesitatingly on the winning side, who did Henry this service, and Shakespeare imagines him doing so with a flourish and a certain condescension:

> Courageous Richmond, well hast thou acquit thee.
> Lo, here this long usurped royalty
> From the dead temples of this bloody wretch
> Have I plucked off, to grace thy brows withal.
> Wear it, enjoy it, and make much of it.

William Hutton, in 1788, put forward the suggestion that it was not Lord Stanley but Sir William Stanley who placed the crown on Henry's head after it had been found on the battlefield.[5] The only supporting evidence for this comes from the quite unreliable ballad 'The Song of Lady Bessy'; strict protocol would not have permitted a mere knight to take precedence over a powerful and opportunist noble such as Lord Thomas Stanley.

That Richard lost his crown in the heat of the battle is entirely believable – indeed, it would be difficult to believe that he did not – but where it was 'found', whether by Reginald Bray as Hutton suggested or by some other survivor of the final melee, has never been reliably ascertained. According to tradition, it was discovered hanging in a thorn bush and this is how the story is portrayed in almost all popular history books, films and television presentations. Even academic studies of the period find it necessary to devote at least a footnote to set out an opinion on this fairly trivial question.

The first intriguing point is that none of the Tudor accounts of the battle make any reference to a hawthorn bush. Vergil and the Croyland Continuation state that the crown was recovered from the 'spoyle of the felde', and Bacon follows in their footsteps with no reference to a hawthorn. Even Shakespeare, who clearly used these chronicles, does not, as one would expect, include such a useful dramatic device in the final scene of *Richard III*. Nor, surprisingly, does the story appear in the catalogue of such anecdotes that feature so strongly in the popular history books of the Victorian era. It was not until the appearance, in 1898, of James Gairdner's *History of the Life and Reign of Richard III* that the hawthorn bush achieved a kind of 'official' endorsement and a permanent place in the Bosworth story. Gairdner states unequivocally that 'the crown which Richard had worn in the field was found after the battle in a hawthorn bush, where apparently, after falling from Richard's head, it had been secreted during the engagement'.

Gairdner gave no references for such a positive assertion and he appended a footnote which begs further questions: 'In memory of this event Henry adopted the device of a crown on a hawthorn bush, which is seen in the great window of Henry VII's Chapel at Westminster.'[6]

Such a device does appear in the Westminster Abbey window and also features elsewhere in Tudor heraldic badges, but there seems to be no evidence to support the suggestion that it was introduced specifically 'in memory of' an incident on Bosworth Field. Feasible perhaps, and romantic, but that is not an adjective one would easily associate with Henry VII – astute, cautious, prudent, austere, aloof, resolute, certainly; romantic, no.

Controversy over Gairdner's comments has continued to divert historians ever since. In 1960, Sydney Anglo came to the conclusion that the whole story was apocryphal since 'there seems to be no sixteenth century authority for connecting this emblem with the Battle of Bosworth', though it is beyond dispute that the Tudors used the hawthorn as a badge.[7] In 1972, S. B. Chrimes in his biography of Henry VII agreed with this, but in 1981 Charles Ross demurred on the grounds that 'it is a somewhat unlikely badge to have been the subject of pure heraldic invention' and 'it is hard to see why it became such a common element of Tudor iconography'.[8] The debate continues.

The hawthorn was much more highly regarded in medieval times than it is today. Indeed, particularly in France and southern England, it was a 'sacred' tree, a potent symbol of the renewal of life and hope for the future, and it featured prominently in May Day celebrations and in other springtime folk customs. In the late fifteenth century, belief was still strong in the symbolic significance of the natural world; emblem books were very much in vogue,[9] and in heraldry – as in folklore – plants, flowers and animals provided a vocabulary with which human qualities, hopes and fears could be described.[10] The hawthorn – or whitethorn, as it was then commonly known – was a widely recognised emblem for all that Henry hoped for, and all but a few die-hard Yorkists yearned for: a new beginning and an end to dynastic faction and political upheaval, a period of stability in which trade could prosper and the law be upheld. If the adoption by Henry of the hawthorn bush as part of his heraldic symbolism could convey this to a people steeped in emblematic folklore, then it could well have been a characteristic and calculated political decision. The story of the crown in the thorn bush is quite a separate issue and, since there is no reference to such a conveniently symbolic accident in any sixteenth-century source, its veracity must remain doubtful.

26

Hugh Latimer:
'The Lighted Candle', 1555

The accession of Queen Mary Tudor marked the beginning of an ideological conflict as she embarked on her attempt to reverse the English Reformation and return her kingdom to the papal fold. Curiously, the central theme of this conflict was not principally one of theology but one of authority in the political relationship between the Church and the Crown and their respective responsibilities towards the people as a whole. Inevitably, this was seen as a struggle for the soul of the nation, a bitter conflict between the Catholic Church of Rome and the Protestant Church in England. In her zeal for her cause, Queen Mary destroyed it. The death by burning of 281 of her subjects from all levels of society ensured the wide acceptance of Elizabeth's Church settlement in 1559 and also an implacable hostility to Roman Catholicism in England for centuries to come. As English Protestants followed one another to the stake they were regarded as more than martyrs dying for their faith; they were helping to mould the 'English nation'. In her popular early twentieth-century history *Our Island Story*, Heather Marshall exhorted her young readers to 'honour them as heroes' for 'these men and women who suffered death so cheerfully for their religion fought for British freedom as much as Caratacus or Harold or any of the other brave men of whom you have heard'.

At the heart of this dramatic episode in English history were the three 'Oxford Martyrs': Thomas Cranmer, Archbishop of Canterbury; Nicholas Ridley, Bishop of London, and Hugh Latimer, Bishop of Worcester under Henry VIII and later fervent and fearless preacher, an eloquent defender of the independence of the Church and the citizen against the 'tyranny' of both the Crown and the Papacy. Ridley and Latimer were burned together and it was the frail seventy-year-old Latimer who encouraged the nervous Ridley to show courage in the face of pain and death: 'Be of good comfort, Master Ridley, and play the man. We shall this day light such a candle, by God's grace, in England, as I trust shall never be put out.'

These were the words ascribed to Latimer by John Foxe in his famous book generally known as *Foxe's Book of Martyrs*, in which he commemorated those who perished in the flames of the Marian persecution. Foxe's account of these events is regarded as a reliable historical record but, as with all other reports of the words spoken by historical characters on notable occasions, we can never be certain that they are accurate in every detail. One has to listen for the ring of truth and Latimer's 'lighted candle' rings as true as any.

The New Oxford Dictionary of National Biography (2004) casts doubt on the authenticity of Foxe's story of Latimer's words to Ridley, and the late Professor Patrick Collinson in his detailed study of the *Book of Martyrs* (P. Collinson, 'Truth and Legend: The Veracity of Foxe's Book of Martyrs', *Elizabethan Essays* (1994)) also discussed the veracity of Foxe's account. The 'lighted candle' story does not appear in the first edition of the book (1563) but was added to the 1570 and later editions. Nor does it appear in other contemporary accounts of the burning of Latimer and Ridley. It is possible that, in a departure from his usual practice, Foxe may have made it up, perhaps following the well-known account by Eusebius of the martyrdom of Bishop Polycarp of Smyrna in the mid-second century. It is, however, one of those inspirational anecdotes that will live on whether false or true for, as M. V. Hughes, our 'London Child of the 1870s', put it, 'they are much more glowing than if they were introduced with the chilling words "It is said that"'.

27

Sir Walter Raleigh:
The Tale of the Cloak, *c.* 1581

He found the Queen walking till, meeting a plashy place, she seemed to scruple going therein. Presently, Raleigh spread his new plush cloak on the ground, whereon the Queen trod gently, rewarding him afterwards with many suits for his so free and seasonable tender of so fair a foot of cloth.

Thomas Fuller, *Worthies of England*, 1662

One day Elizabeth was passing along the streets, and the people as usual came crowding to see her. Among them was Sir Walter Raleigh. The Queen stepped from her coach and, followed by her ladies, was about to cross the road. But in those days the streets were very badly kept, and Elizabeth stopped before a puddle of mud. She was grandly dressed, and how to cross the muddy road without soiling her dainty shoes and skirts, she did not know. As she paused Sir Walter Raleigh sprang forward. He, too, was finely dressed and he was wearing a beautiful new cloak. This he quickly pulled off and, bowing low, threw it upon the ground before the Queen. Elizabeth was very pleased and, as she passed on, she smiled at the handsome young man who had ruined his beautiful cloak to save her dainty shoes, and ordered him to attend her at court. Raleigh's fortune was made.

H. T. Marshall, *Our Island Story*

In 1581, Walter Raleigh was twenty-nine, brazenly ambitious, swashbucklingly self-confident, and already well experienced in war, overseas discovery and piracy against the Spaniards, and in the brutal and tangled affairs of Ireland.[1] He was determined to make his mark at the court of Queen Elizabeth, the centre of power and influence, a place of constant worldly entertainments and enjoyment, a scene of almost ludicrous gallantry speaking the language of chivalry and love, an intricate knot garden of gossip, intrigue and danger, an irresistible magnet to a young, impetuous adventurer anxious to make his name and fortune. Raleigh had many other qualities to commend him to the court: he came from a line of long-established gentry families with distinguished contacts throughout the West Country, he was well read and cultured with a marked intellectual curiosity; his interest in science and navigation enabled Thomas Hariot, a much-neglected pioneer in mathematical theory and optics, to prepare the ground for Newton; he was also the chief patron of Jacques le Moyne, a painter whose *La Clef des Champs* was the first study of the flora of North America; John Hooker's new edition of Holinshed's Chronicles was dedicated to Raleigh, who also characteristically contributed a substantial sum to the funds that helped Thomas Bodley to found his great library at Oxford; and there were few at court who could pen a true line of poetry so well as he – even Spencer, in a flight of poetic fancy, referred to him as 'the summer's nightingale'.

All this was not enough: Raleigh may have been a gentleman but he was not of noble birth. He badly needed an aristocratic sponsor who would secure his acceptance at the queen's court. We do not know whom Raleigh persuaded to perform this service for him; it was certainly not Lord Grey, Lord-Deputy of Ireland during Raleigh's service there (and who had declared that he 'neither liked Captain Rawley's carriage nor his company'), but it could have been Thomas Radcliffe, Earl of Sussex, whose long experience may have led him to see in the young Raleigh a promising counter to what he saw as the excessive and dangerous influence on the queen of Robert Dudley, Earl of Leicester.

Sussex, Leicester or any other useful noble courtier – for Raleigh, an introduction to court life was just the first step, and he had no intention of wasting time slowly climbing the slippery ladder that led to royal favour. The queen had to be made aware of his presence instantly and, adventurer and opportunist as he was, he seized an early occasion to make a dramatic entrance on stage. The story of the queen and Raleigh's cloak was to become one of the favourite anecdotes of English history.

The tale was first told by Thomas Fuller in his *History of the Worthies of England*, published after his death but probably written well within the living memory of those who were able to recall Raleigh's eventful life and unpopular trial and execution. Fuller's version may never be put to the test of verifying evidence, but from all that we know of Raleigh's character and personality – and especially his talent for theatrical publicity and for taking time by the forelock – it undoubtedly has the ring of truth. It is noteworthy that the custom of spreading a cloak for a lady to walk on was well known in France, where Raleigh had spent some time a few years earlier.[2]

It was Sir Walter Scott who put the flesh on the bare bones of the story in his novel *Kenilworth*. With his brilliant literary imagination and his unrivalled grasp of historical detail, Scott creates a story so entirely authentic and convincing that it is small wonder that from this trifling incident Sir Walter Raleigh will forever be known, probably correctly, as the 'Knight of the Cloak'.[3]

Less convincing is Fuller's continuation of the story, where he relates that after the cloak incident, as the queen continued on her way (now, we are asked to believe, with Raleigh as a close companion), Raleigh halted the procession and with a diamond ring scratched on a window the line 'Fain would I climb, yet I fear to fall', and Elizabeth, apparently not at all piqued by the presumptuous antics of the young upstart, calmly borrowed the ring and added a well-judged piece of advice: 'If thy heart fail thee, climb not at all.'

Raleigh certainly had a remarkable ability to know how to please Elizabeth and, given the spirited personality and sparkling intellect of both the queen and her young cavalier, even this legendary tale has a certain plausibility; but, unlike the story of the cloak, it is probably apocryphal.[4]

28

Sir Philip Sidney:
The Glass of Water at Zutphen, 1586

The Earl of Leicester's campaign in the Netherlands would probably have been forgotten, but for its occasioning the death of one of the best writers, the best knights, and the best gentlemen of that or any other age. This was Sir Philip Sidney, who was wounded by a musket ball in the thigh as he mounted a fresh horse, after having his own killed under him. He had to ride back wounded a long distance, and was very faint with fatigue and loss of blood, when some water, for which he had eagerly asked, was handed to him. But he was so good and gentle, even then, that seeing a poor badly wounded common soldier lying on the ground, looking at the water with longing eyes, he said, 'thy necessity is greater than mine' and gave it up to him. This touching action of a noble man is perhaps as well known as any incident in history ... so delightful is an act of humanity, and so glad are mankind to remember it.

Charles Dickens, *A Child's History of England*

Philip Sidney was born in 1554 and died in 1586 at the age of thirty-one. Yet in his short life he acquired a position of pre-eminence throughout Europe as the ideal 'Renaissance Man', the 'uomo universale', a man of many parts with outstanding ability in all of them. His personal charm and skills as a courtier and diplomat were universally acknowledged; his stature as a scholar and poet was recognised in every European university; as a leader of men he was looked upon as the great hope of European Protestantism. As the son of Henry Sidney, Elizabeth's effective governor of Ireland and Wales, and as the grandson of John Dudley, Earl of Warwick and Duke of Northumberland, as the nephew and likely heir of Robert Dudley, Earl of Leicester, and as the godson of King Philip of Spain and John Russell, Earl of Bedford, he was a figure of some prominence, power and influence at the court of Elizabeth I and in the counsels of most of the princely courts of Europe. Indeed, his queen thought he had too much influence and charisma and was often very cool in her relations with him, but in Europe his magnetic personality and political skills elevated him to heroic status – even the haughty Don John of Austria 'gave more honour and respect to this hopeful young gentleman than the ambassadors of mighty princes'.[1]

Sidney's place in English literature was assured with the (posthumous) publication of his major works such as *Astrophil and Stella* and *Arcadia*. Contemporary poets were lavish in their admiration – Richard Carew called him 'the miracle of our age'; Edward Dyer echoed this when he saw Sidney as 'the wonder of our age'; a modern biographer wrote that with the literary works of Sidney and Spenser, 'at one bound English was established among the great literatures of Europe'.[2] It is not surprising that the death in battle of such a man in the prime of life gave rise to so many panegyrical anecdotes, one of which – the story of the dying soldier and the glass of water – appears in most history books and is a standard point of reference in many a Sunday sermon. It is told with its powerful moral message in many books for children, as Maria Callcott told it to her grandson – 'because you will wish to be like him when you grow up'.

In 1584 the Protestant towns and provinces of the Netherlands were under severe pressure from the Spanish armies under the Duke of Parma. With the assassination of William of Orange, the Dutch were now leaderless and it seemed only a matter of time before they had finally to succumb to the Spanish Catholic yoke. The French refused to help and a reluctant Elizabeth of England decided to intervene with a force of 6,000 foot soldiers and 1,000 cavalry under the command of the Earl of Leicester. It was widely believed that the queen would appoint Sidney as the governor of the key port and fort of Flushing, guarding the mouth of the River Scheldt. This was, in effect, a military appointment and would be an acknowledgement of Sidney's already proven abilities as a soldier.

In the event, to general surprise and the obvious chagrin of Sidney himself, Elizabeth favoured William Davison, one of her secretaries who also had knowledge and experience of the Low Countries. This apparent snub by the queen almost changed the entire course of Sidney's life; he immediately left the court and began negotiations with Sir Francis Drake to join in a venture to establish a colony in North America.

This was not a sudden new pursuit for Sidney. He had taken a keen interest in several earlier ventures, so much so that in 1582 Richard Hakluyt had dedicated his *Divers Voyages Towards the Discovery of America* to 'that most virtuous gentleman master Philip Sidney esquire'. As a participant in Humphrey Gilbert's expedition, Sidney had been granted 3 million acres of undiscovered land in America. The queen's decision to deny him Flushing was an opportunity to accompany Drake in 1585.

Sidney's office as Master of Ordnance proved to be of great advantage to this enterprise. Arrangements were soon being made for quantities of guns, powder and munitions to be delivered to Drake, who was busy fitting out the ships at Woolwich; Sidney knew that the queen would not give him permission to embark on such a venture and it was therefore secretly agreed with Drake that he would join the fleet only when it set sail from Plymouth. Such secret plotting was not easy to keep from the ears of Elizabeth and her intelligence agents, and the fleet had been at sea only a few hours when a message arrived ordering Sidney's immediate return to take up 'instant employment under his uncle (the Earl of Leicester) ... in the Low Countries'. Greville in his *Life of Sir Philip Sidney* states that 'Philip would gladly have demurred' but 'duty of obedience' to the queen prevailed.[3] So Sidney went to Flushing to fight the Spanish. One can only speculate on the course history might have taken if his dream of colonising America had ever come to pass.

The Earl of Leicester proved to be an inept general; the queen was frustratingly parsimonious with men and money; the Netherlands States General were obstructive. It was largely left to Sidney and a few able commanders to organise a campaign to check the Spanish advance as fort after fort fell to Parma's troops. A daring and successful night action seized the town of Axel, an operation of no great military significance in which Sidney played only a minor part. This did not deter Fulke Greville from exalting the achievements of his hero: 'How like a soldier did he behave himself, first, in contriving then in executing, the surprise of Axel.'

A subsequent attempt to take Gravelines was thwarted by misleading intelligence, and Sidney had to withdraw before a hail of gunshot leaving forty-four of his men as prisoners, all of whom were murdered by their Spanish captors. Even this could not halt Fulke Greville's panegyric pen: 'How providently again did he preserve the lives and honour of our English army at that enterprise.'[4]

In desperation, Sidney went over Leicester's head and appealed directly to Walsingham, and so to the queen, for reinforcements and especially for funds to pay his increasingly restless soldiers. Meanwhile Parma's armies marched on and the threat of total defeat stared Sidney clearly in the face. Flushing was the only port on the Netherlands coast with the anchorage needed by a Spanish fleet planning to invade England; Sidney had emphatically made this point to Walsingham: 'without it', he wrote, the King of Spain's force 'should never be able to invade England'.

To relieve the now very real threat to Holland, Sidney decided to attack the Spanish garrisons in the forts along the River Issel. Doesburg was captured after a formidable assault and the English force, now with Leicester in command, turned its attention to Deventer and Zutphen some miles to the north. Deventer was taken with little opposition, but Zutphen, defended by a system of forts deemed to be impregnable, had already successfully defied a ten-month siege. Its supplies were now seriously depleted, but a Spanish force was marching to its relief. The English plan was to lay siege to the forts and prepare to ambush the relief convoy, which was expected to be accompanied by the usual small military escort. A small force was therefore assigned to the task of preventing this relief for Zutphen from achieving its objective.

It was 22 September; early-morning autumn mist shrouded the landscape and hid from view the approaching Spanish convoy. With the sudden lifting of the fog, the tiny English force found itself confronted with 3,000 Spanish foot soldiers and 1,500 horsemen. Undeterred, Sir John Norris's cavalry charged the Spanish driving them back until intense musket shot checked any further advance. Two further charges again threw the enemy into disarray but were again halted by the Spanish musketeers. Even their opponents paid tribute to the bravery of the English cavalrymen in this engagement, from which they had to withdraw when the Zutphen garrison sent out 2,000 more troops to escort their vital supplies safely into the town. The English had gained only a hollow success at a cost of twenty-two foot soldiers and a dozen cavalrymen.

Sir Philip Sidney suffered a musket shot in his thigh during the third charge and was taken by barge down the River Ijssel to Arnhem for medical treatment. Fulke Greville, who was not present at Zutphen – having been ordered by the queen not to leave England, nevertheless wrote a detailed account of events there describing how the musket shot 'brake a bone of Sir Philip's thigh' and how he was borne from the field, bleeding profusely, on the back of his horse, 'the noblest and fittest biere to carry a Martiall Commander to his grave'. He then relates the famous story of the glass of water:

> In that sad progress...being thirstie with excess of bleeding, he called for a drink, which was presently brought to him; but as he was putting the bottle to his mouth, he saw a poor Souldier carried along ... gastly casting up his eyes at the bottle. Which Sir Philip perceiving, took it from his head, before he drank, and delivered it to the poor man, with these words, 'Thy necessity is yet greater than mine.' And when he had pledged this poor souldier, he was presently carried to Arnhem.[5]

Such a tale appears entirely convincing as it accords so completely with the character of Sidney as portrayed in the contemporary biographical eulogies of Fulke Greville and Thomas Moffet and in the outpouring of idealised tributes emanating from the universities of Oxford and Cambridge. However, a more objective interpretation of the evidence[6] makes it quite clear that at first no one – and certainly not Sidney himself – expected him to die; his injury was not considered to be life-threatening and, on 27 September, four days after he was wounded the surgeons sent a note to the Earl of Leicester stating that Sidney 'found himself very well and free from any ague'. This was followed five days later by a statement from Leicester himself that 'the worst days be past, as both surgeons and physicians have informed me, he amends as well as is possible in the time. He sleeps and rests well and has a good stomach to eat'; a bulletin confirmed in similar terms four days later still – a fortnight after he was wounded. None of the eyewitness accounts make any reference to the incident of the glass of water, and when Sidney went into a sudden decline just 24 hours before he died there was fear and desperation in his actions – 'Get me a doctor quickly' – as he hurriedly completed his will and penned an urgent appeal for help to a German doctor, Johan Vier. It seems likely that his wound had become infected and gangrene had set in, a condition for which at that time there was no known treatment. This would not have been the time for gentlemanly altruism.

If the incident of the glass of water took place at all, it must have been in the immediate aftermath of the battle when Sidney's wound did not seem to put his life in danger and this would greatly diminish the heroism of the gesture to the 'poor souldier'. Fulke Greville is a valuable source for information on Sidney's life but when his account of events is unsupported by other evidence, it is, as a recent biographer has said, 'usually best taken with a considerable pinch of salt'. For this reason, serious doubts must be cast on the legendary glass of water, a moral tale that 'seems to owe more to Greville's classical reading than to the events at Zutphen'.[7] This, presumably, is a reference to a similar tale told of Alexander the Great. Plutarch's cautionary words should, perhaps, be kept in mind when reading Greville's version of Sidney's career: 'I am writing biography, not history.'

Thus the unsuccessful skirmish at Zutphen (where Sidney played only a minor role) became a glorious victory, his often lukewarm relationship with the queen was transformed into the intimacy of a close confidant, whereas, in fact, Sidney spent little time at court – his limited financial resources forced him to live in the country for much of the year. Even his literary fame arrived posthumously, for none of his major poetic works were published in his lifetime. Even so, on the eve of Sidney's death, Dr John James, his chief physician, wrote a poignant tribute in his journal: 'So rare a gentleman and so accomplished with all kind of virtue and true nobility, as few ages have ever brought forth his equal, and the very hope of our age seemeth to be utterly extinguished.'[8] With or without the tale of the glass of water, Sidney was clearly held in high esteem and he was given a spectacular state funeral, an honour since bestowed only on Horatio Nelson and Winston Churchill.

Sidney's death also has a moral for those who slavishly follow current fashion. It seems that young cavalry officers considered it unmanly to wear full armour and it had become almost obligatory to enter the fray without protection for the hands, arms and legs. According to John Smythe, a military expert of the time,

> The imitating of which their unsoldierlike and fond arming, cost the noble and worthy gentleman Sir Philip Sidney his life, by not wearing his cuisses (thigh armour) ... if he had that day worn his cuisses the bullet had not brake his thigh bone, by reason that the chief force of the bullet ... was in a manner past.[7]

29

Sir Francis Drake:
The Game of Bowls on Plymouth Hoe, 1588

A pinnace came scudding into Plymouth with the astounding news that the Armada was off the Lizard ... The old story goes that Howard and his officers were playing bowls on the Hoe, when Captain Fleming of the 'Golden Hind' burst into their game with his staggering tale. In the general consternation all looked to Drake for the word, and all he would say was that he meant to finish his game. 'There's time for that,' he said, 'and to beat the Spaniards after'.

J. S. Corbett, *Drake and the Tudor Navy*, 1898

Then on Friday, July 29th after dinner, Captain Thomas Fleming, of the bark 'Golden Hind' ... arrived to report that he had sighted a large group of Spanish ships near the Scilly Isles with sails struck, apparently waiting for the rest of the fleet to come up. According to the legend Drake was playing bowls on Plymouth Hoe when Fleming brought the news. Presumably Howard was there too since Fleming although attached originally to Drake's western squadron would have reported to the Lord Admiral, not to Drake; but there is little room in the legend of the Armada for anyone but Drake. At any rate, in the legend it is Drake who replied (one fancies the leisurely bowler's stance as he hefts his wood and eyes the jack, one hears the echo of the west-country drawl): 'We have time enough to finish the game and beat the Spaniards, too.'

Garrett Mattingly, *The Defeat of the Spanish Armada* (Cape: 1959)

A wonderful story has been told and retold about Drake's equanimity during this time of stress. When word arrived that the Spanish Armada had been sighted, the captains of the fleet were supposedly playing bowls on the Hoe at Plymouth, where there was a good view of the harbour and the fleet. Rather than going immediately to his ship, Drake said that there was sufficient time to finish the game, and then to finish the Spaniards. His exact words vary from one telling to the next, primarily because no eyewitness account of the incident has ever been found.

Harry Kelsey, *Sir Francis Drake: The Queen's Pirate* (Yale: 2000)

The death of Sir Francis Drake off Porto Bello in 1596 caused more of a stir in Spain than in his own country. The Spanish commander who had brought Drake's last expedition to nought described him as 'one of the most famous men of his profession that have existed in the world, very courteous and honourable with those who have surrendered, of great humility and gentleness'. In 1598, the poet Lope de Vega wrote his epic poem 'La Dragontea' celebrating the career of the 'dragon' who had harassed Spanish ports and shipping and denigrated the Holy Catholic Church for a generation; and a few years later the historian Antonin de Herrara included accounts of Drake's various exploits in his *General History of the World*. In the England of James I, Drake was recognised as one among many outstanding seamen of the Elizabethan age but no more: it is significant that the only biographies to appear in the seventeenth century all bore as part of their title the words 'Sir Francis Drake revived'.[1] Thomas Fuller portrayed Drake as a patriot and Protestant hero, whose plundering of Spain's ports and treasure ships was to be applauded as he was striking a blow against the Catholic enemy and in support of Elizabeth his queen.[2] A lone and virtually ignored eighteenth-century work attempted to tarnish this interpretation of Drake's exploits by emphasising those aspects of his expeditions that involved conduct that was brutal, illegal, un-Christian and brazen piracy against Spanish ports and shipping.[3]

This was not how Drake or his queen, or most of his countrymen, saw it: he went against the Spaniard with the full authority of Elizabeth to avenge the wrongs committed by Spain against England, to avenge the Spanish treachery against Hawkins at San Juan in 1568, to avenge the Spanish treatment of Protestants in Europe and to strike a blow against the growing Spanish threat to invade England, overthrow the queen and forcibly bring the country back to the rule of the Catholic Church. If, in the course of achieving this end, he made a fortune for himself and his queen at Spain's expense this could readily be justified if the greater end were achieved. The historical fact is that, although England and Spain were not officially at war before 1585, a state of war had prevailed for many years before that, disguised only by the formalities of a pragmatic diplomacy.

Long before the arrival of the Armada, Drake was feared in Spain as the 'dragon' who had so daringly 'singed the King of Spain's beard' at Cadiz and had given Spanish captains a bloody nose in the Indies and on the high seas for almost twenty years. 'A single purpose animates all his exploits and the chart of his movements is like a cord laced round the throat of the Spanish monarchy.'[4] In Spain, Drake was held in awe: he was the embodiment of England's power at sea, a naval captain of fearsome ability, a ruthless and implacable foe who could be overcome only by an overwhelming array of Spanish naval and military might. The English fleet that awaited the Armada was 'Drake's fleet' – he was the dragon they had to destroy and they had not yet tamed him.

Eulogised by G. M. Trevelyan in the 1920s as 'first the greatest of privateers and afterwards the greatest of Royal Admirals', Drake had languished for over 200 years in the historical shadows. It was not until Victorian times that he was restored to the ranks of English national heroes. In an age when Britannia ruled the waves and British gunboats were an ever-ready instrument to enforce British interests from China to Gibraltar, it was patriotic to believe that this was no more than England's traditional role in world affairs and that the dashing officers and jolly sailor boys of the 'Queen's navee' were the true heirs of the great Francis Drake. 'It is, it is a glorious thing, To be a pirate king' chorused the Pirates of Penzance; Drake's drum, kept in his home at Buckland, was repaired and spruced up to become a national treasure immortalised in Sir Henry Newbolt's eponymous poem, which assured the nation that 'If the Dons sight Devon' Drake himself would 'quit the port of Heaven, An' drum them up the Channel as we drummed them long ago'.

In those heady days of imperialistic splendour, when the legendary tales of English history were children's bedtime reading, the story of Drake and the Armada was dug out from dusty documents, embellished and told and retold until it was incorporated into the corpus of the national history. The confident nonchalance demonstrated by Drake in the story of the game of bowls seemed to epitomise that imperturbable sangfroid and assured superiority that was popularly believed to be the hallmark of every British officer. The story appeared in 1898 in J. S. Corbett's authoritative work *Drake and the Tudor Navy*, and it has found a place in almost every important book on Drake ever since.

Any historical anecdote without trustworthy eyewitness confirmation and that also purports to record words spoken at the time has to be treated with caution: Garrett Mattingly in his 1959 account of the defeat of the Spanish Armada comments,

> Of course it need not have happened. There is no contemporary authority for it; the earliest record is more than forty years after the event. But forty years is within the limits of fairly reliable oral transmission. It could have happened. The words are like Drake; they have his touch of swagger and flair for the homely jest to relieve a moment of tension. Also it would be like Drake to say the first word, even though his commander-in-chief stood at his elbow.[5]

This echoes Corbett's comment that 'the story may well be true. It is quite natural that the admirals may have been seeking diversion from their toil after the midday dinner, as the custom was, and such a piece of posing to produce an enheartening moral effect was quite in accordance with Drake's methods and character.'[6] This, too, was the view taken by J. A. Williamson in his 1938 *Age of Drake* and by most other writers on the period; even Harry Kelsey in his book *Sir Francis Drake: The Queen's Pirate*, which is almost unremittingly hostile to Drake, agrees that it is 'a wonderful story' that 'may be true', but doubts whether there is any factual basis for it.[7]

The earliest reference to the occasion is in 1600 in John Stow's *Annales of England*, where we learn that 'Officers and others kept revels on the shore, dancing, bowling and making merry when at the instant of the foe's approach'. This was only twelve years after the event and so would readily be remembered. In 1624 there appeared a tract entitled 'The Second Part of Vox Populi', the work of Thomas Scott, chaplain to James I. This was primarily an attack on the Spanish ambassador, Count Gondomar, who was pressing for a marriage between King James's son Charles and the Spanish Infanta. Included in the tract was an account of a meeting of the Spanish council to discuss relations with England, during which the Duke of Braganza is alleged to have said, 'Did we not in '88 carry our business for England so secretly ... as in bringing our navy to their shores while their commanders and captains were at bowls upon the Hoe at Plymouth?'[8] This, too, would have been within living memory. Scott is unlikely to have known so precisely what went on in a meeting of the council in Madrid; the important fact is that he so effortlessly alludes to a game of bowls, probably referring to a popular anecdote from the time of the Armada. It would be curious if he had plucked the idea out of the air, especially as it had little relevance to the thrust of his political argument.

These near-contemporary sources may seem to lend credibility to the story of a game of bowls being played as the Armada approached, but neither mentions Drake by name, although it is not unreasonable to assume that, as Vice Admiral, he would be among the 'officers and others' referred to by Stow. Drake's name first appears in this context in 1736 when Sir William Oldys published his edition of *Sir Walter Raleigh's History of the World*, and in the preface he wrote the oft-quoted passage:

> Captain Thomas Fleming brought (news) into the harbour on the 19th of July that he had discovered the enemy approaching from the Lizard Point in Cornwall. The captains and commanders were then, it seems, at bowls upon the Hoe at Plymouth; and the tradition goes that Drake would needs see the game up; but was soon prevailed on to go and play out the rubbers with the Spaniards.[9]

This is also the earliest source for any comment Drake may have made, but Oldys refers only to 'a tradition that Drake would needs see the game up' – he does not put words into Drake's mouth. Even in 1855 when Charles Kingsley wrote his *Westward Ho!*, this part of the legend was still unformed. Indeed, Kingsley puts the words into the mouth of Hawkins: 'Come, Frank Drake, we'll play the game out before we move.'[10] It was not until Cobbett's great work in 1898 that precise words were given to Drake: 'In general consternation all looked to Drake for the word, and all he would say was that he meant to finish the game. "There's time for that," he said, "and to beat the Spaniards after."'[11] Corbett's invention so quickly became part of the legend that a version of it was incorporated into the authoritative *Dictionary of National Biography* just a few years later; all later versions are no more than variations on it. It would be surprising if Drake had not made some audacious comment or displayed a certain bravura at that moment, if only to calm the nerves of his fellow officers, but precisely what that was we do not know.

We can, however, be reasonably certain, as John Stow informs us, that Admiral Howard and Drake and others were engaged in a game of bowls. This had been a popular sport for many years: a thirteenth-century royal archive at Windsor refers to two men bowling towards a cone, and a bowling green is known to have existed at Southampton in 1299. By the reign of Edward III, the pastime had become so widespread that the king considered it to be a threat to archery practice and the game was officially banned – with little effect.[12] Shakespeare was certainly familiar not only with the game but also with the new 'bias': in *Richard II* the queen and her ladies are seeking relaxation in the garden and the following exchange takes place:

Queen: What sport shall we devise here in this garden
         To drive away the heavy thought of care?
Lady: Madam, we'll play at bowls.
Queen: 'Twill make me think the world is full of rubs,
         And that my fortune runs against the bias.[13]

None of the 'bowls' used in the Elizabethan game has survived but it is known that the bias was introduced in the mid-sixteenth century, probably by the Duke of Suffolk. No formal manicured greens had yet arrived and the Elizabethan lawns and grassy areas where the game was played were, indeed, full of rubs, so the open headland of Plymouth Hoe would have been regarded as just as suitable as any royal garden. John Stow's reference in 1600 to officers dancing and bowling 'on the shore', and Thomas Scott's assertion in 1624 that they were 'at bowls upon the Hoe', were both within living memory of the actual event. Yet there are those who believe that a bowling alley at an inn would have been a more probable venue as the ships' officers would have frequented such a place; Kingsley created the whole scene at 'the little terrace bowling green behind the Pelican Inn', which 'commanded a view of the Sound and the shipping far below'. Unfortunately, the only historical evidence for this is an obscure seventeenth-century reference to a Pelican Inn at Plymouth.

The absence of any eyewitness account of this famous game of bowls has led some commentators to doubt its authenticity but, as Robert Birley demonstrated in his lecture 'The Undergrowth of History', 'if a story takes some time to become visible, as it were, that is not in itself proof that it is false'.[14] Nor should we underestimate the value of oral tradition, especially when an event is recorded (even indirectly) well within the lifetime of those who were adult citizens at the time. It seems clear that conclusive proof of the truth of this story cannot be deduced from the evidence so far available, but the balance of probabilities suggest that it is authentic, although some doubt must remain concerning the traditional site on Plymouth Hoe. It would be perversely sceptical not to accept that Drake was present among those participating in the game but, equally, it would be naive to believe that we have any knowledge of what he actually said when the Armada was sighted.[15]

30

Oliver Cromwell:
'Cruel Necessity', 1649

The night after King Charles the first was beheaded, my Lord Southampton and a friend of his got leave to sit up with the body, in the banqueting-house at Whitehall. As they were sitting very melancholy there, about two o'clock in the morning, they heard the tread of somebody coming very slowly up stairs. By-and-by the door opened, and a man entered, very much muffled up in his cloak; and his face quite hid by it. He approached the body, considered it, very attentively, for some time: and then shook his head and sighed out the words, 'cruel necessity'. He then departed in the same slow and concealed manner as he had come in. Lord Southampton used to say, that he could not distinguish anything of his face; but that by his voice and gait, he took him to be Oliver Cromwell.

> Joseph Spence (1699–1768), *Observations, Anecdotes and Characters of Books and Men* (unpublished until 1820 but known to Samuel Johnson)

The story of a nocturnal visitation to the coffin of Charles I by Oliver Cromwell was well established by the early decades of the eighteenth century. Soon after the Restoration of the monarchy in 1660, James Heath published his *Flagellum or The Life and Death, Birth and Burial of Oliver Cromwell, the Late Usurper*, where the story first appeared. A few details differ slightly from Spence's version, chiefly the words allegedly spoken by Cromwell as he inspected the king's body: 'If he had not been King he might have lived longer.' In 1787, the Reverend Mark Noble in his *Memoirs of the Protectoral-House of Cromwell* stated that it was 'certain that he went to feast his eyes on the murdered King' and contributed his own embellishments to the versions of Heath and Spence. Here we are given the name of one of the guards – Bowtell – whose sword

Cromwell borrowed to prise open the coffin lid; we learn that, in the course of his inspection, Cromwell placed his finger to Charles's neck to discover if the head had been completely severed; and again the words spoken are different. Bowtell apparently asked Cromwell, 'What government they should have now?' to which Cromwell replied, 'The same that was now'. All three accounts have the ring of authenticity, especially in the convincingly Cromwellian tone of the words he is said to have uttered. None of these details can now be verified, but the persistence of the belief, from a short time after the event, that Cromwell did make a visitation to the body of the dead king suggests, synoptically, that this at least may actually have taken place. In his 1955 lecture to the Historical Association entitled 'The Undergrowth of History', Robert Birley offered the suggestion that, while such tales can rarely be proved to be historical fact, they often 'emphasised something especially dramatic in history' – in this case 'the impossible dilemma of Oliver Cromwell'. If such events were so important to the popular imagination of their time, then they should be of significance to the historian.[1]

Shakespeare's loud-mouthed rogue, Ensign Pistol, may have pronounced that 'oaths are straws, men's faiths are wafer-cakes', but this was not the prevailing opinion among the country gentry and learned lawyers who made up the 493 members of the Long Parliament that met in 1640. To most of them – and certainly to Oliver Cromwell – to swear a solemn oath was to place your conscience at the mercy of a living, vengeful God, who would jealously judge your future actions accordingly.

In 1643/4 the members of the House of Commons swore a solemn oath to adhere to the principles set out in The Solemn League and Covenant. In the light of later events, the importance of this has been diminished by many historians – and certain sections of the document did have political implications – but a recent study has suggested that 'the importance of such an oath cannot be over-estimated' and, especially, the 'key Commitment' made in Clause III, whereby the Commons swore that

> We shall with the same sincerity, reality and constancy, in our several
> vocations, endeavour with our estates and lives mutually to preserve the
> rights and privileges of Parliaments, and the liberties of the kingdoms,

and to preserve and defend the King's Majesty's person and authority, in the preservation and defence of the true religion and liberties of the kingdoms, that the world may bear witness with our consciences of our loyalty, and that we have no thought or intentions to diminish His Majesty's just power and greatness.

It is this conscientious and specific commitment, the desire not to break a solemn engagement which dominated Cromwell's political conduct through the post-war crisis. A settlement which protected civil and religious liberty had also to preserve Parliament, the King's person and his just power and greatness.[2]

Unfortunately, the king also had a conscience, which would not allow him to compromise with his opponents whom he always regarded as 'rebels' against their lawful king, a king moreover who ruled by divine right – a doctrine that held that the authority of a lawful monarch was derived directly from God; that rebellion was, therefore, a crime against the Almighty and that the king was under no obligation to bargain with or answer to his subjects. Add to this Charles's own authoritarian and intransigent personality, and it is clear that, even when the Royalists had been defeated in war, Charles could not accept the reality of the situation: treason was a crime against God and God's appointed representative, and could not be allowed to go unpunished. On this Charles appeared quite inflexible.

The events that followed the Royalist surrender serve to illustrate how the clash of these two incompatible ideologies and these two uncompromising 'consciences' made an agreed solution to the crisis impossible to achieve. Apparently oblivious to the change in his situation brought about by the total defeat of the Royalist armies, Charles continued to act as if he could still dictate the course of events. He believed that he could successfully exploit the growing discord between Parliament and the Army, between the Presbyterians and the Episcopalians, between the radical and the conservative factions in the Army, between Parliament and the Scots and between the ordinary common folk of England and the religious zealots who would impose a 'moral tyranny' including a draconian sabbatarianism, closing down the theatres, reducing the number of alehouses and abolishing Christmas. Cromwell despaired of this increasingly anarchic situation, which threatened to destroy all that he had fought for in the Civil War, especially a reformed Church with liberty of conscience, a reformed constitutional relationship between King and Parliament and protection for the rights of property. There was no thought of abolishing the monarchy – even the various proposals for a settlement that were put forward between 1646 and 1649 assumed the continuation of the monarchy.

Charles was obdurate; he refused to make any genuine concessions, he was unwilling to compromise, he clung obstinately to his kingly dignity, he rejected the proposals put to him with uncharacteristic rudeness. In 1646, he rejected the Newcastle Propositions and the Heads of the Army Proposals; in 1647 he brushed aside Parliament's 'Four Bills'. While prevaricating over these, he was also engaged in plotting with Royalists who wished to stage an uprising, secretly negotiating with the Scots for an invasion of England – the so-called Engagement – and endlessly involved in futile plans to escape to the Continent. By 1648, Cromwell began to believe that any settlement with Charles was now impossible. The king, he said, had proved himself 'so great a dissembler and so false a man that he was not to be trusted'. He now made the pragmatic decision that further attempts to negotiate with the king would be futile: 'Truly, we declared our intentions for Monarchy, and they still are so, unless necessity force an alteration'; placing his hand on his sword, he proclaimed, quoting the scriptures, 'Thou shalt not suffer a hypocrite to reign.'

The moment of 'necessity' that Cromwell had anticipated came in the summer of 1648 when the Scots invaded England to rescue Charles from his predicament, according to a secret accord agreed to on Boxing Day 1647. The terms were more favourable to Charles than any of the proposals made by Parliament or the Army, but in agreeing to a Scottish invasion Charles had finally alienated both. Within a few weeks the Scots were routed at Preston and Charles now had to face the consequences of provoking a second civil war – and then losing it. One immediate consequence was a resolution by the Army Council 'to call Charles Stuart, that man of blood, to an account for the blood he has shed and mischief he has done to his utmost against the Lord's causes and people'.

Parliament, on the other hand, alarmed at the Scots incursion and the triumph of the Army in defeating it, forgot their earnest vote of 'No Address', and agreed to reopen negotiations with the king, offering him terms far more favourable than on any previous occasion. Charles was released from his unhappy confinement in Carisbrooke Castle and provided with more congenial quarters with a retinue of loyal courtiers, chaplains and servants. Parliament, at least at this stage (August 1648), was not contemplating a royal execution. After more than ten weeks of discussion, the king and the parliamentary commissioners reached an agreement, with important concessions being made by both sides, notably by the king who conceded no less than thirty-eight of Parliament's demands.

Charles was genuinely distressed to surrender so much that he held sacrosanct and the parliamentarians were reluctant to agree to the king's scruples concerning the episcopacy, but the fact was that both king and Parliament were now frightened by the power and intentions of the Army so both were anxious to come to an agreement.[3]

Events quickly proved that they were well advised to fear the Army. Barely had the Newport negotiations ended when a troop of soldiers arrived and unceremoniously seized the king and took him to Hurst Castle on the mainland, a damp, dismal fortress with dark, cell-like rooms and 'all the charm of a modern pillbox'.[4] Meanwhile the Army council had presented its 'Remonstrance' to Parliament, a document which took four hours to read out but with the clear message that the Army would carry out a purge of Parliament to secure acceptance of their specific demand that Charles should be brought to trial. Parliament rejected the 'Remonstrance' decisively by 125 votes to 58. Pride's famous purge followed, leaving only eighty compliant members as a 'Rump Parliament' who duly resolved 'to proceed against the King', and, having declared that they represented all the people of England, voted to establish a special court to put the king on trial, with ill-disguised designs on his life.

Cromwell at first took little part in all this but he quickly understood that such a court would have no lawful standing and began to search for ways 'to bring him to justice with some plausible appearance of legality and consent'.[5] 'There seems no real reason to doubt what many of Cromwell's contemporaries believed: that he was making genuine attempts to settle the kingdom without cutting off the head of the King.'[6] For reasons that have never been clear, all this suddenly changed and, in a speech in Parliament at the end of 1648, Cromwell announced that 'since providence and necessity hath cast them upon it, he should pray God to bless their counsels'. He had finally made up his mind that, with the Army in full cry for blood, with Parliament reduced to the role of puppet to the Army, and with the king's constant prevarication, procrastination and duplicity, there was no alternative. Providence and necessity had marked out the course that must be taken to save the country from anarchy or military and religious tyranny. Once Cromwell had decided that he knew the will of God and that he was to be God's instrument, he proceeded with frenzied determination to force the matter to a conclusion.

So on 26 January 1649, sentence was passed that Charles I should be 'put to death by the severing of his head from his body', sentenced, according to the presiding judge, by a court constituted in the name of the people of England. A lady in the public gallery expressed the widespread doubt about this when she called out: 'Not half the people'.[7] On 30 January, the king was executed. God's will had been done and Cromwell was never heard to regret his part in it. He had made every effort to persuade the king to accept defeat and agree to the terms Parliament put before him but when the Army council took matters into their own hands he realised that only ruthless measures could now avoid a state of affairs that would negate all that he and Parliament had fought for. Necessity determined his course; providence was the hand that guided him.[8]

Necessity and providence can often be cruel; of this Cromwell was well aware, but he saw the execution of the king as the only possible solution to the dilemma of the time. The words 'Cruel Necessity' sum up profoundly the truth of this and, whether apocryphal or not, the tale of Cromwell's night-time visit to the body of Charles reflects the struggle with his conscience that Cromwell endured before the fatal decision was made.

The New Oxford Dictionary of National Biography (2004) comments that the only credible story of all the legends attached to Cromwell is 'the testimony of Phillip Warwick that as Cromwell looked down on the dismembered royal corpse he murmured: "cruel necessity"' (Sir Phillip Warwick, Royalist MP, secretary to King Charles I).

31

Sir Isaac Newton: The Falling Apple and the Law of Gravity, 1666

> After dinner, the weather being warm, we went into the garden and drank tea under the shade of some apple trees, only he and myself. Amidst other discourse, he told me he was just in the same situation as when formerly the notion of gravitation came into his mind. It was occasioned by the fall of an apple as he sat in contemplative mood.
>
> William Stukeley, *Memoirs of Sir Isaac Newton*

In an age of towering intellectuals, Isaac Newton was indisputably the greatest of them all. His work on mathematics produced the binomial theorem, the differential calculus, the integral calculus, the computation of the area of a parabola and the theory of universal gravitation, while his researches into optics led not only to the development of the reflecting telescope and advances in astronomy, but also to new theories of light and colour. His *Principia Mathematica* is one of the most accomplished and masterly treatises of all time, and 'rounded off the fundamental scientific work of the era that began with the Renaissance'.[1] Alexander Pope's epitaph for Newton perfectly summed up his brilliance:

Nature and Nature's Laws lay hid in Night.
God said, Let Newton be and all was Light.

The story of the apple first appeared in 1738 in Voltaire's *Philosophie de Newton*, where he relates that

One day in the year 1666, Newton, having returned to the country and seeing the fruits of a tree fall, fell, according to what his niece, Mrs

Conduitt, has told me, into a deep meditation about the cause that thus attracts bodies in the line which, if produced, would pass nearly through the centre of the Earth.[2]

Voltaire was in England during the years 1726–29 but he never actually met Newton (who died in 1727) and Mrs Conduitt herself was relating an incident that was alleged to have occurred some sixty years earlier, and thus one that she could not have witnessed (she was born only some thirty years later).

William Stukeley's version of the story appeared in 1752 in his *Memoirs of Sir Isaac Newton*, recalling an occasion when Stukeley was visiting Newton at his home in Kensington on 15 April 1726.

Both these sources seem to indicate that the story may have originated with Newton himself and, while this could suggest that it might therefore bear the hallmark of truth, two factors warn against ready acceptance of this. Firstly, Newton was well known for tales of eccentricity and exaggeration and Stukeley was described by one of his friends (Bishop Warburton, no less) as 'a strange compound of simplicity, drollery, absurdity, ingenuity and antiquarianism', and much of his writing is judged to be often fanciful and untrustworthy. Secondly, it is difficult to believe that Newton had not spent some time working at this problem, particularly when Kepler's Third Law had so recently pointed the way; indeed, R. W. Herivel in his study *The Background to Newton's Principia* states that by 1666 all Newton's work and calculations were coming together to the formulation of the law of gravity.[4]

Newton was certainly at his home at Woolsthorpe in the autumn of 1666, since the university at Cambridge was closed as a result of the serious outbreak of the bubonic plague at that time; and it was certainly then that many of his most important theories began to take shape. He seems to have spent a good deal of time in his garden, of which, we learn, he was 'very curious' and he took great care that it was 'never out of order ... not enduring to see a weed in it'.[5] It is quite possible that on an autumn day and 'in contemplative mood', Newton was surprised by the sudden fall of an apple, but that this had more than an incidental connection with the formulation of the law of gravity seems inconceivable. A modern biographer has protested that the story of the apple vulgarises universal gravitation by treating it as no more than a bright idea.[6] It is, perhaps, worth noting that it was not until modern times that the story was further embroidered by the apple actually falling on Newton's head.

A more reliable version of Newton's meditations in his garden is given by his close friend Henry Pemberton, Gresham professor of physics at Cambridge, whom Newton entrusted with the preparation of the third edition of his *Principia*. In 1728, the year following Newton's death, Pemberton published *A View of Sir Isaac Newton's Philosophy*, and in the preface he wrote

> As he sat in the garden he fell into speculation on the power of gravity, that as this power is not sensibly diminished at the remotest distance from the centre of the earth to which we can rise ... it appeared to him reasonable to conclude that this power must extend much further than is usually thought. Why not as high as the moon? said he to himself, and if so, her motion must be influenced by it: perhaps she is retained in her orbit by it.[7]

Newton's remarkable mind was working on a higher plane than the unexceptional fall of an autumn apple. Stephen Hawking has described Newton's *Principia Mathematica* as 'probably the most important single work ever published in the physical sciences'.[8] This awesome treatise, first published in 1687, presented a mathematical exposition of such fundamental and radical theories concerning the universe that they have influenced mankind's understanding of it ever since. To formulate the concept of a force emanating from the centre of Earth and extending its influence 'as high as the Moon' and even further into the infinity of space – and with accurate mathematical predictability – was such a huge scientific and intellectual achievement that, for all practical purposes, we are, 300 years later, still living in a Newtonian universe. Newton's calculations can be used to predict with remarkable accuracy the orbit of the Moon round Earth and the orbits of the planet round the Sun. That apples fell to the ground in Newton's orchard while he sat and pondered these fundamental problems of the universe we may be sure, but that their fall gave him his great insight into the complex forces of gravitation may be discounted. He had been moving towards a mathematical understanding of this for some time before 1666. Indeed, it would be entirely in keeping with Newton's quirky sense of humour to make the most of such a familiar occurrence to embellish – or even to try to explain – the mystery of his profound discovery. The story of the apple (and perhaps other whimsical Newtonian anecdotes) may well have been invented by Newton himself as a simple illustration of a profound mathematical problem. One would like to believe that this interpretation is closer to the truth than the suggestion of a recent biographer that the story is 'a later fabrication or at least an exaggeration, almost certainly to suppress the fact that much of the inspiration for the theory of gravity came from his subsequent alchemical work'.[9]

32

James Stuart, the Old Pretender: The Warming-Pan Baby, 1688

James Stuart (also known as James VIII and III, Old Pretender), 1688-1766, royal pretender. The only surviving son of James II, his birth provided the King with a presumptively Catholic heir, and helped to spark the Glorious Revolution. Some found his birth too convenient to the King to be plausible, and suggested that he had not, in fact, been born to the Queen but had been smuggled in in a warming pan.

The History Today *Who's Who in British History*

'One great check on the king's ardent zeal for the restoration of popery was the knowledge that should his eldest daughter, the wife of the prince of Orange, succeed him, the whole work would be undone, both the princess and her husband being Protestants ... James, therefore, ardently desired a son; and when, on June 10th 1688, a son was born, he thought that everything would prosper to his wishes. This very event, however, in fact, hastened his expulsion from the throne ... Among the many calumnies that were heaped on him and his queen, it was asserted that the young Prince of Wales was not their child, though acknowledged by them for the sake of depriving the princess of Orange of her right to the succession.'

Mrs Markham's *History of England*

Just as the social customs, moral principles and religious and political conventions of the 'great age' of Victoria loomed large in Britain for much of the twentieth century, so did the sun of the 'golden age' of Elizabeth I illuminate the hearts and minds of seventeenth-century England. However deeply society was divided by the bitter conflict of the Civil Wars, general sentiment was still attached to the 'ancient constitution' of a strong monarchy governing with the support of a largely accommodating Parliament. There was also a sense of loyalty to the only recently established 'Anglican' Church, which was popularly seen as the national shield against the perceived threats from both a resurgent European Catholicism and from disruptive domestic non-conformity. A recent study of James II has suggested that 'the "natural" development in later Stuart England would have been towards a stronger monarchy (as in France) rather than towards a stronger Parliament',[1] while it is now believed that the depth of support for the Established Anglican Church in the later seventeenth century has been seriously underestimated and the extent of sympathy for non-conformity has been much exaggerated. Essentially the political and religious sentiments of the country in general were 'conservative', and at the outset of his short reign James II appeared to appreciate this as he announced in Council that he would make it his

> endeavour to preserve this government both in Church and state as it is by law established. I know the principles of the Church of England are for monarchy and the members of it have shown themselves good and loyal subjects; therefore I shall always take care to defend and support it. I know too that the laws of England are sufficient to make the king as great a monarch as I can wish. [2]

On the king's orders, this declaration was printed and published and helped to calm some of the doubts that his subjects may have felt about the possible threat posed by the prospect of a Catholic monarch. Loyal addresses flooded in to congratulate James on his accession. Thoughts of resistance to the lawful monarch were discredited; James had no son and after a series of miscarriages it seemed unlikely that his queen would now produce a Catholic heir.

Within a short time, all this had changed. It soon became clear that James II had inherited his grandfather's belief in the doctrine of the Divine Right of Kings. He saw the monarchy as a sacred trust from God to be used as the king, and only the king, judged best in the service of God. For James II, God's service committed him to the advancement of Catholicism and, in this as in all other decisions of principle, the king had a duty to command and the subject had a duty to obey. It is unlikely that James ever intended to use force to coerce his subjects back into the Catholic fold, but he soon left them in no doubt that his unswerving objective was 'to establish the Catholic religion in England'. James may well have meant no more than that he wished to ensure that Catholics were given equality of citizenship with Protestants, in particular the right to worship freely and the right to hold any public office. He firmly believed that, once the penal laws and the Test Acts were abolished, Catholics would be accepted as loyal subjects and converts would flock from the Church of England to his Church like sheep that have erred and strayed. Barillon, the French ambassador, wrote of James's high hopes: 'He flatters himself that the Anglican Church is so little removed from the Catholic that it should not be difficult to bring the majority of them to declare themselves openly. He has told me several times that they are Roman Catholics without knowing it.'[3] James may have believed this: as Bishop Burnet commented, 'He had no true judgement ... and was obstinate against all other advices.' For the political reality was that most of James's subjects were profoundly suspicious of 'popery', which they associated, instinctively, with arbitrary absolutism and religious persecution (Louis XIV's regime in France was a constant reminder and *Foxe's Book of Martyrs* lay side by side with the Bible in many homes). Hostility to England's commercial activities in the West Indies had convinced Englishmen that Spain was their natural enemy: 'God hath willed it so'. Many among the gentry feared for the safety of the estates their ancestors had acquired after the Dissolution of the Monasteries. James's reassuring words on all these matters carried little weight when his policies were seen in action.

A Catholic ambience at court was quickly established – Catholic priests, a Catholic chapel, a papal nuncio, Catholic schools, a friary and a monastery in London – all harmless symbols, but signifying a sinister defiance of public sentiment. Of greater concern was James's decision to maintain a standing army of almost 20,000 men, including over seventy Catholic officers, whom the king had commissioned in breach of the Test Act and insisted on pardoning and retaining despite parliamentary protests. This was followed by the arbitrary dismissal of six judges who refused to acknowledge that the king had the power to dispense with Statute Law, a stance which a packed bench of judges overruled in a declaration that "'tis an inseparable prerogative of the kings of England to dispense with penal laws in particular cases and upon particular necessary reasons'.[4] This opened the way for James to plan to dispense entirely with the Test and Corporation Acts, since 'any statute which deprived the king of his subjects' services or debarred them from serving him was unjust in itself'. This was the king's justification for the Declaration of Indulgence of 1687, which suspended the penal laws and so allowed admission to public office of any of the king's subjects whom he wished to promote.

James was not satisfied with this: he had set his mind on a total repeal of the penal laws, but Anglicans, Dissenters and above all Parliament had stubbornly refused to countenance such a step. Resistance was strengthened following an assurance from William of Orange and Princess Mary, who now seemed most likely to succeed James on the throne, that they would grant religious toleration to Catholics and Dissenters but would not repeal the Test Acts. James could make no further progress towards such a repeal without a compliant parliament, and he told the papal nuncio that he intended to remove all office-holders whose support he could not rely on.

More than 200 JPs were dismissed and most were replaced by Catholics; many key offices of state were placed in the hands of Catholics and a Jesuit was made a privy councillor; command of the Navy was given to a Catholic; an army led by Catholic officers was stationed close to London; a court of commissioners for ecclesiastical causes, suspiciously similar to the Court of High Commission that had been abolished and declared illegal by the Long Parliament in 1641, was established to govern the Church and the universities, a court James immediately used to deprive the Vice Chancellor of Cambridge of his office for refusing to admit Catholics to the university, and to bully the fellows of Magdalen College, Oxford, into choosing the king's Catholic nominee as President – twenty-five recalcitrant fellows were expelled. James was fully aware that he could not secure the repeal of the penal laws without the election of a favourable House of Commons, and in 1687 he embarked on a campaign to this end: all office-holders – MPs, JPs, State and court officials, Lords-Lieutenant, Deputy-

Lieutenants, all those holding municipal offices in the boroughs and all members of the London livery companies – were required to answer two cardinal questions: 'Would they vote for the repeal of the Test Acts if they were elected to Parliament?' and 'Would they vote for candidates who pledged themselves to do so?' Those whose answers were negative or otherwise unsatisfactory were to be dismissed and replaced by others who were more compliant. Soon afterwards, hundreds of magistrates and other officers were dismissed and 3,500 members of the London livery companies were expelled, while a number of municipal charters were revised in order to give the Crown control over the magistrates. All this was accompanied by a naive propaganda campaign whereby James tried to convince his subjects of all the benefits that could be obtained once liberty of conscience was secured. He was unable to understand why they were so reluctant to embrace his proposals. For their part, his subjects had been confirmed, by the king's arbitrary actions, in their belief that he was planning the forcible conversion of the nation to the Roman Catholic Church and the imposition of a despotic government – a belief strengthened by the popular suspicion that James had a secret understanding with Louis XIV of France that French assistance would, if necessary, be forthcoming to achieve this.

In all this James had forfeited the support of most Anglicans without securing the support of the Nonconformists and, in a desperate attempt to convince the latter of the advantages they would gain by a repeal of the Test Acts, in 1687 he issued a second Declaration of Indulgence granting full freedom of worship and a suspension of the penal Acts. This sudden proposal to make use of a royal power to suspend parliamentary legislation, rather than the more selective dispensing power, increased suspicions. When James then ordered that the Declaration should be read out in every church on two successive Sundays, seven bishops petitioned the king to withdraw the order on the ground that such a use of the dispensing power was illegal. They were placed under arrest, imprisoned in the Tower, brought to trial and charged with publishing a seditious libel.

The vociferous popular acclaim that greeted their acquittal was a reflection of the tension that had been created by James's policy of undermining the established Protestant society and institutions of his kingdom in the misguided belief that Englishmen would readily return to the Catholic Church if the opportunity were offered by a benevolent monarch. He entirely misjudged the mood of his subjects. A wiser and less sectarian monarch would have taken note of the reaction to the rumours of a 'Popish Plot' less than ten years earlier – an eruption of popular hostility to Catholicism verging on paranoia, in the course of which numerous public figures were falsely accused of popish plotting and thirty-five innocent men were judicially murdered. The 1605 Gunpowder Plot was immediately recalled when a mysterious knocking caused alarm when the House of Commons was sitting; almost any anti-Catholic rumour was readily believed, repeated and embroidered; Protestants preferred to suffer pain and fever rather than be treated with the new drug, quinine, then known as Jesuits' powder, brought by these Catholic priests from Peru; and even Nell Gwynn became a popular figure when she declared that she was the Protestant whore. James was totally deluded in his obsessive belief that the great majority of his English subjects were longing for an opportunity to return to the Catholic faith. He never understood that their patience with his provocative policies was founded on a fear of rebellion and renewed civil war, and on the hope that they could look forward, since James had no Catholic heir, to a return to stable Protestant government with the anticipated accession to the throne of James's daughter, Mary, wife of William of Orange.

In the autumn of 1687, these hopes received a rude shock when it was announced that, after many years, the queen was pregnant: James and zealous Catholics hailed the news as a miracle; suspicious Protestants cast doubt on the story and even concocted a rumour that, even if it were true, whatever the sex of the baby, there was a plot to produce a boy to be passed off as a royal child. On 10 June 1688, the queen gave birth to James Edward Stuart and Protestant hopes seemed finally crushed.

The story quickly spread that the queen had again miscarried and a substitute infant had been introduced into the queen's chamber, a rumour reinforced by the sinister reports that only Catholic ladies had been present to witness the birth; Princess Anne, James's Protestant daughter, having been sent to Bath after being refused permission to 'feel [the queen's] belly', and all the Protestant ladies, un-forewarned of the imminence of the child's birth, were at church. Bishop Gilbert Burnet, in his informative but very partisan *History of My Own Time*, wrote a long and detailed account of all the subsequent court gossip, which, when it was published some forty years later at a time of real and imagined Jacobite plots, gave a certain credibility to the popular belief that, in order to ensure a Catholic succession, a monstrous conspiracy had been devised to foist a Catholic Prince of Wales on a country already praying that the Protestant William of Orange and his wife, Mary, James's elder daughter and heir presumptive to his throne, would soon relieve them of the perceived threat of a Roman Catholic tyranny. English Protestants were not willing to believe that a son had been born to James and his queen; this would mean the sudden shattering of their dearest dreams and they were prepared to listen to any fragment of gossip that might suggest that it could not be true.

Bishop Burnet, who bore a great deal of personal animus against James II, had been in exile in Holland for several years, and the most likely source for his information about affairs in England was correspondence, often written in code or in invisible ink, sent from London by a certain James Johnstone to Hans William Bentinck, aide and confidant of William of Orange and later 1st Earl of Portland. It is from these 'spy-in-the-house' letters that we can obtain a sense of the fraught tension at court and among the Protestant establishment in the days following 10 June 1688.

Johnstone's letters – preserved for us in the Portland Welbeck Papers – record in intimate detail almost every moment in the circumstances surrounding the birth of James's son, recounting every incident that could fuel Protestant suspicions. There was a sudden change in the queen's calculations of the expected date of birth – by early June the danger of invasion from Holland was becoming acute, so a son and heir was needed urgently; Catholic priests openly and confidently predicted that a son would be born; only Catholics were present in the birth chamber; the newborn child did not cry and 'was wrapped up and hurried away instead of being shown to the Counsellors'; only the king went into the next room, returning briefly to announce that he had a son; the others present were then told 'they had no more business there'; the king 'cryed all night'; 'some took note that Mrs Touraine, the Queen's favourite, came and went away with somewhat in her lap to the bed when the Queen was in labour. She says it was only linnen upon the occasion; they tell the story of the child convey'd in a bed-pan which a Lady on her death-bed acknowledged and the child was disinherited'; the child was deformed and was 'black and blue' after the queen's hard labour and had breathing difficulties; the surgeon and midwife did not expect it to live; it had been stillborn and another child, ready waiting in the next room, had been substituted; some said the child was sick, the king said it was 'a strong and lively Prince', too strong according to 'one who saw the child two days after ... not like a child so newly born'.

According to James Johnstone, there was official acknowledgement that 'the thing was imprudently managed' but, even so, he came to the conclusion that 'the truth is this; nothing is more evident than that a trick was designed, otherwise they would not have acted like mad people, in making the thing look disputable, but if they really put the trick in execution or not, God Knows'.[5]

This is all very much the stuff of the conspiracy theory of history; as the 1897 editor of *Burnet's History* commented, there is none of this circumstantial evidence that cannot be explained in other ways.[6] The simple fact is that English Protestants did not want to believe that there was now, suddenly and unexpectedly, a Catholic heir to the throne: 'Be it true child or not,' wrote Bentinck's correspondent, 'the People will never believe it'.[7]

James, with his customary lack of understanding of the political and religious sensitivities of his English subjects, found it difficult to believe that they could be so obtuse as to cast scandalous doubt on the birth of his son and heir. Indeed, he proceeded to make matters worse by declaring that 'if there are not Englishmen loyal enough to maintain him, 30000 strangers may be had on call' and by further extracting from the King of France a promise of sixteen men-of-war to assist him.[8] He also inflamed public opinion by denying a pardon for the seven bishops whom he had put in the Tower for refusing to read out his Declaration illegally dispensing with the Test Acts. When the court acquitted the bishops, there were rejoicings and bonfires in the City of London, which ought to have warned James of the dangerous course he was pursuing. One of the judges, Sir Francis Pemberton, is quoted as saying, 'If the King can dispense in Church matters he can do it too in matters of property and the liberty of men's persons, so that thus the Protestant religion, the Laws and Rights of the People of England are all blown up at one blow.'[9]

Meanwhile, the life of the king's newborn son was being put in serious danger by the royal doctors, who had formed the eccentric theory that human milk was bad for babies and had prescribed a diet of gruel with boiled bread laced with canary wine, and a concoction known as Dr Goddard's drops described as a volatile spirit of raw silk. It was only after the child had nearly died that, as Johnstone duly reported, he was put 'in the hands of a Whore, a Tailor's wife' who clearly provided him with more appropriate sustenance.[10]

The young prince's survival only served to foster the rumours concerning his legitimacy and James's attempt to scotch them was yet another unfortunate misjudgement. He decided to make public the Solemn Depositions made in council on Monday 22 October 1688, relating to the birth of his son. Among these Depositions appeared a question that was in itself more significant than any answer to it, for it was seized upon by those who believed, or wished to believe, that the child whom James claimed to be his son was, in fact, supposititious. 'Do you,' the questioner asked, 'think it [i.e. the child] was conveyed there in a Warming-pan or otherwise?' This served to strengthen the tide of suspicion and animosity against the king and gave birth to a legend.

It was not long before a pamphlet appeared purporting to give details of 'A Warming-pan Plot worse than Cellier's Meal-Tub' (a reference to the Meal-Tub Plot of 1679, when a Thomas Dangerfield claimed to have uncovered a plot to murder King Charles II and his brother – later James II – producing documents alleged to have been hidden in a meal-tub in the house of Elizabeth Cellier. This created a public stir as it seemed to be part of a wider popish plot then causing so much apprehension, but Dangerfield was exposed as a former convict and condemned for perjury. He was pilloried, whipped and fined, and soon afterwards assassinated); Jacobites were given the nickname 'warming-pans' and a popular anti-Jacobite song contained the lines

> Let those rebels if they can,
> Make us forget the warming-pan
> Which first conveyed that pretty man
> Into the Chamber Royal.

The story was given an aura of respectable authority with the publication of Bishop Burnet's *History* in the years between the Jacobite rebellions, when public apprehension and private suspicion of Jacobitism ran high. Burnet produced no evidence, but it is not difficult to understand why his words were seen to lend support to a story already well established in popular mythology: 'The Queen lay all the while abed; and, in order to the warming one side of it, a warming-pan was brought, but it was not opened, that it might be seen that there was fire and nothing else in it; so here was matter for suspicion, with which all people were filled.'[11]

It is not at all surprising to find this intriguing tale in almost every popular history, with its sinister elements of secret conspiracy, mysterious intimacy and sense of a nation's history at a decisive crossroads. But modern historians see no reason to question the legitimacy of James's son, for there is no real historically acceptable evidence to suggest that the boy was not the queen's and much to suggest that he was. Perhaps one day DNA technology will resolve the issue.

33

Captain Jenkins's Ear, 1731

I was in hopes that you would have made use of your power to have detected and discouraged the violence and villainies which has for a long time been practiced by those whom you distinguish by the name of Guarda Costas; but as you don't take the least notice to answer that part of my letter, and that I have repeated assurances that you allow vessels to be fitted out of your harbour, particularly one Fandino, and others who have committed the most cruel piratical outrages on several ships and vessels of the king my master's subjects, particularly about the 20th April last sailed out of your harbour in one of those Guarda Costas, and met a ship of this island bound for England; and after using the captain in a most barbarous inhuman manner, taking all his money, cutting off one of his ears, plundering him of those necessaries which were to carry the ship safe home, without doubt that she should perish in her passage ...

Despatch from Rear Admiral Charles Stewart (Commander-in-Chief at Jamaica) to His Excellency Dionisio Martinez de la Vega, Governor of Havana, 12 September 1731

The fifteenth-century Portuguese explorations southwards along the coast of Africa, and the discovery of the West Indies by Columbus in 1492, opened a new era of overseas trade and imperial expansion, monopolised by Portugal and Spain. To maintain this monopoly and to avert future conflict between the two countries, in 1493 the Spanish Pope, Alexander VI, in the 'Bull Inter Caetera' awarded Spain exclusive rights over all Spanish discoveries in the New World; and in the following year the papal-inspired Treaty of Tordesillas divided the undiscovered parts of the world between Portugal and Spain. Everything 370 leagues (a Spanish league was 6.781 km, thus giving the distance specified in the treaty as approximately 2500 km, i.e. all the known 'New World') to the west of a line passing through the Cape Verde Islands and the Azores would be declared to be Spanish and everything to the east should belong to Portugal. With only slight departure from this arrangement, Spain eventually laid claim to Central America, Mexico, the whole of South America and unlimited areas of territory in North America, of which occupation of a wide belt of land from Florida to California was a token. Access to this empire was legally restricted to Spaniards only and it was the attempt of successive Spanish governments and their colonial governors to exclude foreign shipping, most of which was English, which was one of the causes of dissension and open warfare between Spain and England for over 200 years.

The treaties, known collectively as the Treaty of Utrecht, which in 1713 brought to an end the War of the Spanish Succession, marked the first significant legal concessions made by Spain in this long campaign to seal off their empire against foreign traders – and they were concessions made with the utmost reluctance even in the face of overwhelming defeat. By these treaties, Spain ceded Minorca and Gibraltar to Britain – the latter still, in the twenty-first century, a cause of dissension between these two members of the European Union – and granted Britain what were seen at the time as significant privileges in their colonial trade. Most important of these concessions were the Asiento or contract to supply 4,800 slaves annually to the Spanish colonies and the right to send one ship of 500 tons laden with English goods each year to the fairs held at Vera Cruz and Cartagena.

The Spanish government may have looked upon these concessions as special privileges conferred reluctantly upon a victorious enemy but they were, in practice, regarded as totally inadequate by both English merchants and Spanish colonists. The Spaniards needed far more than 4,800 slaves per annum and far more manufactured goods than could be provided by their home country or by just one English ship each year – and English merchants were only too anxious to make up the shortfall. The Spanish government's insistence on the precise terms of the treaty made it inevitable that the deficit would be supplied by illicit trade, and that there would be frequent clashes between these English freebooters and the Spanish *guarda costas*, licensed by the Spanish governors to keep them out.

Both parties bore some responsibility for these incidents. The *guarda costas* were often little better than pirates, attacking without discrimination any English ships they came across, even those plying a legitimate trade – mainly sugar, tobacco and rum – with the English colonies in the area, notably Jamaica, Barbados, St Kitts and the Bahamas. Between 1713 and 1731, some 180 English ships were plundered or confiscated and their captains and crews captured and often ill-treated. The English merchants, for their part, not only indulged in what they saw as appropriate reprisals but also circumvented the restrictions of the legal permission to trade with only one ship per annum by the device of sending with the legitimate ship a flotilla of smaller vessels, from which the ship was reloaded when its original cargo had been discharged, thus ensuring, as a French observer noted, that 'le vaisseau ne desemplit jamais' (the ship is never entirely empty).[2]

There was clearly a great deal of provocation in the conduct of both the Spanish *guarda costas*, many of whom according to Commodore Edward St Lo's report to the Admiralty in 1728, were 'no better than pirates', and the English merchants, who blatantly engaged in illicit trade with the Spanish colonies contrary to the concessions extorted from Spain at Utrecht. It may have been obdurate on the part of the Spanish government to persist in attempting to exclude the rest of the trading community from their colonies in an age of rapidly expanding commerce, but as Rear Admiral Stewart, Commander-in-Chief at Jamaica, stated in an outspoken despatch to the Duke of Newcastle who, together with William Pitt, was openly supporting the disgruntled English merchants, 'The question will be whether we, by carrying on the clandestine trade, are not ourselves the authors of our complaints.' Stewart, furthermore, informed Newcastle that the ships that 'sailed from this island, manned and armed on that illicit trade, have more than once bragged to me of their having murdered seven or eight Spaniards on their own shore'. On the other hand, Stewart also reported to the Admiralty all the incidents of piracy and cruelty involving the Spanish *guarda costas* and the unlicensed pirates who acted with them, and he remonstrated firmly but diplomatically with the Spanish governor of Havana whenever such incidents occurred. He was particularly unequivocal in his despatch to the governor over the treatment of Captain Jenkins after his ship, the *Rebecca*, was seized by the notorious Fandino in April 1731, commenting that 'the king my master [has] too much reason to believe that these repeated insults on his subjects could never be continued but by the connivance of several Spanish governors in these parts'. The governor's response was to reiterate his complaints about the number of English trading vessels infringing the terms of the trading convention between Britain and Spain and to warn that the continuance of the friendly relations between the two countries 'will with difficulty be effected while the English nation prejudices the Spanish commerce by their continual illicit trade'.[3]

But this, it seems, was precisely what the 'English nation' proposed to do, in spite of Walpole's warning that war with Spain 'would on our part be unjust, and if it is unjust, it must be impolitic and dishonourable'. In the 1730s, demands for war against Spain increased year by year as popular chauvinism and the making of political capital accompanied every reported incident of Spanish seizure of English ships and ill-treatment of English sailors. In its issue for June 1731, the *Gentleman's Magazine* gave prominence to reports of several such incidents including a detailed account of the treatment of Captain Jenkins whom the Spanish 'hang'd up three times, once with the cabin boy at his feet; they then cut off one of his ears, took away his candles and instruments and detained him a whole day' before setting him adrift.[4]

Jenkins was received at court and 'laid his case before His Majesty', a privilege which in itself endowed his injury with a special significance and guaranteed it national publicity. Clamour for action against Spain among the merchant traders and the political opportunists grew steadily in the 1730s, and in 1738 Jenkins was given permission to appear before the House of Commons; he produced what he alleged was his severed ear pickled in a glass jar and gave a colourful account of his ill-treatment seven years earlier. When asked what his feelings were at the time, he declared that he 'committed his soul to God and his cause to his country', a reply which stirred up such a patriotic storm that

Walpole's peace policy lay in ruins and a fleet was ordered to the West Indies to attack Porto Bello, Cuba and Cartagena. War was formally declared in October 1739, a war often dubbed 'The War of Captain Jenkins's Ear', a war in which England became uselessly embroiled in the confused dynastic and petty territorial feuds of European kings and princes, and especially those of King George II's Electorate of Hanover. The national debt, which stood at £47 million in 1739, had risen to £76 million by 1748 when the Treaty of Aix-la-Chapelle did nothing whatsoever to settle differences between Britain and Spain. On the contrary, the annual ship and the Asiento were renewed exactly as before but only for four years. Robert Walpole's bitter response to the delirious rejoicings of the London populace and the ringing of church bells when the war began was now fully justified: 'They now ring the bells but they will soon wring their hands.'[5]

In 1790 when the French Revolutionary mob was loudly demanding war, the Comte de Mirabeau held up the example of this futile and costly war as a warning against permitting popular clamour to determine questions of war and peace.

The story of Captain Jenkins and his ear, and its unfortunate impact on English public opinion, was disregarded in accounts of English history for much of the nineteenth century, as it was generally believed to be a fabrication invented to win support for war against the Spanish. The publication in 1889 of the Naval despatches of the time confirmed the truth of the story and revealed the full extent of bitter hostility that prevailed between Spain and English traders in the West Indies, a rivalry which had begun with Hawkins and Drake and did not end until the late eighteenth century when Spain finally realised that the concept of a closed empire was not a feasible basis for international relations.

34

General James Wolfe: Gray's Elegy and the Capture of Quebec, 1759

Quebec was a very strong town. It was built upon rocks high above the river, and was defended by the great French general, Montcalm.

For a long time Wolfe tried in vain to take the town. Montcalm was too clever and watchful. Day by day passed and Wolfe grew ill with care and weariness.

Many of his soldiers were killed, and the fresh troops which he expected did not arrive. At last he decided on a bold and daring plan.

There was one place which the French did not guard very strongly, because they thought it was quite impossible for the British to attack them there. This was a steep cliff. But Wolfe had noticed that there was a narrow pathway up this cliff, and he decided to take his soldiers by that path...

One dark night the British soldiers were rowed over the river. No one spoke, every one moved as quietly as possible. The oars were muffled, so that the sound of the rowing might not be heard by the French. Only Wolfe, as his boat went silently down the river, repeated a poem to his officers in a low voice. The poem was called 'An Elegy in a Country Churchyard,' and it had been written a few years before by an English poet called Gray...

It is a long poem and very beautiful, and, when Wolfe had finished repeating it, he turned to his officers and said, 'Now, gentlemen, I would rather be the author of that poem than take Quebec,'

H. T. Marshall, *Our Island Story*

An anecdote which he also used to tell deserves to be remembered. He happened to be on duty in the boat in which General Wolfe went to visit some of his posts the night before the battle, which was expected to be decisive of the fate of the campaign. The evening was fine, and the scene, considering the work they were engaged in, and the morning to which they were looking forward, sufficiently impressive. As they rowed along, the general with much feeling repeated nearly the whole of Grays 'Elegy' (which had appeared not long before, and was yet but little known) to an officer who sat with him in the stern of the boat; adding, as he concluded, that 'he would prefer being the author of that poem to the glory of beating the French to-morrow'.

J. Playfair, 'A Biographical Account of the late Professor
Robinson', *Transactions of the Royal Society
of Edinburgh*, 1814, Vol. 7, p. 499

Author's note: John Robison, scientist and mathematician, left no eyewitness account of the events in which he participated, and much of what is known of his experiences is derived from the biographical lecture given to the Royal Society of Edinburgh in 1814 by John Playfair, his successor as professor of natural philosophy at Edinburgh. Robison was a young midshipman aboard the admiral's ship in the St Lawrence River during the campaign that led to the capture of Quebec in 1759. The story he used to tell is the original version of the famous tale of Wolfe and Gray's 'Elegy' and, with a variety of modifications – notably Carlyle's colourful reconstruction, it has been the source of all subsequent accounts.[1]

The Seven Years' War, which began in 1756, had not gone well for the British and Prussian cause. A succession of military defeats in Europe, the loss of several key forts in North America and a series of costly and ineffective naval actions against the French coast (described by the French as breaking their windows with guineas) had allowed the Russians to occupy Berlin, and the French to take the initiative in America and, more menacingly, to seize Ostend and threaten Britain with invasion. The year 1759, however, was soon to be hailed as the *annus mirabilis*, as news of victories in all the scattered theatres of conflict spread through the London coffee houses.

The French were driven back over the Rhine and decisively defeated at Minden by the newly formed Royal Regiment of Artillery and by six spirited regiments of infantry; the French

Mediterranean fleet was destroyed at Lagos by Admiral Boscawen and their Atlantic fleet by Hawke at Quiberon Bay, while their invasion fleet of flat-bottomed boats was disposed of by Rodney. In the colonial conflict, French control in India was effectively ended by the successes of Clive, Eyre-Coote and Admiral Pocock. Well-coordinated military and naval operations captured the French West African ports of Goree and Senegal, and the sugar island of Guadeloupe in the West Indies. In North America, General Wolfe began his campaign by capturing Louisburg, 'the Gibraltar of the West', as a preliminary to the challenging assault on the French fort of Quebec, strongly protected by 16,000 men and over 100 guns and by the natural barrier of the precipitous cliffs known as the Heights of Abraham.

Ill with fever and opposed by most of his senior officers, Wolfe conceived the idea of landing a force of several thousand men in a cove on the bank of the River St Lawrence and scaling the formidable cliffs above by means of a steep and narrow goat track, which he had spotted in an earlier reconnaissance patrol. Reprimanding his officers for their reluctance to accept his orders and issuing an Order of the Day not dissimilar to Nelson's before Trafalgar, Wolfe embarked on the 'fine evening' of 12 September to join his flotilla to the chosen landing point at what is now known as Wolfe's Cove. At 2 a.m. on the morning of 13 September the assault began, and by dawn 4,500 men were deployed on the Plains of Abraham, having taken the French General Montcalm by surprise, as he had believed that such an attempt on his defences was impossible. Within a few hours, the battle was over; both Wolfe and Montcalm were dead and the fort of Quebec was in English hands.

There seems no reason to doubt that the account given by John Robison and quoted by John Playfair is entirely reliable. Those who have cast doubt on the story of Wolfe's recitation of Gray's Elegy have pointed to the specific order issued by Wolfe that strict silence was to be observed during the operation – even the oars of the boats and the men's boots were muffled – in order not to alert the French to the forthcoming attack. If Wolfe had then proceeded to recite Gray's poem he would have been guilty of violating his own orders and endangering the whole enterprise. In an effort to absolve Wolfe from such unprofessional conduct, some historians have explained that he spoke only in a hushed whisper. Lord Stanhope's mid-nineteenth-century *History of England* relates that 'not a word was spoken, not a sound was heard beyond the rippling of the stream. Wolfe alone – thus tradition has told us – repeated in a low voice to the other officers in his boat those beautiful stanzas with which a country churchyard inspired the muse of Gray', and supports this by citing James Grahame's recent *History of the United States* in which Wolfe is made to speak 'in accents barely audible'. Carlyle, in one of his imaginative passages, describes Wolfe's recitation as 'silently conversing with his people'.[2]

In these, as in many other versions, it is assumed that this moving occasion took place when the assault force was actually on its way up-river to scale the formidable cliffs of the Heights of Abraham. But a close examination of Playfair's account reveals that this was not so. Wolfe, we read, went by boat with a few of his officers, 'to visit some of his posts the night before the battle'. It was a fine evening, still light enough to enable them to admire the 'impressive' scenery, and having recited Gray's Elegy, Wolfe added that 'he would prefer being the author of that poem to the glory of beating the French to-morrow'.[3] This clearly implies that the whole episode occurred on the evening of 12 September, and not during the 4-mile row 'in strict silence' across the St Lawrence River in the early hours of the morning of 13 September.

We can safely accept Professor Playfair's eyewitness account of this famous occasion and, at the same time, express astonishment and admiration that, in such fateful circumstances, Wolfe could repeat 'nearly the whole' of the 128 lines of Gray's poem (James Grahame notes that Wolfe had received a copy of the poem 'by the last packet from England'), which includes the poignant and prophetic line: 'The paths of glory lead but to the grave.'

35

George Washington:
The Cherry Tree

Of all the great men in history he was the most invariably judicious, and there is scarcely a rash word or action or judgement recorded of him … He was in the highest sense of the words a gentleman and a man of honour, and carried into public life the severest standard of private morals. It was at first the constant dread of large sections of the American people, that if the old government were overthrown, they would fall into the hands of military adventurers, and undergo the yoke of military despotism. It was mainly the transparent integrity of the character of Washington that dispelled the fear. It was always known by his friends and it was soon acknowledged by the whole nation and by the English themselves, that in Washington America had found a leader who could be induced by no earthly motive to tell a falsehood, or to break an engagement, or to commit any dishonourable act.

W. H. Lecky, *History of England in the Eighteenth Century*

This extract from Lecky's paean of praise for George Washington reflects the nineteenth-century view of Washington as the embodiment of the eighteenth-century American ideal of republican virtue, which emphasised duty, sacrifice, integrity, moral fortitude and honourable conduct at all times. These are not the qualities that usually accompany historical heroes; they are usually expected to be flamboyant, glamorous, irascible, ruthless, eccentric and even rather wicked. Washington was none of these; an early biography had portrayed him as cold and colourless, a hero certainly but a rather dull, prosaic one. *A History of the Life and Death, Virtues and Exploits of General George Washington* was published in 1800, the year after Washington's death. A second edition appeared in 1806 with a new and revealing title: *The Life of George Washington, with Curious Anecdotes Laudable to Himself and Exemplary to His Countrymen.* The author was Mason Locke Weems who claimed, with no evidence to support him, that he had been formerly rector of Washington's parish of Mount Vernon, and in this new version of his book he was determined to 'flesh out a believable and interesting figure ... to humanise Washington'.[1] He allowed his imagination full rein, even as far as a description of Washington's ascent into Heaven where, it seems, 'at the sight of him, even those blessed spirits seemed to feel new raptures'.[2] Weems was to create a portrait that bore only a passing resemblance to reality, but that embodied many of the virtues cherished by the citizens of the new republic that Washington had brought into being – and of these, moral fortitude and integrity were paramount.

The story of Washington and the cherry tree is probably all that many pupils in British schools remember of the brief glance at the history of America they are allowed, and it still features in some schools in the States. It appeared first in the 1806 edition of Weems's biography and was introduced as an anecdote 'too valuable to be lost and too true to be doubted, for it was communicated to me by the same excellent lady to whom I am indebted for the last', an aged lady who, according to Weems, was 'a distant relative of Washington'. The entire rigmarole was pure fiction, but Weems told it with aplomb – so much so that a recent author quotes an American woman who remembered every word of the story from her schooldays and commented, 'If the tale isn't true, it should be. It is too pretty to be classified with the myths.'[3] This is how Weems told the story:

When George was about six years old, he was made the wealthy master of a hatchet of which, like most little boys, he was immoderately fond; and he was constantly going about chopping everything that came his way. One day, in the garden, where he often amused himself hacking his mother's pea-sticks, he unluckily tried the edge of his axe on the body of a beautiful young English cherry tree, which he barked so terribly, that I don't believe the tree ever got better of it. The next morning the old gentleman, finding out what had befallen his tree, which, by the by, was a great favourite, came into the house, and with much warmth asked for the mischievous author, declaring at the same time that he would not have taken five guineas for his tree. Nobody could tell him anything about it. Presently George and his hatchet made their appearance. 'George', said his father, 'do you know who killed that beautiful little cherry tree yonder in the garden?' This was a tough question; and George staggered under it for a moment; but quickly recovered himself; and looking at his father with the sweet face of youth brightened with the inexpressible charm of all-conquering truth, he bravely cried out, 'I can't tell a lie, Pa; you know I can't tell a lie. I did cut it with my hatchet'. 'Run to my arms, you dearest boy' cried his father in transports, 'Run to my arms; glad am I, George, that you killed my tree; for you have paid me for it a thousand fold. Such an act of heroism in my son is more worth than a thousand trees, though they blossomed with silver, and their fruits of purest gold.'[4]

Somewhat overblown to pass muster in a later age, maybe, but regarded as inspirational in the bliss of the new dawn of independent America.

Weems confessed in a letter to a friend that he had invented the anecdotes in his Washington biography[5] and included them for effect. In this, he certainly succeeded, for it was to be several generations before serious questioning began, and by that time most of them had become irrevocably etched in American memory, a process further ingrained by much-admired paintings in the 1860s – notably, John McRae's engraving of G. G. White's painting *Father I Can Not Tell a Lie, I Cut the Tree*, and Henry Brueckner's *Washington praying at Valley Forge* (Weems's story, which inspired this painting, conveniently ignored the fact that Washington was not a pious man. He attended church but he was always a deist rather than a Christian).

The result of Weems's fertile imagination has been that, even after a century of serious historical study, the real George Washington is still to some extent obscured by the legend. As a recent commentator put it, 'He has become entombed in his own myth – a metaphorical Washington Monument that hides from us the lineaments of the real man.'[6]

The final word on the cherry tree story should, perhaps, go to Mark Twain, who in 1867 wrote his *Brief Biographical Sketch of George Washington* and, with characteristic ironic humour, noted that 'George Washington, as a boy, was ignorant of the commonest accomplishments of youth. He could not even lie'.

36

Admiral Horatio Nelson: 'I Really Do not See the Signal', Copenhagen, 1801

Scene: The Battle of Copenhagen, 2nd April 1801. Nelson's fleet closely engaged with the Danish fleet and with the Trekroner battery. Severe losses and damage on both sides. Time 1.30 p.m. Outcome of the battle uncertain.

About this time the signal lieutenant called out that No. 39 (the signal for discontinuing the action) was thrown out by the commander-in-chief. He (Nelson) continued to walk the deck, and appeared to take no notice of it. The signal officer met him at the next turn, and asked if he should repeat it. 'No', he replied: 'Acknowledge it.' Presently he called after him, to know if the signal for close action was still hoisted, and being answered in the affirmative, said 'Mind you keep it so.' He now paced the deck, moving the stump of his lost arm in a manner which always indicated great emotion, 'Do you know,' said he to Mr Ferguson, 'what is shown on board the commander-in-chief? No. 39!' Mr Ferguson asked what that meant. 'Why, to leave off action!' Then shrugging up his shoulders, he repeated the words – 'Leave off the action! Now damn me if I do! You know Foley,' turning to the captain, 'I have only one eye, – I have a right to be blind sometimes,' – and then putting the glass to his blind eye, in that mood of mind which sports with bitterness, he exclaimed, 'I really do not see the signal.' Presently he exclaimed, 'Damn the signal! Keep mine for closer battle flying! That's the way I answer such signals. Nail mine to the mast!'

Robert Southey, *Life of Nelson*, 1813

Britain had little to celebrate as the nineteenth century dawned. At home there was growing unrest: riots were breaking out as a succession of bad harvests and a rapidly increasing population caused local bread shortages; the emergence of radical groups, sympathetic to the French Revolutionaries, was alarming the Establishment, resulting in a series of repressive Acts of Parliament such as the Combination Acts, the Seditious Meetings Acts, the Treasonable Practices Acts and the Newspaper Publication Act, all rigorously enforced. The huge costs of the war against France, including massive subsidies to allies and heavy payments for the import of supplementary grain supplies, had brought about a 15 per cent depreciation in the value of the currency and had turned a healthy trade surplus into a deficit. The national debt had doubled; income tax had just been introduced for the first time and was highly unpopular; inflation in the price of basic goods was made worse when country banks indulged in a threefold increase in their issues of paper money. Real poverty in both town and country was widespread.

At the same time, in Europe the war against Napoleon was going badly: French successes at Marengo and Hohenlinden had eliminated Britain's allies from the conflict; the Czar of Russia had gone over to Bonaparte; Spain threatened to attack Britain's ally, Portugal; Prussian troops had occupied the British Crown possession of Hanover; Denmark had seized the key port of Hamburg. Most ominous of all, Russia, Prussia, Sweden and Denmark were conspiring to form a Northern League of Armed Neutrality against British shipping in the Baltic, thus threatening, with their formidable navies, Britain's vital trade route to the principal sources of naval supplies – timber, pitch, hemp and flax – and substantial grain imports now more urgently needed than ever.[1]

Prompt and effective action was required to meet this mounting danger to Britain's security, commercial prosperity and domestic stability. The Baltic was the key, and the point of conflict here was the challenge by the Northern League to the internationally accepted right of British ships to stop and search neutral ships in time of war and to seize cargoes of contraband goods intended for an enemy.[2] The Baltic countries had already made clear their resentment at British seizures of their ships carrying cargoes (including naval supplies) to France, and their combined fleets, based in Copenhagen, Karlskrona, Kronstadt and Revel (now Tallinn), put them in a strong position to close the Baltic to British trade. After some procrastination and a change of government, it was eventually decided to send a fleet of eighteen ships-of-the-line and thirty-five smaller vessels to persuade Denmark to abandon the Northern League or suffer an attack on Copenhagen and the destruction of her fleet. This was to be the first step in the eventual elimination of the three Baltic fleets that posed a threat to British interests.

Nelson was appointed second-in-command of the expedition under Admiral Hyde Parker, an officer with a distinguished record in various Naval operations but not cast in the same mould as Nelson – who had established a reputation at Cape St Vincent and the Nile for daring, unorthodox manoeuvres and a firm belief in directly engaging the enemy. Nelson's proposal to deal with the Russian fleet at Revel first was rejected by Hyde Parker, but he did accept his audacious plan for a direct assault on the formidable Danish fleet drawn-up under the defensive batteries of Copenhagen, an operation which initially involved sailing a force of forty-five ships through intricate, narrow and shallow channels from which all marker buoys had been removed, to approach to within three-quarters of a mile of the enemy's line of battle.

After two days and nights of meticulous planning and laborious marking of a navigable channel through the shoals, Nelson was ready to send his ships into battle. In a remarkable display of seamanship, his captains took their vessels to their appointed positions, less than half a cable's length (*c.* 100 m) from each other with their broadsides facing the Danish line. The first shots were fired just after ten o'clock on the morning of 2 April and a ferocious fight ensued, in which combatants on both sides showed prodigious courage as their comrades and their ships were shot to pieces round them. So horrific was the carnage and so doubtful the outcome, that after three hours Hyde Parker, unable to send support because of contrary winds and currents, decided, after much debate, to hoist the signal (No. 39) to discontinue the battle.

This unexpected signal led to what has been described as 'one of the most astounding incidents in the history of naval warfare'[3] and eventually gave rise to one of the best-known anecdotes of Naval history. This only is certain: Hyde Parker gave the signal and Nelson disobeyed it. The version of the story that became, and has remained, the most familiar, was that written by the Poet Laureate Robert Southey in his *Life of Nelson*, first published in 1813 and since then published in more than a hundred editions. So revered was Nelson as a national hero, and so popular did the legend become, that it was not long before the phrase 'to turn a blind eye to' entered the English language.

The most reliable account we have of the entire battle is that written by Colonel the Hon. William Stewart, the officer commanding a landing party of 600 troops, who was with Nelson on board the *Elephant* and who compiled a long and detailed journal of the operation. Stewart met Robert Otway, Captain of Hyde Parker's flagship, who managed to reach the *Elephant* with a message from the Admiral that Nelson should continue the action if he saw the possibility of a successful outcome. This serves to indicate Hyde Parker's confused state of mind at the time, because his signal was not permissive since it was not flown, according to naval regulations, under a red pendant. Only this would have given Nelson freedom to exercise his discretion. As it turned out, the signal precipitated an immediate tragedy: Captain Edward Riou was killed instantly as he came under enemy fire when turning his ship, the *Amazon*, to obey Parker's order – 'thus', wrote Stewart, 'was the British service deprived of one of its greatest ornaments, and society of a character of singular worth'. Others later commented critically on Parker's signal: Rear-Admiral Graves wrote, 'If we had discontinued the action before the enemy struck, we should all have gone aground and been destroyed', and Vice-Admiral William Young stated that Parker's signal 'could not have been obeyed without exposing the whole to certain destruction'. Parker was too far away to assess the precise state of the battle, whereas Nelson correctly judged that the engagement had reached a critical point and that the Danish resistance was beginning to weaken. Within an hour, victory was assured. Nelson was proved right, but he had disobeyed his commanding officer's orders and kept his own signal for continued close action flying – that part of the story is established fact.

Robert Southey's *Life* may have become the most widely read of all the many biographies of Nelson but it was not the first. In

1806, the year following Trafalgar, there appeared a *Life* by James Harrison, strongly influenced by Emma Hamilton, in which Mr Ferguson, the surgeon on board the *Elephant*, is quoted as the authority for Nelson's alleged quip that since he had lost an eye he had a right to be blind sometimes and therefore he could not see Parker's signal. Harrison does not refer to Nelson actually putting his glass to his blind eye. This appeared three years later with the publication of an 'official' biography by James Clarke and John M'Arthur, which was little more than a hagiography – inaccurate and totally controlled and censored by Nelson's hypocritical, self-serving brother, William. This is a thoroughly unreliable work whose authors were said to have 'omitted, interpolated, transposed, improved' in their use of their manuscript sources. Even so, the version they gave of the signal incident was said to be the account given 'by an officer who was with Lord Nelson'. Robert Southey based his *Life* largely on these earlier biographies and apparently assumed that this officer was Mr Ferguson and that it was he who heard Nelson's insubordinate exclamations and witnessed the episode of the telescope to the blind eye. This seems improbable since Ferguson was the ship's surgeon and would not have been with Nelson but below decks attending to the many dying and wounded. The publication in the 1840s of *Nelson's Dispatches and Letters*, edited by Sir Nicholas Nicolas, revealed that this officer was none other than Colonel James Stewart, who appears to have accepted Clarke and M'Arthur's invitation to contribute his own reminiscences. Nicolas took this account to be as trustworthy as Stewart's earlier versions in his journal and in a letter to Sir Henry Clinton, and printed it in this official publication of Nelson's documents.[5] A recent biographer, however, has expressed a view that Stewart had a poor opinion of Clarke and M'Arthur's work and was content to repeat the details that first appeared in Harrison's biography of a few years earlier and that Southey followed.[6] It is improbable, however, that Colonel Stewart – a close friend of Nelson, a distinguished soldier, a Member of Parliament and a reliable witness – who was on the quarter-deck with Nelson, would wish to lend his name to an account that he knew to be untrue. It would be injudicious to dismiss this anecdote as a fairy tale, and at least one modern biographer accepts it as a fact with Colonel Stewart firmly in place as the eyewitness.[7]

Meanwhile, in 1828, James Ralfe had produced his monumental work *The Naval Biography of Great Britain*, in which he claimed that Hyde Parker had sent Nelson a private message that his signal should be considered optional, to be obeyed or not, at Nelson's discretion.[8] This was probably the same message that Captain Robert Otway was conveying to Nelson but was unable to deliver before Parker lost his nerve and hoisted Signal No. 39 without waiting for his messenger to arrive. In any event, as has been mentioned, the signal was not presented as permissive, thus leading to all the subsequent confused, enthralling, captivating tale of a national hero defiantly disobeying orders, a telescope placed impishly to a blind eye and a remarkable Naval victory against a formidable and courageous foe.[9]

37

Florence Nightingale:
The Lady with the Lamp, 1854–56

Lo in that hour of misery
A lady with a lamp I see
Pass through the glimmering gloom
And flit from room to room
And slow, as in a dream of bliss,
The speechless sufferer turns to kiss
Her shadow, as it falls.
A Lady with a Lamp shall stand
In the great history of the land
A noble type of good
Heroic womanhood.

H. W. Longfellow, 'Santa Philomena', 1857

Longfellow's poem set in stone the legend of Florence Nightingale as 'The Lady with the Lamp', the dedicated nurse caring for the suffering wounded in the appalling hospital-barracks of the Crimean War. It was written in the flurry of publicity and popular enthusiasm generated by the reports from the Crimea by the commissioner of *The Times* Fund for the sick and wounded. He had decided that the large sums of money at his disposal would be best utilised and administered by being placed in the hands of Miss Nightingale to facilitate the sweeping improvements she was making in the medical and sanitary conditions in the hospital at Scutari.[1] Her efforts were regarded less enthusiastically by obdurate and complacent officialdom, but fortunately she had the support of Sidney Herbert, Secretary of State at the War Office, who spoke at a public rally to raise funds for the Crimean wounded. He read to the large crowd letters written by soldiers who had personal experience of Florence

Nightingale's work at Scutari: 'What comfort it was to see her pass even. She would speak to one and nod and smile to as many more … We lay there by hundreds, but we could kiss her shadow as it fell, and lay our heads on the pillow again, content.'[2]

In the House of Lords the report of *The Times* Fund commissioner was read out:

> Wherever there is disease in its most dangerous form and the hand of the despoiler distressingly nigh, there is that incomparable woman sure to be seen. Her benignant presence is an influence for good comfort, even amid the' struggles of expiring nature. She is a 'ministering angel' without any exaggeration in these hospitals, and as her slender form glides quietly along each corridor, every poor fellow's face softens with gratitude at the sight of her. When all the medical officers have retired for the night and silence and darkness have settled down upon these miles of prostrate sick, she may be observed alone, with a little lamp in her hand, making her silent rounds.[3]

As with so many legends of history's heroic figures, the story of the 'Lady with the Lamp' acquired an aura of sentimental romanticism. Florence did not see herself as a 'ministering angel', and neither did the bemused and incompetent officials of the War Office and the Army Medical Board, whom she unceasingly harassed for essential supplies and for desperately needed improvements in hospital administration, sanitation and hygiene. For her, this unremitting battering against the stone wall of official obscurantism to achieve the reforms she saw were so urgently required was just as important as the task of attending to the needs of the sick and the dying. If we were to seek signs of angelic quality in Florence Nightingale it might be found in the disarming, persuasive logic of her reports to commissions, committees and Government ministers: in the preface to her seminal *Notes on Hospitals* she wrote disarmingly, 'It may seem a strange principle to enunciate as the very first requirement in a Hospital that it should do the sick no harm.'

There were, of course, many other nurses working in the dreadful conditions that prevailed in the military hospitals of the Crimean War. Most of them were rough, untrained, uncompassionate, earthy women, cast in the mould of Charles Dickens's Sarah Gamp; but a remarkable exception was a black Jamaican nurse, Mary Seacole, a skilled and caring nurse with notable administrative abilities who spent the years of the war in the hospital at Spring Hill, just a few miles from the Front near Sebastapol. Here she faced the same appalling conditions as Florence Nightingale at Scutari and tackled them with the same drive and dedication. From the soldiers she cared for, she earned the same respect and adoration as that accorded to Florence Nightingale. She, too, patrolled her wards at night bearing her lamp, but she had no influence in high places and she did not win the politician's praise nor catch the poet's eye. Mary Seacole was neither an uncouth Mrs Gamp nor a daughter of high society; she did not fit easily into the rigid social categories of Victorian society. Indeed, it was considered extraordinary for someone of Florence Nightingale's upper-class background to devote her life to nursing and such unsavoury matters as sanitation and hospital hygiene. Because of this only she could be the 'Lady with the Lamp'; but Mary Seacole should not be forgotten (the story of Mary Seacole is best read in her autobiography *The Wonderful Adventures of Mrs Seacole in Many Lands*, first published in 1857 to much acclaim and republished in 1984. Although overshadowed – and much disapproved of – by Florence Nightingale, this remarkable woman was feted by the military establishment, adored by the public and accepted into the household of Alexandra, Princess of Wales).

Despite the efforts of several admirable biographers, beginning with the outstanding two-volume work by Sir Edward Cook, the achievements of Florence Nightingale in the sixty years after she returned from the Crimea are generally little known. Yet all that she had achieved there was to her no more than a stepping stone.

Fighting ill health and official complacency and indifference, she worked tirelessly to bring about a revolution in the standards of medical practice and administration in hospitals. She raised the status of nursing to that of an honourable vocation that the daughters of the upper classes adopted with enthusiasm, particularly when it was favoured with the patronage of Princess (later Queen) Alexandra. The opening in 1860 of the Nightingale Training School and Home for Nurses at St Thomas's Hospital in London in effect marked the beginning of modern nursing; the numerous editions of her *Notes on Nursing* set the standard for modern nursing practice. Nursing schools and nursing homes were established in East London and Liverpool, and the Golden Jubilee of 1887 was marked by the foundation of the Queen's Jubilee Nursing Institute. Her work to reform the administration of hospitals was prodigious and, against the weight of opposition from the political and military establishment, she eventually secured a Royal Commission, which accepted almost all her recommendations. New hospitals were built to the standards she had outlined in her *Notes on Hospitals*, the Army Medical School was founded and the Army Medical Department, which had caused her so much vexation in the Crimean War, had to endure wholesale reorganisation. These were remarkable achievements and, as one of her more candid biographers commented, 'What she accomplished in those years of unknown labour could, indeed, hardly have been more glorious than her Crimean triumphs; but it was certainly more important.'[5]

In her later years, Florence Nightingale was a formidable figure, honoured by the queen, feared by politicians and obsessed with the work of reform she had set herself; she became manipulative, dictatorial, omniscient and, occasionally, bitterly angry at the restrictions placed upon women in nineteenth-century society: 'Her fierce pen shaking with intimate anger, depicts in biting sentences the fearful fate of an unmarried girl in a wealthy household. It is a *cri de coeur*.'[6]

But the image of this extraordinary and courageous woman remains indelibly etched in popular historical knowledge only as the 'Lady with the Lamp'.

The New Oxford Dictionary of National Biography (2004) notes that the term 'The Lady with the Lamp' was coined by *The Times* newspaper following a report from its correspondent working as an almoner in the hospitals in the Crimea, who 'described her midnight vigils and defined what quickly became her iconic stature'.

Addendum

A new biography of Mary Seacole gives a full and sympathetic portrait of the life and character of this flamboyant Jamaican nurse, who in 2004 was voted the 'top black Briton of all time': Jane Robinson, *Mary Seacole* (Constable: 2005).

38

Queen Victoria: 'We Are Not Amused'

Finding herself on the throne, Queen Victoria immediately announced her intention of being Good and plural but not amused. This challenge was joyfully accepted by her subjects, and throughout her reign loyal and indefatigable attempts to amuse her were made by Her Majesty's eminently Victorian ministers and generals.

W. C. Sellar and R. J. Yeatman, *1066 and All That*

Sellar and Yeatman, in their own inimitable way, have captured the image that, for most of us, still clings to our historical memory of Queen Victoria – morally strait-laced, overly conscious of her public duty as monarch, punctilious in matters of etiquette and decorum and strictly disciplinarian in the upbringing of her children and in the regime of her household. The well-known portraits and photographs of Victoria serve only to reinforce this impression of a queen with a mission – whether it is Winterhalter's portrait of the forty-year-old sovereign with her imperious, determined presence arrayed in her robes of state, or von Angeli's dark portrayal in 1875 of a tight-lipped, black-clad widow gazing out almost defiantly at an unkind world, or the famous Diamond Jubilee photograph of a sad, serious old lady covered in lace and half-turned away from a world she no longer feels part of – all helping to confirm the common dictionary definition of 'Victorian' as implying moral rectitude and a life of strict austerity with connotations of prudery and solemnity. Victoria's contemporaries did, indeed, invent an unlovely word, 'Balmorality', to define the outward reality of this in the daily life of the Royal Household. Victoria was, however, a character of innumerable contradictions and all this presents but one side of her immensely complex personality.

Soon after her accession to the throne, she had a long discussion with Lord Melbourne about the role of the monarchy in British society, and from this she emerged with a determination to repair the damage done by the scandals and extravagance of the Prince Regent's time and by the dubious constitutional procedures and 'vulgar' popularity of the sailor king, William IV. The monarchy must now be seen to be dignified, serious, exemplary and respected. There were, inevitably, errors of judgement on the way – the queen was after all only just eighteen when she began her reign – and the royal dignity often trod heavily on the sensitivities of innocent subjects; but few would deny that by the middle of the century these aims had been entirely fulfilled.

This was the public image of Victoria the queen; as one so often discovers, the private person could be very different. Within the family circle Victoria took part in and, according to her journals and letters, thoroughly enjoyed simple jokes, games and most entertainments. She had a standard phrase for her journal to mark a happy day: 'I was very much amused.' She was kind and affectionate and, contrary to popular belief, was fond of children even if, understandably, she could not 'bear their being idolised and made too great objects of – or having a number of them about me making a great noise'.[1]

Victoria's sense of humour was not quite as restricted as Lord Granville, at one time her Foreign Secretary, in a famous comment, would have us believe. Nothing made her laugh so much, he observed, as hearing that one had trapped a finger in a door. It is certainly true that the queen considered it a great joke when Lord Kinnoul fell head over heels down a steep slope, and when an embarrassed Duke of Argyll dropped the crown and delivered it to her 'like a pudding that had sat down'. She also found it highly amusing to describe how her mother processed from the dining room wielding a fork in mistake for her fan. The queen loved to tell the tale of the medals struck to mark the Ashanti campaign, relating how shocked some of her court had been at the design: 'Roman soldiers with nothing – nothing at all – but helmets on.'[2] Then what is one to make of her gift to Prince Albert of a small sculpture of a naked Lady Godiva on horseback?

When it came to the queen as sovereign, there was no relaxation of the strict protocol Victoria had determined should be observed by all. The majesty of the Crown would be upheld at all times and on all occasions. Even Prince Albert had to insist that it was 'Victoria, his wife', and not 'Her Majesty, the Queen', who requested admittance to his room. Pity the poor librarian, who, on the occasion of the queen's visit, thought to take the opportunity to introduce his daughter, only to receive the crushing reply, 'I came to see the library'; or the elderly gentleman suffering from gout, whom she kept standing for hours in her presence.[3] Prime ministers, lord chancellors, field-marshalls, admirals and generals, foreign dignitaries – all were expected to treat Majesty as Majesty had decreed. Even the 'gentle raillery' advocated by Archbishop Randall Davidson as a means to cheer up his queen in her moments of depression would be likely to be received in a similar vein.[4] 'No-one could deliver more effectively than Queen Victoria the look that froze or the phrase that made men and women shrivel: "We are not amused."'[5]

There are many anecdotes purporting to explain Victoria's use of this phrase, almost all of them with no supporting evidence. One of the most often-quoted of these tales appeared in a collection of royal anecdotal essays published in New York in 1977 under the title *Queen Victoria Was Amused*. This described how, during a visit to the queen by several of her grandchildren, she heard a good deal of noisy laughter from the room where they were playing and went to investigate. Her questions met at first with an embarrassed silence but eventually one of the youngsters, presumably understanding that a royal command was not to be disobeyed, admitted that the immoderate laughter was in response to a risqué joke one of them had told. On hearing the nature of the joke, the queen put on her air of offended majesty and, with the sharp rebuke – 'We are not amused' – left the room.[6] No evidence has been forthcoming to support this story.

More convincing is the entry in Lady Caroline Holland's *Notebooks of a Spinster Lady* for 2 January 1900, where we read that this was the queen's rebuke to the Honourable Alexander Grantham Yorke, one of her grooms-in-waiting, whom she had unexpectedly seen entertaining his companions by giving an imitation of Her Majesty. This has the ring of truth, but it still seems probable, in the light of the regular entry of a balancing phrase in her early journals (referred to above), that 'We are not amused' was her stock response to any conversation or incident that she judged too inappropriate or too indelicate to be acceptable, either because of the company present or because it affronted the dignity of the Crown.

The New Oxford Dictionary of National Biography (2004), after briefly commenting that the provenance of the 'We are not amused' story is 'unclear', makes the point that 'Victoria's determination to present a regal face to posterity did her a great disservice, for a readiness to be pleased, and indeed, even amused, was one of her more endearing characteristics'. The queen 'felt it undignified and unqueenly to be painted or photographed smiling'. All her public statues, too, represent her as stern and matriarchal.

39

The Angels of Mons, 1914

Early on the morning of 4 August 1914, a bright and clear summer's day, German forces crossed the Belgian frontier. They had been assured that the Belgians would put up no opposition to the German advance. Five days later, the invading army, surprised and frustrated by the fierce resistance of these 'chocolate soldiers', was brought to a halt before the forts of Liège.

In London, Sir Edward Grey, the Foreign Secretary, persuaded a half-hearted House of Commons that if Britain stood aside from the coming conflict, reneged on our moral commitment to support France and Belgium if they were attacked, not only would Western Europe fall under the domination of Germany but 'we should … sacrifice our respect and good name and reputation before the world'. An ultimatum was sent to the German government to stop the invasion of Belgium within twenty-four hours or a declaration of war would ensue.

After much discussion and disagreement in the British War Council[1] a British Expeditionary Force of four divisions embarked for France on 9 August. It was officially described as 'incomparably the best-trained, best-organised, and best-equipped British Army that ever went forth to war'.[2] It may well have been all of these – and its fighting capacity was soon to be proved beyond doubt – but most of those who sent it into France in 1914 were shamefully ignorant of the enemy forces opposed to it, in what became known as The Battle of the Frontiers. The German 1st Army, under von Kluck, continued its advance through Belgium with 160,000 troops and 600 guns; the BEF facing them along the line of the Mons canal comprised 70,000 men and 300 guns, including just twenty-four machine guns, or two per battalion. The British force at first had no field telephones or wireless equipment and was wholly deficient in siege- and trench-warfare materials; it had few motor vehicles, but (splendid anachronism) it had 30,000 horses bearing cavalry officers whose swords had been officially newly sharpened. Unfortunately, this was not to be just a continuation of war on the veldt.

On 23 August 1914, two British divisions prepared to do battle with six German divisions at Mons. They were ignorant of the enemy's strength, at odds with their French allies and handicapped by the rigidity of military planning, which would brook no change even when the new RAF air reconnaissance reported a German enveloping movement. Beguiled by military nostalgia as they marched past Malplaquet, the scene of an earlier British triumph, by the rapturous reception they were given by the local inhabitants and by the confident assurances that they would be home victorious by Christmas, these men believed that it would, indeed, be 'roses, roses all the way'.

They were now plunged into a scene of carnage and destruction hitherto unknown in warfare. The machine gun and new developments in artillery had transformed the field of battle: the Germans had overwhelming superiority in both. Even so, the British force at Mons fought the enemy to a standstill with such accurate, concentrated, rapid fire from their Lee-Enfield rifles that the Germans believed that they were facing massed machine guns. The battle lasted for nine hours; casualties on both sides were heavy; there were many acts of individual bravery and every regiment taking part had its moments of glory. Mons was a bloody baptism of fire. Even so, it was not von Kluck who forced the British into the 'glorious retreat' from Mons, but a sudden change of plan by the French High Command.

The French Fifth Army on the British right flank had suffered a serious reverse at Charleroi and had taken heavy losses; it was now in danger of encirclement, bringing back memories of the disaster at Sedan in 1870. Just as Kitchener was anxious to avoid the annihilation of the BEF at Mons, so Joffre saw that another Sedan would mean almost certain defeat for France. Retreat was the only option, and when the French moved back the British had to follow or face certain destruction. The Germans had resumed their advance on all fronts and were confident of a quick victory. Only a successful retreat could save both French and British from imminent surrender or annihilation.

The retreat from Mons was an impressive military exercise; its importance lies less in its demonstration of the courage and discipline of the small British force than in the fact that this force lived to fight another day, to hold the enemy at bay while Kitchener's conscript 'army of millions' was brought into being.

The Battle of Mons, then, was not one of Britain's major military victories, comparable to Agincourt, Blenheim, Waterloo or El Alamein, but men everywhere fought bravely and sustained grievous losses. The temporary check to the German advance through Belgium and the successful extrication of both British and French forces from encirclement may have contributed to the eventual victory of the Allies; the BEF had proved itself to be anything but 'General French's contemptible little army'.[3]

Yet Mons has become a legend, a legend which began only a few days after the battle, with a despatch from Arthur Moore, *The Times* correspondent in France. This became known as the Amiens Despatch and was published in a special Sunday edition of the paper; it was the first indication the British public had received of the reality of events at the Front. Moore did not minimise the extent of the military reverse suffered by the British regiments in 'the action of Mons': he wrote of a 'retreating and broken army', in which some units had 'lost nearly all their officers'; yet there had been 'no failure of discipline, no panic and no throwing up the sponge'. Even so, Britain had to face the fact that 'the first great German effort had succeeded'.

All this was a terrible shock to the British public, which had entered the war with an excessive measure of imperialist elan. Censorship had been so strictly imposed that the newspapers had printed little more than bland assurances about the military action in France and Belgium, and it was assumed that the Kaiser was being taught a severe lesson. The news from Mons was the end of a dream. Mr Britling, in the novel by H. G. Wells, aptly summed up public reaction to the Amiens Despatch: 'It was as if David had flung his pebble – and missed.'[4]

Thus far Moore's report was reasonably close to the facts, but he then proceeded to enter the realms of fantasy and, in so doing, laid the foundation of a popular legend surrounding the Battle of Mons. It was, he wrote, the BEF that 'bore the weight of the blow' (thus totally ignoring the key role of France's formidable Fifth Army) and, having fought the Germans to a standstill, they then accomplished a 'Glorious Retreat', events which, as the legend gathered momentum, soon created a widespread belief that at Mons the BEF had saved France, Europe and Western Civilisation.

It was in this heady atmosphere that Londoners read their *London Evening News* just a few weeks later. The edition of 29 September 1914 contained a short story by Arthur Machen entitled *The Bowmen*, written as if it were an eyewitness account of the Battle of Mons.

Machen described how 'three hundred thousand men in arms with all their artillery swelled like a flood against the little English army' defending a vital salient. 'All the morning the German guns had thundered and shrieked against this corner and against the thousand or so of men who held it', and the shells 'tore good Englishmen limb from limb … There was no help it seemed … The English artillery was good' but 'it was being steadily battered into scrap iron.' Only 500 men remained and although the advancing Germans fell in 'companies and battalions', others swarmed after them 'column upon column, a grey world of men … There was no hope at all'. In the midst of this inferno a British soldier suddenly remembered 'a queer vegetarian restaurant in London' where on all the plates 'was printed a figure of St George in blue, with the motto "Adsit Anglis Sanctus Georgius" – may St George be present to help the English'. The soldier continued to fire at the advancing Germans as he called out this invocation, but he felt something like an electric shock pass through his body and 'it seemed to him that a tumult of voices answered this summons. He heard or seemed to hear thousands shouting "St George! St George!"'; and he 'saw a long line of shapes, with a shining about them. They were like men who drew the bow, and with another shout, their cloud of arrows flew singing and tingling through the air towards the German host'. To the astonishment of the hard-pressed English soldiers, they saw the Germans fall by the thousand as 'line after line crashed to the earth'. As the singing of arrows darkened the air, voices were heard crying: 'Harrow! Harrow! Monsignor St George succour us.' German soldiers numbering 10,000 lay dead before that salient, and no wounds could be found on their bodies. 'St George had brought his Agincourt bowmen to help the English.'[5]

Thus the legend of the Angels of Mons was born. Arthur Machen himself was rather embarrassed to see his flight of imagination assume the status of actual fact, but he was, it seems, assured by churchmen that he had been truly granted a supernatural insight into a genuine divine intervention in the affairs of men – his 'Agincourt bowmen' were indeed angels sent to defend a just cause in its time of peril. Fifty years later, a more sceptical age, distanced by time from the emotions of 1914, was more concerned to put this bloody but minor engagement into historical context than to examine the role of celestial beings in the conflict. In his *English History 1914–1945*, A. J. P. Taylor drily commented, 'Mons achieved legendary importance if only because it was the one occasion when Heavenly Powers intervened in the war. The Angels of Mons, varying in number from two to a platoon, fought on the British side.'[6]

In September 1914, the people of Britain were in shock at the realisation that German military power was not to be humbled within three months as was popularly believed. Heavy censorship had obscured from the press and the public the extent of the reverse suffered at Mons. When *The Times* published the Amiens Despatch describing the defeat of the BEF, helplessly outnumbered by the enemy and faced with the overwhelming firepower of the German machine guns, leaving the shattered British regiments as 'a retreating and broken army', the nation was in a mood to clutch at any straw that rumour blew its way. Within days of *The Times* despatch, the country was swept with reports that thousands of Russian troops had landed in Aberdeen and were coming to the aid of the Allied cause. The rumour gathered pace as each day went by: a porter at Edinburgh railway station had swept away the snow that had fallen from Cossack boots; delays in the rail service from Edinburgh to London were attributed to the demands on accommodation to transport the Russians south; a Scottish landowner claimed that 125,000 Russians had passed through his estate; Londoners had seen 10,000 of them marching along the Thames Embankment in the early hours on their way to Victoria Station; an Oxford professor had been summoned to act as interpreter; in Paris a welcoming party was being arranged to greet their arrival; almost everyone knew someone who knew something about them.[7] By the time an official denial of such an improbable 'rescue' army was issued, the story was firmly embedded in the public mood of near hysteria. In such an atmosphere, Arthur Machen's dramatic story of the 'Angels of Mons' was readily believed. Throughout our history, hope, credulity and despair have often walked hand in hand.

40

Forbidden Fruit in
the Garden of Eden

> Of man's first disobedience, and the fruit
> Of that forbidden tree, whose mortal taste
> Brought death into the world, and all our woe,
> With loss of Eden.

The opening words of Milton's *Paradise Lost* accurately reflect the words that appear in the Book of Genesis, newly translated into English in 1611 – just a few years after Milton was born. Genesis refers to 'the tree of knowledge of good and evil, thou shalt not eat it'. There is no indication whatever of the nature of this tree. In many parts of the Middle East, and according to Muslim tradition, the tree was widely assumed to be the banyan, or Indian fig tree – a belief that would seem to be supported by a verse in the same chapter of Genesis: 'and they sewed fig leaves together, and made themselves aprons'. In a manuscript from the eighth-century Carolingian period, the tree appears as a palm tree with Adam and Eve eating dates. Apple trees did not flourish in the soil and climate of the biblical lands and so are unlikely to have been singled out for such a momentous occasion. Yet in the Western world it is almost universally believed that the forbidden fruit was an apple.

English literature throughout the centuries abounds with references to the apple as the forbidden fruit that led to the Fall of Man. This interpretation was generally accepted in the Middle Ages: the fourteenth-century *Cursor Mundi* tells us that 'Adam brake goddis co-mandment of the appel', and a popular Christmas carol has for 500 years reminded us that 'Adam lay i'bowndyn, And al was for an appil, an that he tok'. In the seventeenth century,

Milton himself, towards the end of *Paradise Lost*, records Satan's triumph with the line 'Him by fraud have I seduc'd with an apple'. Modern writers and poets have constantly returned to the same theme: from Robert Southey to Emily Dickinson to Ted Hughes, the imagery of the apple in the Garden of Eden is put to poetic use. Mark Twain gave his own perceptive interpretation: 'Adam was but human – this explains it all. He did not want the apple for the apple's sake; he wanted it only because it was forbidden.'

Whatever the forbidden fruit may have been – and the fig appears the most likely candidate (it was under a banyan, or fig tree, that Buddha experienced his great 'Enlightenment') – it seems certain that it became an apple in our own tradition as the result of an error in the translation. In the fourth-century Latin Vulgate translation of Genesis from Hebrew, the world 'evil', in the expression 'the tree of knowledge of good and evil', is translated by the Latin word 'malum', which is also the Latin word for 'apple', and this gave rise to the idea that the fruit was from an apple tree.

Precisely when this error first appeared in English is difficult to determine, but the seventh-century poet Caedmon, in his translation of the Book of Genesis into Anglo-Saxon, used the phrase 'the loathsome apple'. Two centuries later, King Alfred, in his translation of Pope Gregory's 'Cura Pastoralis', also translated the tree of evil as an apple tree. By the early middle ages this interpretation had become firmly rooted in our religious culture and literary tradition and has remained so ever since.

Notes

Introduction

1 M. V. Hughes, *A London Child of the 1870s* (1934), pp. 48–9.
2 K. Magnus, *The First Makers of England* (1901), p. vii.
3 G. Hosking and G. Schopflin, *Myth and Nationhood* (1977), quoted in S. Barczewski, *Myth and Identity in Nineteenth-Century Britain* (OUP: 2000), p. 46.
4 G. A'Beckett, *The Comic History of England*, Vol. 1 (1846), p. 276, quoted in R. Mitchell, *Picturing the Past* (OUP: 2000).
5 *The Oxford Thackeray*, Vol. ix, p. 166 and Vol. xiii, pp. 542–3.
6 J. Lingard, *History of England*, Vol. viii (1854–5), p.157.
7 *The British Critic*, Vol. 9, pp. 19–21, quoted in S. Barczewski, *op. cit.*, p. 98.
8 J. Austen, *Northanger Abbey*, Chapter 14.
9 R. Birley, *The Undergrowth of History* (The Historical Association: 1955), pp. 28–9.
10 F. Barlow, *William Rufus* (Yale: 2000), Preface, p. xv.
11 G. M. Trevelyan, *History and the Reader* (CUP: 1945), pp. 17 and 24.
12 Horace, *Ars Poetica*, Lines 343–4.

1 Caratacus in Rome

1 Suetonius, *Gaius*, p. xlvi.
2 *Ibid.*, p. xliv

3 P. Solway, *Roman Britain* (OUP: 1981), p. 103.

4 Tacitus, *Annals* xii, p. 33 (trans. M. Grant: Penguin Classics).

5 Tacitus, *Annals* xii, pp. 35–6 (trans. M. Grant: Penguin Classics).

6 Tacitus also provided a speech for Calgacus, leader of the Caledonia resistance to Agricola, following the Battle of Mons Graupius in AD 84, which is less convincing than that attributed to Caratacus. It was in this speech that Tacitus used the famous sentence 'They rob, kill and rape and this they call Roman rule. They make a desert and call it peace.' *Agricola* xxxi-ii (OUP: 1967).

2 St Gregory

1 B. Colgrave and R. A. B. Mynors, (eds) *Bede's Ecclesiastical History of the English People* (OUP: 1969), p. 122n.

2 *Ibid.*, p. 123n.

3 *Ibid.*, pp. 132–5.

4 *Ibid.*, p. 567.

5 See Tony Auguarde, *The Oxford Guide to Word Games* (OUP: 2003), pp. 1 and 248.

6 F. M. Stenton, *Anglo-Saxon England* (OUP: 1943), p. 103.

7 P. Wormald, *The Venerable Bede and the 'Church of the English'* (1992), p. 26.

3 Edmund, King of East Anglia

1 Bishop Asser, *Life of Alfred*, ed. W. H. Stevenson (OUP: 1904), p. 26.

2 G. C. Brooke, *English Coins* (1932), p. 30 and Plate VIII.

3 R. L. Gregory (ed.), *Oxford Companion to the Mind* (OUP: 1987), p. 457.

4 W. W. Skeat (ed.), *Aelfric's Lives of the Saints* (Early English Text Society: 1891), pp. 314–35.

5 Bede in his *Historia Ecclesiastica* tells of the similar fate that befell Edwin and Oswald, *Kings of Northumbria in the Seventh Century* Vol. II, p. 20 and Vol. III, p. 12.

6 H. O. Coxe, *Roger of Wendover – Chronica i.*, pp. 303–15.
7 *The Bury Post*, 11 October 1848 (with acknowledgement to the Bury St Edmunds Record Office).

4 King Alfred

1 William of Malmesbury, *De Gestis Regum Anglorum*, Rolls Series, Vol. I, p. 125. Ed. W. Stubbs, 1887–9.
2 Adapted from the translation by Robert Birley, *The Undergrowth of History* (Historical Association: 1955), p. 6.
3 W. H. Stevenson, *Asser's Life of King Alfred Together with the Annals of St Neots* (OUP: 1904), p. 261.
4 Adapted from the translation by Robert Birley, *op. cit.*, p. 8. Manuscript printed in Anglia III, p. 104.

5 King Edgar

1 F. M. Stenton, *Anglo-Saxon England* (OUP: 1943), p. 363.
2 *Ibid.*, pp. 365–6.
3 W. H. Stevenson, *English Historical Review*, Vol. 13, 1898, p. 505.
4 *Ibid.*, p. 506.
5 F. M. Stenton, *op. cit.*, p. 364.
6 Florence of Worcester, *Chronicon ex Chronicis* (ed.) B. Thorpe (English History Society: 1848–9), i, pp. 142–3.
7 R. H. M. Dolley and D. M. Metcalf, 'The Reform of the English Coinage under Eadgar' in *Anglo-Saxon Coins: Studies Presented to F. M. Stenton* (1961).

6 King Cnut

1 F. M. Stenton, Anglo-Saxon England (OUP: 1943), p. 391.
2 M. K. Lawson, *Cnut: The Danes in England in the Early Eleventh Century* (Longman: 1993), p. 133.

3 F. M. Stenton, *op. cit.*, p. 390.

4 D. Hume, *History of England* (1778), Chapter III, p. 152.

5 A. Campbell (ed.), *Encomium Emmae Reginae* (RHS Camden Society, 3rd Series, Vol. lxxii, 1949), ii, 20, p. 36.

6 Henry of Huntingdon, *Historia Anglorum*, ed. T. Arnold (Rolls Series: 1879), Vol. I, p. 189.

7 G. Gaimar, *L'Estorie des Engles*, ed. A. Bell (Oxford: 1960), pp. 149–50.

8 D. Hume, *op. cit.*, Chapter III, pp. 153–4.

9 F. M. Stenton, *op. cit.*, p. 404.

10 M. K. Lawson, *op. cit.*, p. 133.

7 Lady Godiva

1 Alfred Tennyson, *Godiva*, Lines 19–31.

2 D. Donaghue, *Lady Godiva – A Literary History of the Legend* (Blackwell: 2003), p. 129.

3 V. H. Galbraith, *Roger of Wendover and Matthew Paris*; David Murray Lecture (1944); R. Vaughan, *Matthew Paris* (CUP: 1958).

4 Roger of Wendover, *Flores Historiarum*, ed. H. O. Coxe (English Historical Society: 1841–2), pp. 497–8; (Author's translation) Matthew Paris, *Chronica Majora*, ed. H. L. Luard (Rolls Series: 1872–4), Vol. I, pp. 526–7.

5 F. Barlow, *The English Church 1000–1066* (1979), pp. 56–7.

6 R. Grafton, *Grafton's Chronicle,* ed. H. Ellis (1809), pp. 147–8.

7 H. R. Ellis Davidson, 'The Ride in Folk Tradition', in J. C. Lancaster (ed.), *Godiva of Coventry* (1967), pp. 61–73.

8 D. Donaghue, *op. cit.* p. 39.

9 *Ibid.*, p. 129. Professor Donaghue's book has a wealth of information on the history and interpretation of the Godiva legend. The author acknowledges his debt to this work for some of the detail given in this chapter.

8 William II

1   E. A. Freeman, *The Reign of William Rufus* (1882), Vol. 2, p. 336.
2   Sellar and Yeatman, *1066 and All That*.
3   F. E. Barlow, *William Rufus* (Yale: 2000), p. 261.
4   *Ibid*., pp. 102–4.
5   *Sir Gawain and the Green Knight*, translated by B. Stone (1975), p. 64ff.
6   William of Malmesbury, *De Gestis Regum Anglorum*, ed. W. Stubbs (Rolls Series: 1887–90), II, pp. 377–9.
7   The collapse of the tower of Winchester Cathedral in 1107 was also attributed to the wrath of God that such a sinner should be buried there. A more realistic explanation by William of Malmesbury later admitted that the structure was unstable and due to fall down at any time.
8   J. H. Round, *Feudal England* (1895), p. 472.
9   A. L. Poole, *From Domesday Book to Magna Carta* (OUP: 1951), p. 114.
10 C. W. Hollister, *Monarchy, Magnates and Institutions in the Anglo-Norman World* (1986), pp. 57–75.
11 E. Mason, 'William Rufus: Myth and Reality' in *Journal of Medieval History*, 1977, iii, p. 18n.
12 F. Barlow, *op. cit.*, p. 425; C. W. Hollister, *Henry I* (Yale: 2000), p. 104.

9 Henry I: The Loss of the *White Ship*

1   Stephen of Blois had already boarded the *White Ship* intending to join Prince William's party but he disembarked just before the ship set sail, complaining of diarrhoea. His indisposition was to have a profound effect on the course of English history when his claim to the throne on Henry's death plunged the country into civil war.
2   Accounts of the disaster may be found in Orderic Vitalis, *Historia Ecclesiastica*; William of Malmesbury, *Gesta Regum Anglorum*; Hugh the Chanter, *History of the Church of*

York 1066–1127; Symeon of Durham, *Historia Ecclesiae Dunelmensis*. Details are given in C. W. Hollister, *Henry I* (Yale: 2001), p. 277.

3 Orderic Vitalis, *Historia Ecclesiastica*, trans. M. Chibnall (OUP: 1969–80), Vol. 6, p. 300.

4 R. Southern, *Medieval Humanism and Other Studies* (OUP: 1970), p. 230; Walter Map, *De Nugis Curialum*, ed. and trans. M. R. James et al. (1983), pp. 438 and 470; Geoffrey Gaimar, *L'Estoire des Engleis* (OUP: 1960), p. 206; Henry of Huntingdon, *op. cit.*, pp. 464–6. For these references, see Hollister, *op. cit.*, pp. 216 and 281; A. L. Poole, *From Domesday to Magna Carta* (OUP: 1952), p. 129.

5 Paul de Rapin, *History of England* (1727), trans. N. Tindal, Vol. I, de Thoyras, p. 197.

10 Henry I: Death from 'a Surfeit of Lampreys'

1 Orderic Vitalis, *Ecclesiastical History*, ed./trans. M. Chibnall (OUP: 1969–80), Vol. 6, p. 448 et seq.

2 Henry of Huntingdon, *Historia Anglorum*, ed. T. Arnold (1879), Vol. I, p. 254 or ed. D. Greenway (OUP: 1996), p. 490.

3 Robert Fabyan, *New Chronicles of England and France* (1516), ed. H. Ellis (1811), p. 260.

4 Ranulph Higden, *Polychronicon*, ed. J. R. Lumby, translated by John Trevisa (1367) (Rolls Series) VII, p. 476.

12 Fair Rosamund

1 Gerald of Wales, *Opera* Vol. VIII, ed. J. S. Brewer (Rolls Series), p. 165.

2 T. Hearne, introduction to his edition of *William of Newburgh* (1718). Supplement to his edition of J. Leland's *Itinerary* (1718).

3 W. L. Warren, *Henry II* (Yale: 2000), p. 119. A powerful and controversial personality such as Eleanor of Aquitaine became

an inevitable source for the creation of rumour, gossip and, eventually, legendary tales: v. F. W. Chambers, 'Some legends concerning Eleanor of Aquitaine' in *Speculum*, xvi, 1941, 459–68.

4 R. Fabyan, *Chronicle* (1516), ed. H. Ellis, pp. 276–7.

5 T. Percy, *Reliques of Ancient English Poetry* (1765), Vol. II, p. 145.

6 *Monasticon Anglicanum*, ed. Caley, Ellis and Bandiel (1817–30), p. 366.

7 T. Hearne, introduction to his edition of William of Newburgh's *Historia Rerum Anglicarum* (1198, 1718); R. Higden, *Polychronicon*, ed. H. Lumby, VIII, p. 52.

8 J. Leland, *Itinerary*, ed. T. Hearne (1718), Vol. II, p. 77.

9 Roger of Hoveden, *Chronica III*, ed. W. Stubbs (Rolls Series: 1861–91), pp. 167–8.

10 T. Hearne, *A Discourse about Fair Rosamund and the Nunnery of Godstow* (1718).

11 *Dives et Pauper* (1493), 14 vi.

13 Richard I and Blondel

1 Gerald of Wales, *Opera*, Vol. VIII (Rolls Series: 1861–71), p. 247.

2 W. L. Warren, *King John* (Eyre Methuen: 1978), p. 6.

3 Ralph Coggeshall, *Chronicon Anglicanum*, (Rolls Series: 1875), pp. 97–8.

4 *Itinerarium Peregrinorum*, ed. W. Stubbs (1864).

5 *Gesta Regis Henrici Secundi* (Rolls Series: 1867), i, 346.

6 A. L. Poole, *From Domesday Book to Magna Carta* (OUP: 1951), p. 367.

7 K. Norgate, *Richard the Lionheart* (1924), Chapter V.

8 '*Le Récit d'un Ménestrel*' ed. N. Wailly, p. 41 et seq., translated E. N. de Reims Stone in *Three Old French Chronicles of the Crusades* (1939).

9 Claude Fauchet, '*Receuil de L'Origine de la Langue et Poésie Françoise, Ryme et Romans*' in *Fauchet's Oeuvres* (1580).

10 Oliver Goldsmith, *History of England*, Vol. 1, p. 236.

11 Grove's *Dictionary of Opera* (1992), Vol. 3, p. 1314.

12 E. Penrose, *Mrs Markham's History of England*, XIII, p. 105.

13 J. Gillingham, *Richard I* (Yale: 2002), p. 233.

14 Blondel de Nesle, *Oeuvres*, ed. P. Dubois (1862), *Die Lieder des Blondel de Nesle*, ed. L. Weise (1904).

14 Prince Arthur of Brittany

1 A. L. Poole, *From Domesday to Magna Carta* (OUP: 1951), p. 3.

2 W. L. Warren, *King John* (Eyre Methuen: 1978), pp. 48–9.

3 King John's own account, as reported by Ralph Coggeshall in his *Chronicon Anglicanum*, ed. J. Stevenson (Rolls Series: 1875), pp. 137–8. Quoted in W. L. Warren, *op. cit.*, p. 79.

4 *History of William the Marshall*, ed. P. Meyer (Paris: 1891–1901). Quoted in W. L. Warren, *op. cit.*, p. 81.

5 W. Shakespeare, *King John*, Act 4, Scene III. Maria Callcott's story of Arthur begging de Burgh not to blind him is from Act 4, Scene I.

6 *Annals of Margam Abbey* in *Annales Monastici*, ed. H. R. Luard (Rolls Series: 1864–6), iii, Vol. i, p. 27.

7 J. R. Green, *Short History of the English People* (1874), Vol. II, p. 114.

8 A. L. Poole, *op. cit.*, p. 425.

15 King John

1 See A. V. Jenkinson, 'The Jewels Lost in the Wash' in *History*, Vol. 8 (1923).

2 Coggeshall's *Chronicon Angliicanum*, p. 184, reports the rumour that a priest who was at Newark to say a Mass for a dead king had seen men leaving the town loaded with loot, with the implication that some of the treasure had been salvaged but then stolen from the king's deathbed. Rumour,

betrayal and suspicion were all so rife in those unsettled times that this can only be noted as a possibility. Coggeshall himself refers only to the loss of John's 'chapel with his relics', but these would, of course, be the items of most interest to an abbot.

3 An analysis of the most important research into this topic may be found in Appendix C of W. L. Warren's biographical study of King John (Yale: 1997).

4 Coggeshall, *Chronicum Anglicanum*, pp. 183–4.

5 This improbable story is found in several minor chronicles of the thirteenth century, e.g Walter Gisburn and Thomas Wykes of Osney. The latter chronicle was edited by H. R. Luard for the Rolls Series, 1869, *Annales Monastici*, iv, pp. 1–319.

16 The Death of King John

1 J. R. Green, *A Short History of the English People* (1874).
2 J. W. Stubbs, *A Constitutional History of England* (1875).
3 K. Norgate, *John Lackland* (1902).
4 See also S. D. Church (ed.), *King John: New Interpretations* (1999).

17 Queen Eleanor of Castile

1 M. Prestwich, *Edward I* (Yale: 1990), p. 60.
2 M. Powicke, *The Thirteenth Century* (OUP: 1953), p. 268.
3 M. Prestwich, *op. cit.*, pp. 132–3.
4 Ptolemy of Lucca, *Historia Ecclesiastica*, (ed. L. A. Muratori, *Rerum Italicarum Scriptores*, 1723–1751, Vol. xi, p. 1168); Johannis Longi, *Chronica S. Bertini, Monumenta Germaniae historica*, xxv, p. 856. These sources are given in M. Prestwich, *op. cit.*, p. 78.
5 Walter of Guisborough, *Chronicle*, ed. H. Rothwell (Camden Society), 3rd Series, Vol. lxxxix, pp. 209–10 (untranslated version).

18 Robert Bruce and the Spider

1 G. W. S. Barrow, *Robert Bruce* (1976), pp. 237–40.

2 Quoted in *Scotland: the Story of a Nation* by Magnus Magnusson (1999), pp. 169–70 where reference is made to a Clan Douglas family document, which appears to give historical confirmation to this story.

19 Edward III

Much of the information in this chapter is derived from an article published in the *University of Birmingham Historical Journal* for 1947/8 (pp. 12–50) written by Margaret Galway entitled 'Joan of Kent and the Order of the Garter'. With the exception of Reference 1, all references may be found in this article, as indicated below.

1 M. McKisack, *The Fourteenth Century* (OUP: 1959), p. 250.

2 Jean Froissart, *Chronicle*, Berners' translation, Vol. I, pp. 42 and 149; Galway, p. 18.

3 J. Selden, *Titles of Honour* (1614), Vol. II, pp. 657–8; Galway, p. 27.

4 J. Froissart, *op. cit.*, Vol. II, p. 243; Galway, p. 14; G. Chaucer, *The Squire's Tale*, Lines 34–5.

5 H. N. Nicolas, *Orders of Knighthood* (1826), Vol. I, p. 11ff; Galway, p. 32.

6 M. Galway, *op. cit.*, p. 34.

7 M. Galway, *op. cit.*, pp. 41–8.

8 J. Selden, *op. cit.*, Vol. II, p. 658; Galway, p. 34.

9 H. N. Nicolas, *op. cit.*, Vol. I, pp. 17–20; Galway, p. 34.

20 Dick Whittington and His Cat

1 Samuel Pepys, *Diary*, 21 September 1668.

2 Samuel Lysons, *The Model Merchant of the Middle Ages* (1860); *Monasticon Anglicanum*, ed. J. Caley, H. Ellis, B. Bandiel (1817–30), Vol. VI, p. 740.

3 H. T. Riley, *Memorials of London and London Life in the 13th, 14th, and 15th centuries* (1868), pp. 534–5 and 676. Lysons, *op. cit.*, states that Whittington was elected MP for London in 1416 but there is no official record of this.

4 E. F. Jacob, *The Fifteenth Century* (OUP: 1961), pp. 76, 86 and 440.

5 *Stow's Survey of London* (Oxford: 1908).

6 J. Granger, *Biographical History of England* (1775) Vol. I. p. 62. Quoted in H. B. Wheatley, *History of Sir Richard Whittington by T. H.* (Thomas Heywood?) (1885), Introduction, p. xxix.

7 H. B. Wheatley, *op. cit.*, p. i.

8 K. Thomas, *Man and the Natural World* (Allen Lane: 1983), pp. 109–10.

9 S. Lysons, *op. cit.*, p. 42.

10 R. Johnson, *A Song of Sir Richard Whittington* published in the *Crowne Garland of Roses*, Goulden (1612), reprinted in *A Collection of Old Ballads* (1830). Quoted in full in H. Wheatley *op. cit.*, Introduction, pp. ix–xiv.

11 K. Thomas, *op. cit.*, p. 109.

12 Sir William Ouseley, *Travels* (1819), quoted in H. B. Wheatley, *op. cit.*, Introduction, p. vi.

21 The Wars of the Roses

1 Bernard André, 'Les Douze Triomphes de Henry VII'in *Memorials of King Henry VII* (Rolls Series: 1858).

2 David Hume, *History of England*, 1761. Hume's *History* was described by Francis Palgrave, the early Victorian historian, as 'History for the Million', a judgement confirmed by its vast number of editions and by its use as the source for most nineteenth-century history textbooks.

3 J. S. Brewer, *The Student's Hume* (1880), p. 210.

4 Walter Scott, *Anne of Geierstein* (A. & C. Black: 1829), p. 56 in 1863 ed.

5 Maria Callcott, *Little Arthur's History of England* (1835). This was one of the most influential history books for children

written in the nineteenth century, during which it was issued in seventy editions and sold almost a million copies.

6 B. P. Wolffe, *Henry VI* (Methuen: 1983 ed.), p. 289.

22 Queen Margaret of Anjou

1 J. J. Bagley, *Margaret of Anjou* (1948), p. 26.
2 W. Shakespeare, *Henry VI*, Part III, Act 1, Scene IV.
3 For much of the detail that follows see *Archaeologia*, Vol. 47, 1883, pp. 286–94.
4 J. J. Bagley, *op. cit.*, p. 48.
5 Agnes Strickland, *Lives of the Queens of England* (1840s), Vol. III, 'Margaret of Anjou'.
6 Quoted in *Archaeologica*, *op. cit.*, pp. 291–2.

23 George, Duke of Clarence

1 J. R. Lander, *England 1450–1509* (Arnold: 1980), p. 296.
2 *Rotuli Parliamentorum* VI 193, quoted in C. Ross, *Edward IV* (Eyre Methuen: 1974), p. 187n. Also Yale: 1997.
3 This was not only Edward IV's problem. It stemmed largely from the weakness of the monarchy following the death of Henry V, and was not solved until the Tudor monarchy was firmly established.
4 *Calendar of Patent Rolls 1467–77*, pp. 251–2, Quoted in C. Ross, *op. cit.*, p. 157.
5 'Croyland Chronicle' in *Rerum Anglicarum Scriptores Veterum*, ed. W. Fulman (1684), trans. H. T. Riley (1893), p. 592.
6 *Chronicle of London*, ed. C. L. Kingsford (1905), p. 108.
7 D. Mancini, *The Usurpation of Richard III*, ed. C. A. J. Armstrong (1969), p. 63; Polydore Vergil, *English History*, ed. and trans. D. Hay (R. H. S. Camden series: 1950) lxxiv, p. 167; Thomas More, *Richard III*, ed. R. S. Sylvester (1963), p. 7. Edward Hall, *Chronicle*, ed. H. Ellis (1809), p. 326.

8   Robert Fabyan, *The New Chronicle of England and France* (1516), ed. H. Ellis (1811), Vol. II '1478', p. 666.

9   W. Shakespeare, *The Tragedy of Richard III*, Act I, Scene IV.

10 Jean Molinet, *Chroniques 1476–1506*, ed. J. A. Buchon, p. 377.

11 Olivier de la Marche, *Memoires*, Vol. iii, ed. H. Beaune and J. d'Arbaumont, p. 70.

12 Thomas More, 'History of Richard III', ed. R. S. Sylvester in *Complete Works* (1963), pp. 8–9.

24 Richard III

1   *The Great Chronicle of London*, ed. A. H. Thomas and I. D. Thornley (1938), Introduction. Quoted in C. Ross, *Richard III*, p. xxxviii.

2   J. Rous, *History of the Kings of England* (*c.* 1486). Printed in Alison Hanham, *Richard III and His Early Historians* (1975).

3   *York Civic Records*, ed. A. Raine, Vol. II, pp. 71–3. Quoted in C. Ross, *op. cit.*, p. 140.

4   Thomas More, *History of King Richard III*, ed. R. S. Sylvester (Yale: 1963), pp. 7–8.

5   Polydore Vergil, *Anglica Historica,* ed. Q. D. Hay (Camden Society Series: 1950) lxxiv, pp. 226–7.

6   James Gairdner, *History of the Life and Reign of Richard III* (CUP: 1898), pp. xi–xiii.

7   P. Tudor-Craig, *Richard III* (National Portrait Gallery: 1973), pp. 80 and 92–3.

8   P. Rhodes, 'The Physical Deformity of Richard III' in *British Medical Journal*, 1977, Vol. 2, 1650–2.

9   M. Hicks, *Richard III* (Tempus: 2000), p. 192. On Bosworth Field, Richard's body was stripped naked, thrown across a horse, carried to a nearby convent where it was exposed to public view for several days and then buried without a stone or epitaph.

25 The Battle of Bosworth

1   C. Ross, *Richard III* (Eyre Methuen: 1981), p. 216.
2   J. Gairdner, *A History of the Life and Reign of Richard III* (CUP: 1898), Appendix.
3   Polydore Vergil, *English History*, ed. H. Ellis (Camden Society: 1844); Edward Hall, *Chronicle* (1584), ed. H. Ellis (1809); Raphael Holinshed, *Chronicles 1577*, ed. H. Ellis (1807–8).
4   Sir John Fortescue (d. 1479) had stated that such a manifestation of God's will was confirmation of the Right of Kingship in his treatise on the nature of English governance.
5   William Hutton, *The Battle of Bosworth Field* (1788), p. 132.
6   J. Gairdner, *op. cit.*, p. 244.
7   S. Anglo, *The Foundation of the Tudor Dynasty* (Guildhall Miscellany II: 1960), p. 3.
8   S. B. Chrimes, *Henry VII* (Eyre Methuen: 1972), p. 49 (1981 ed.); C. Ross, *op. cit.*, p. 225; see also Plate 12 in C. Ross, *The Wars of the Roses* (Thames and Hudson: 1976).
9   R. Freeman, *English Emblem Books* (1967).
10 K. Thomas, *Man and the Natural World* (Allen Lane: 1983), pp. 64 and 77.

27 Sir Walter Raleigh

1   At the age of seventeen, Raleigh joined the Huguenot army fighting in the French Wars of Religion and was present at the decisive battle of Jarnac and Montcontour; in 1578, he went with Sir Humphrey Gilbert's expedition to explore the possibility of an English settlement in North America, but this ended less than successfully at the Cape Verde Islands; in 1580 he was in Ireland as Captain of a company of 100 men during the Fitzmaurice rebellion and he was involved in the slaughter at Smerwick and in the brutal suppression of the rebels in Munster.
2   M. W. Willard, *Sir Walter Raleigh* (Princeton: 1959), p. 21; Raleigh Trevelyan, *Sir Walter Raleigh* (Penguin Books: 2002), p. 48, notes that the seals Raleigh adopted in 1584 as Captain

of the Queen's Guard and as Governor of Virginia clearly show a cloak spread like wings over his Coat of Arms above the tactfully chosen motto 'Amore et Virtute'.

3 Sir Walter Scott, *Kenilworth*, Chapter 15.

4 Thomas Fuller, *The Worthies of England* (1662), p. 133.

28 Sir Philip Sidney

1 Fulke Greville, *Life of Sir Philip Sidney* (1652), (OUP: ed. 1907), p. 120.

2 John Buxton, *Sir Philip Sidney and the English Renaissance* (OUP: 1964), p. 112.

3 Fulke Greville, *op. cit.*, p. 124.

4 Fulke Greville, *op. cit.*, pp. 126–7.

5 Fulke Greville, *op. cit.* pp. 129–30.

6 See the studies by Katherine Duncan-Jones (*Sir Philip Sidney, Courtier Poet*) and Jan van Dorsten (*The Final Year*).

7 Alan Stewart, *Philip Sidney, A Double Life* (Chatto & Windus: 2000), pp. 265 and 313.

8 *Ibid.*, p. 320.

9 *Ibid.*, pp. 312–13

29 Sir Francis Drake

1 For example, Philip Nichols, *Sir Francis Drake Revived* (1624); Nathaniel Crouch, *The English Hero or Sir Francis Drake Revived* (1681).

2 Thomas Fuller, *The Holy and Profane State* (1642), p. 132 et seq.

3 G. W. Anderson, *A New Authentic and Complete Collection of Voyages Round the World* (1781), p. 371 et seq.

4 Sir Walter Raleigh, *English Voyages of the Sixteenth century* (1906). p. 84. Quoted in J. B. Black, *The Reign of Elizabeth* (OUP: 1959), p. 247.

5 G. Mattingly, *The Defeat of the Spanish Armada* (Cape: 1959), p. 229.

6 J. S. Corbett, *Drake and the Tudor Navy* (Longman: 1898), Vol. II, p. 188.

7 H. Kelsey, *Sir Francis Drake: The Queen's Pirate* (Yale: 2000), p. 322.

8 T. Scott, 'The Second Part of Vox Populi or Notes from Spain' (1624), printed in J. Morgan, *Phoenix Britannicus* (1732), pp. 345–6.

9 W. Oldys, preface to his 1736 edition of *Sir Walter Raleigh's History of the World*, p. xliv.

10 C. Kingsley, *Westward Ho!* (1855), Chapter XXX.

11 J. S. Corbett, *op. cit.* p. 188.

12 T. Auguarde, *Oxford Companion to Sports and Games* (OUP: 1975), p. 99.

13 W. Shakespeare, *Richard II*, Act 3, Scene IV.

14 R. Birley, *The Undergrowth of History* (Historical Association: 1955), p. 21.

15 A summary of the development of the story may be found in C. W. Bracken's *History of Plymouth* (Underhill Press, Plymouth: 1931), p. 90 et seq., and in his article in the *Western Morning News* for 30 November 1938, available in the Clipping Files of the West Country Studies Library, Plymouth.

30 Oliver Cromwell

1 Robert Birley, *The Undergrowth of History* (Historical Association: 1955); James Heath, *Flagellum …* (1663), p. 70; Joseph Spence, *Anecdotes, Observations, and Characters of Books and Men* (John Murray: 1820), p. 286; Mark Noble, *Memoirs of the Protectoral House of Cromwell* (1787), Vol. I, p. 118.

2 J. C. Davis, *Oliver Cromwell* (Arnold: 2001), pp. 197–8.

3 C. Carlton, *Charles I, The Personal Monarch* (Routledge: 1995), pp. 331–3.

4 *Ibid.*, pp. 335–6.

5 C. V. Wedgwood, *The Trial of Charles I* (Collins: 1964), p. 77.

6 A. Fraser, *Cromwell, Our Chief of Men* (Phoenix Press: 2002) ed., p. 274.

7 *Ibid.*, p. 288.

8 A salutary comment on this justification for one's actions was made by a member of Cromwell's parliaments: the doctrine of Providence and Necessity can be a two-edged sword – a thief might lay as good a title to every purse he took upon the highway. (Keith Thomas, *Religion and the Decline of Magic* (Allen Lane: 1973 ed.), p. 125.

31 Sir Isaac Newton

1 G. N. Clark, *The Later Stuarts* (OUP: 1940), p. 360.
2 F. M. Voltaire, *Philosophie de Newton* (1738), Part III, Chapter 3.
3 W. Stukeley, *Memoirs of Sir Isaac Newton,* ed. A. Hastings-White (1936), pp. 19–20.
4 R. W. Herivel, *The Background to Newton's Principia* (1965), p. 65.
5 F. E. Manuel, *A Portrait of Isaac Newton* (Harvard U. P.: 1968), p. 105.
6 R. S. Westfall, *Never at Rest: A Biography of Isaac Newton* (CUP: 1980), p. 155.
7 H. Pemberton, *A View of Sir Isaac Newton's Philosophy* (1728), Preface.
8 Stephen Hawking, *A Brief History of Time* (Space Time Publications: 1990), p. 4.
9 M. White, *Sir Isaac Newton* (Fourth Estate: 1997), p. 87.

32 James Stuart, the Old Pretender

1 J. Miller, *James II* (Yale: 2000), p. xv.
2 Quoted in J. Miller, *op. cit.* p. 120.
3 *Ibid.*, p. 127.
4 *Ibid.*, p. 157.
5 G. Burnet, *History of My Own Time* (pub. 1723–34), pp. 475–9 (1857 ed.); Portland Welbeck Collection in Nottingham University Library: PWA 2165, 2167, 2171, 2173, 2175.
6 G. Burnet, *op. cit.*

7 PWA 2171
8 PWA 2171; J. Miller, *op. cit.* p. 190.
9 PWA 2175
10 PWA 2167, 2177
11 G. Burnet, *op. cit.*

33 Captain Jenkins's Ear

1 J. K. Laughton, *English Historical Review iv*, 1889, p. 742.
2 Quoted in B. Williams, *The Whig Supremacy* (OUP: 1942), p. 297
3 J. K. Laughton, *op. cit.*, pp. 743–7.
4 *The Gentleman's Magazine*, No. VI, June 1731, p. 265.
5 William Coxe, *Memoirs of Sir Robert Walpole* (1798), Vol. I.

34 General James Wolfe

1 E. E. Morris, 'Wolfe and Gray's Elegy' in *English Historical Review*, xv, 1900, pp. 125–9.
2 *Ibid.*, p. 126, quoting P. H. Stanhope, Viscount Mahon, *History of England from the Peace of Utrecht to the Peace of Versailles*, *1713–83* (1836–54), Vol. IV, p. 244; Carlyle *Frederick the Great*, Vol. V, p. 555 (Library Edition).
3 *Ibid.*, p. 127.

35 George Washington

1 K. A. Marling, quoted in a Virginia educational website (2002) under the title 'The Moral Washington'.
2 M. L. Weems, *The Life of George Washington* (1806), p. 60
3 K. A. Marling, *George Washington Slept Here: Colonial Revivals and American Culture 1876–1988* (Harvard U. P 1988), p. 310.
4 M. L. Weems, *op. cit.*, Chapter II.
5 Rupert Hughes, *George Washington 1736–1762* (Hutchinson 1926), p. 501.

6 M. Cunliffe, *George Washington, Man and Monument* (Collins: 1959), p. 12.

36 Admiral Horatio Nelson

1 Over 75 per cent of the grain imported into Britain at that time came from the Baltic ports, representing almost 20 per cent of the country's total consumption.

2 This was the so-called Rule of 1756, agreed during the Seven Years' War.

3 O. Warner, *Nelson's Battles* (Pen and Sword Military Classics: 2003), p. 121.

4 *Ibid.*, p. 122.

5 Nicholas Nicolas, *The Dispatches and Letters of Vice-Admiral Lord Viscount Nelson, 1844–1846*, Vol. IV, pp. 308–9. Quoted in G. J. Marcus, *A Naval History of England, Vol 2: The Age of Nelson* (Allen and Unwin: 1971), pp. 184–5.

6 T. Coleman, *Nelson* (Bloomsbury: 2001), pp. 258–60.

7 T. Pocock, *Horatio Nelson* (Random House: 1987). The Nelson Society Website, 2001, also follows this version.

8 James Ralfe, *The Naval Biography of Great Britain* (1828), Vol. IV, p. 12.

9 Tributes were paid by both sides to the courage and tenacity shown by both British and Danish participants in this bloody and destructive engagement. Casualties were severe; precise numbers are difficult to ascertain but in his 1960 *A Social History of the British Navy*, Michael Lewis gave these figures: Killed – British 253; Danish 790. Wounded – British 688; Danish 910.

37 Florence Nightingale

1 V. Lytton Strachey, *Eminent Victorians* (Penguin ed.: 1986), p. 121.

2 E. Cook, *The Life of Florence Nightingale* (1913), Vol. I, p. 237.

3 E. Cook, *op. cit.*, pp. 236–7.

4 E. Cook, passim.
5 Lytton Strachey, *op. cit.*, p. 133.
6 Lytton Strachey, *op. cit.*, p. 155.

38 Queen Victoria

1 Elizabeth Longford, *Victoria R. I.* (Weidenfeld & Nicolson: 1971), p. 377.
2 *Ibid.*, pp. 399 and 574.
3 *Ibid.*, pp. 568 and 570.
4 G. A. K. Bell, *Randall Davidson* (1935), Vol. I., p. 85.
5 Elizabeth Longford, *op. cit.*, p. 64.
6 Alan Hardy, *Queen Victoria Was Amused* (Taplinger, New York: 1977); contributed essay by A. H. Bevan entitled 'Popular Royalty'.
7 Caroline Holland, *Notebooks of a Spinster Lady* (1919), 2 January 1900.

39 The Angels of Mons

1 These debates are admirably outlined in Barbara Tuchman's *August 1914*, Chapter 12.
2 *Official History: Military Operations: France and Belgium 1914*, Vol. i, p.10. Quoted in A. J. P. Taylor's *English History 1914–1945* (OUP: 1965), p. 8.
3 This famous remark is usually attributed to Kaiser Wilhelm II, but it appears in an Annexe to BEF Routine Orders for 24 September 1914, and it may have been part of a propaganda campaign. See Arthur Ponsonby's *Falsehood in Wartime* (1928), Chapter 10.
4 H. G. Wells, *Mr Britling Sees It Through* (1916).
5 *London Evening News*, Tuesday September 29 1914 (by courtesy of the British Library Newspaper Library).
6 A. J. P. Taylor, *op. cit.*, p. 9.
7 M. MacDonagh, *In London During the Great War* (1935),